PRAISE FOR

# The Undercurrents

"From the first moment I heard Kirsty Bell read from her writing, I have yearned for the book she was then working on. And now here it is, perfect and perfectly balanced, a clear-eyed and beautifully written account about place, about consciousness. I treasure *The Undercurrents*, and so will you."          —Hilton Als, author of *White Girls*

"An enthralling book about how finding the truth of a city's story means finding the truth of your own . . . the author skillfully weaves the narrative threads into an elegant tapestry . . . A remarkably absorbing work that requires close attention—and repays in full."
—*Kirkus Reviews* (starred review)

"With *The Undercurrents*, Kirsty Bell does for Berlin what Luc Sante has done for New York and Rebecca Solnit for San Francisco; she tells the stories recorded in the city's stone and water, and in the hearts of its inhabitants. Her profound and idiosyncratic chronicle of Berlin is an act of hydromancy, divining a history of love and loss from the water that flows beneath and between the city's bricks."
—Dan Fox, author of *Limbo*

"Kirsty Bell's approach to Berlin, the mixing of the personal with the historical, is fascinating. I read her book with great interest and pleasure."

—Norman Ohler, author of *Blitzed: Drugs in the Third Reich*

"I read this watery, engrossing book in the bath, following along as Kirsty Bell's reflective curiosity leads her onward along the Landwehr Canal, in and out of the archives, novels, memoirs and stories of her building and her neighborhood. Evocative and fascinating, *The Undercurrents* is a liquid psychogeography of Berlin that had me mulling over the psychic charge of place not only where Bell lives, but where I live too."

—Lauren Elkin, author of *Flâneuse: Women Walk the City in Paris, New York, Tokyo, Venice, and London*

"It is easy to be carried along by these submerged currents, by the momentum of the prose, the motion through a resisting city. As in other classics of urban discovery, the personal becomes universal, and the past that demands to live in the present is revealed like a shining new reef. As we return, time and again, to the solitary figure at the window."

—Iain Sinclair, author of *London Orbital*

"Kirsty Bell has achieved a real work of art: She tells of Berlin's sunken past as a freshly emerged present—and she explains the energy of this city from the history of the people, the streets and the hopes that have shaped it."

—Florian Illies, author of *1913: The Year Before the Storm*

"With sleuthing interest and novelistic flair, Kirsty Bell's *The Undercurrents* has ruptured familiar terrain...an associative thesis on the dangers of repression, from gargantuan acts of genocide to the comparatively subtle shames of familial collapse...An enchanting and sometimes disturbing symbolism runs through *The Undercurrents*, as Bell imaginatively weaves the city's hard factuality with the emotional and physical experience of living in it."                                   —*frieze*

"With her extraordinary new book, *The Undercurrents*, Kirsty Bell brilliantly shows us that not only is history all around us, but it is also something that we actively live alongside and are continuously becoming part of...Bell takes us on an enthralling tour of Berlin's recent history...As well as breaking down barriers between the past and present, Bell also breaks down barriers between forms; a hybrid of memoir, history and literary exploration, *The Undercurrents* defies easy, fixed definition, the same way that history does."          —*Buzz Magazine*

"[Bell] mixes personal reflections with historical and literary research in her lively investigation of the city and its contemporary built environment."          —*Exberliner*

"A captivating portrait of the German capital. . . . Bell's book derives its tension from the way in which everything is interwoven: personal and private with the familiar names and great sweep of history, as well as the many testimonies and voices of those rarely read about in conventional accounts."
          —Katharina Rudolph, *Franfurter Allgemeine Zeitung*

# The Undercurrents

ALSO BY KIRSTY BELL

*The Artist's House: From Workplace to Artwork*

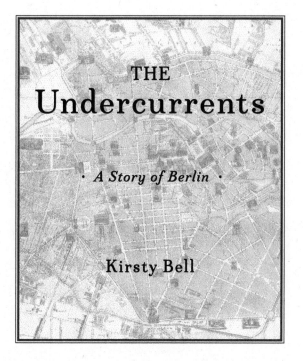

THE
# Undercurrents

· *A Story of Berlin* ·

## Kirsty Bell

**Other Press**

NEW YORK

*Production editor: Yvonne E. Cárdenas*
*Text designer: Jennifer Daddio / Bookmark Design & Media Inc.*
*This book was set in Marcia*
*by Alpha Design & Composition of Pittsfield, NH*

1 3 5 7 9 10 8 6 4 2

Library of Congress Cataloging-in-Publication Data
Names: Bell, Kirsty, author.
Title: The undercurrents : a story of Berlin / Kirsty Bell.
Description: New York : Other Press, [2022] |
Includes bibliographical references.
Identifiers: LCCN 2022003275 (print) | LCCN 2022003276 (ebook) |
ISBN 9781635423440 (paperback) | ISBN 9781635423457 (ebook)
Subjects: LCSH: Berlin (Germany)—Biography. | Berlin (Germany)—
Social life and customs. | Berlin (Germany)—History. |
Berlin (Germany)—Buildings, structures, etc. |
Berlin (Germany)—In literature. | Bell, Kirsty.
Classification: LCC DD857.A2 B437 2022 (print) |
LCC DD857.A2 (ebook) | DDC 943/.155—dc23/eng/20220415
LC record available at https://lccn.loc.gov/2022003275
LC ebook record available at https://lccn.loc.gov/2022003276

# Contents

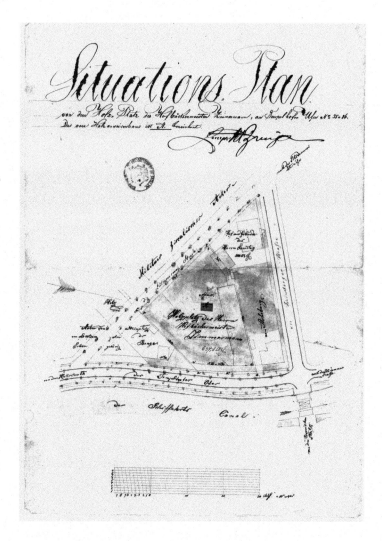

# Prelude

*A large pool of water* had appeared overnight on our kitchen floor, so silent and unexpected it seemed to be a mirage. Tap water had been dribbling from a loose pipe beneath the sink and leaking noiselessly down through the two stories below us. This scene, which we woke up to on the morning of our son's ninth birthday, was the most dramatic but not the only incident of water damage. For several months before and after, a collection of plastic buckets and basins had become a semi-permanent, wandering feature, brought out to catch leaks in different parts of our home. One evening, a few months after the kitchen flood, our elder son noticed water dripping from the plasterwork rosette in the center of the living-room ceiling. Looking up, we saw an ominous spreading patch of brown as water leaking from upstairs traversed the terrain above our heads. Water always finds its way. My sons and I fetched the buckets and basins once more and laid out towels to soak it up. It was as if our new apartment was trying to tell us something.

The apartment we had lived in before on the east side of the city, with an Edenic plasterwork of vines, fruits and flowers twisting around the columns of its façade, exerted no such influence. We were there for ten years – husband and wife, two sons, two cats – and throughout this time, regardless of our difficulties, that apartment was consistently neutral. It did not make its presence felt or stir up any overt feelings. It was simply a container, benevolent if anything, in enabling the maintenance of the status quo. Our new apartment, closer to the boys' school in the west, was awkward from day one. Aggravating and interfering, it kept producing warning signals that could not be ignored. It intervened and forced itself into the role of the protagonist.

There are things you can see and others you can only feel, that you sense in a different way, as a whisper in your mind, or a weight in your bones. A nugget of doubt had crystallized and been disturbing the everyday flow of my thoughts for weeks already. Like a silty clot of debris, its vague contours had gained definition when we moved east to west across the axis of the city. Its shape was of unhappiness. And now here it was, clotting up my mind as I paced between the many rooms of our extravagantly proportioned new home. A cultivated emptiness in the mind can allow for rippling, drift and snag. It can draw out things that don't want to be seen.

That early morning encounter with a glassy pool of water on the kitchen floor was an unequivocal sign of rupture. Something had broken its banks and could no longer be contained. After years of emotional repression, subconsciously practiced to maintain a functional family life, this spontaneous display, this uncalled-for outburst – *this flood* – was a symbol of almost hysterical clarity. It asked for an equally extreme response, which duly came in a sudden, brutal and final break. A severing of the family unit, whereby one part was broken off and the other three parts remained together. My husband went away for work and never came back to our home.

Water always finds its way. Winding through the crevices of this old building. Seeping into smoothly plastered and painted surfaces. Appearing suddenly in damp bruises of mold in high-up corners. Inducing patches of plasterwork to blister off external walls. There was always a logical explanation, a cause to put it down to. Heavy rainfall on unsealed roof tiles; pipes drilled into or fixed up faultily; blocked drains in overflowing showers. The builders at work on the penthouse upstairs were clearly a slapdash bunch. Still, the relentlessness of these various cases began to feel oppressive. It was as if the surfaces of the apartment refused to be sealed; its infrastructure would not hold tight. Whenever it rained, I was anxious. As the months progressed, I felt an urge to map out the stains and marks that had been left on the ceilings, walls and floors. If I were to plot out their topography, could I devise a map to read and make sense of these minor domestic disasters?

I had a persistent and uneasy feeling of intent behind these incidents. One that could not be seen straight on, but rather accessed sidelong through some form of divination. Like the hydromantic method of scrying, reading the ripples on a surface of water, lit by the light of the moon at best. As the boundaries of the apartment became porous, containment was no longer an option, and neither was silence. There would be no more holding things at bay. External events, emotional truths, historical incidents, all would find a way to make themselves known.

By the time the pool of water appeared on the kitchen floor, our marriage was already broken, but this occurrence induced its final rupture. In contrast to the steady drip of sadness that we had both grown accustomed to and comfortably ignored over the years, the break was violent. The flood precipitated a crisis that extended beyond the many hours spent mopping up. A crisis for which the apartment seemed to share responsibility, brought to a head through its very own plumbing. I was grateful for this sign of what seemed to me like solidarity, a compassionate act that fortunately caused no lasting physical damage. Our own wooden floorboards dried out fast and no trace on them was left behind. The apartment below us, which bore the brunt of the leakage, was in between tenants and empty. The enormous dehumidifiers, brought in to dry the walls and air, could do their noisy work without disturbing anyone. In the painter's studio on the first floor, the flood ran down the only wall on which no canvas was hanging. Miraculously the huge paintings on the other two walls, which she had spent the last six months painstakingly composing, were spared. The glass globe lamp in the ground floor entrance hall, in which the last dregs collected, was simply unscrewed and emptied out, like a goldfish bowl no longer needed.

"Sometimes when water is flowing it means the house is mourning," I read online. "There is an excess of emotion that needs to be expelled." The image that formed on the surface of the pool of water did not just reflect a broken home, it also reflected the house itself.

These tears of mourning were the building's own. It would soon become my subject.

At the same time as all this water damage was troubling the apartment, I began to notice how insistently the view from my kitchen window was presenting itself. It seemed to draw me to it, away from the calamities occurring inside and towards its offer of a broad sky, treetops and buildings leading towards the horizon. This position became a recurrent refrain in the passage of working days at home. A female figure at the window, seen from the back and looking out. Motionless at this threshold, the body separate from its thoughts, as the inside is separate from the outside. In the building's vernacular, the window is the cut.

The first ever photographic image, taken by Joseph Niépce in 1826, was the view from the window of his studio. It shows a shadowy arrangement of soft grey planes and solids, the angle of a roof. Twelve years later, in 1838, the first photograph of a human being, by Louis Daguerre, was the view outside his window. A sweeping vista down a tree-lined street, flanked with imposing buildings but otherwise deserted, save two static, ghostly figures. These early photographs were a form of basic research, an examination of material facts that started at the most obvious point: the view, from the inside looking out. A location of self within a place, a certain kind of anchoring. Christopher Isherwood in *Goodbye to Berlin* famously adopts the same approach. "From my window, the deep solemn massive street," begins the chapter titled "Berlin Diary" from 1930. Isherwood himself becomes the photographic apparatus: "I am a camera with its shutter open, quite passive, recording, not thinking." But the female figure at my window isn't quite so passive as she looks across at Berlin's cityscape. She is wondering about orientation, just how did she come to end up in this place? And what is this place in any case, whose surface seems so fraught with secrets?

The building we moved into in the summer of 2014 stands on the banks of Berlin's Landwehr Canal: with its feet in the west, it looks across the water towards the east. In Berlin, this city of extremes and interrupted histories, the simple denominations of east and west are loaded with ideological import. Location, literally, is make or break. The plot on which my building stands was peripheral in the mid-1800s when it came to first be built upon, lying just beyond the customs wall that had circled the center for a good hundred years. But in the fast-paced industrial development of the decades that followed, the city's axes were refigured, and this plot came to occupy a ringside seat looking onto its theater of action: the center of government, journalism, transport and metropolitan life. When Berlin was divided into sectors in the second half of the twentieth century, it shifted again to the desolate outskirts. But now in the early 2000s, its position in a capital city still adjusting to unification has come to be re-centered.

Berlin's sharply defined residential districts each possess a distinctive character, but while this building straddles several, it doesn't fit squarely in any one. Though officially in Kreuzberg, it occupies its northernmost tip, a block from the border with the Tiergarten district, while Schöneberg spreads out behind. This area is not densely inhabited, but spacious and full of hesitant gaps, temporal jumps and wild moments of greenery. The canal banks are called the Ufer, and ours the Tempelhofer Ufer, the banks that originally lead to the village of Tempelhof. Despite the area's comparative spaciousness, the view from my third-floor kitchen window is dense with a patchwork of city history. But beyond its visible components, something else seems to be at work. An unsettling sense of a past that snags attention but won't let itself be clearly seen. A downward pull that seems to halt the present.

I begin searching out historical photographs, literature and archives, combing them for evidence of this place. Books about its architecture and early urban development. Literature from a century ago that took place in the streets around me. Grim online address books from the 1930s, inventories of all the houses with Jewish occupants. Eyewitness accounts from the last street battles of the Second World War. I watch Wim Wenders's *Wings of Desire*, which I saw as a teenager when it first came out, in Manchester's art-house cinema in 1987. Now I scan the screen for places I recognize and views familiar from my current daily life. They are there: the train tracks that run behind my house, the swans afloat on the canal, the ruined railway station I can see from my window in the middle distance. I begin to plot my own experience onto these accumulated layers of time, words and images. This is a beginning.

In the summer of 2001, I had arrived in Berlin from New York, one more in the most recent swell of newcomers to a city formed historically by its successive waves of immigrants. Following a strong gut instinct that overrode cautions of the rational mind, I had left my job, my friends, my New York studio and moved in with my German boyfriend, to his vast Berlin apartment. All high ceilings, pale grey linoleum, barely any furniture, and the biggest bathroom I'd ever seen. Landing a good ten years after the city's unification, I already felt belated. Artists, musicians, writers, filmmakers, actors, designers had been flocking here for years by then, inhabiting Berlin's derelict apartments, setting up studios and turning any abandoned building into a bar, club or gallery. The sheer space was a palpable relief after the density and compression of life in New York City. There was a wildness here bordering at times on desolation. So much was empty, so much uncertainty. I had just turned thirty and was looking for change. The availability and undefined potential of this place seemed to offer an openness in which one could act. Perhaps it could help me start to write. I packed two suitcases, sublet my New York studio with everything that was in it, and left to begin a new chapter in this unknown place.

When I arrived on his doorstep, my boyfriend was living on Mauerstraße, near Checkpoint Charlie, in the dropped-pin center of the city. A strangely forlorn neighborhood, it seemed devoid of purpose or atmosphere, populated mainly by straggling bunches of tourists, and not a tree in sight. Even the buildings here appeared withdrawn, eyes downcast to their own foundations. It seemed ironic to live on a street named *Wall Street*, in this city bent on self-invention following the fall of the Berlin Wall, but the *Mauer* its street name referred to was a different wall: the eighteenth-century customs wall that once had stood nearby. The view from my boyfriend's bedroom window was taken up entirely by an enormous brand-new office block, designed by Philip Johnson and finished in 1997 in Berlin's post-unification boom. There was something awkward about this slick and massive building, as if it had been put down in the wrong place. I didn't know it then, but the American Business Center, as it was called, was built on the site of the Bethlehemskirche, an eighteenth-century church – one of the city's oldest, until it was destroyed by bombs in 1943. In 2012, a Spanish artist installed a steel framework outlining the form of the disappeared church, but when we lived there, I knew nothing of the disappeared building, this missing puzzle piece. A similar unease and silence surrounded that house and the one I live in now. Something reticent and dislocated. An uncanny weight hanging in the air.

Shortly after I arrived in Berlin, my boyfriend and I left Mauerstraße and moved to the more accommodating neighborhood of Prenzlauer Berg in the city's former East. In an area about to be reconfigured by the homogenizing forces of gentrification, we unwittingly ticked all the relevant boxes. Within six months I was pregnant, and we became one of this neighborhood's many young families. Here we had our babies, bought our first flat, tied the knot and adopted pets. Caught up in the ongoing task of welding family and work into one seamless whole, we got distracted and lost sight of each other. We let our marriage run aground. A fact that was not yet apparent, however, when twelve years later, we moved across the city, from center east to center west.

Whoever "seeks to approach his own buried past must conduct himself like a man digging," advises Walter Benjamin, Berlin-born and a resident on and off until his exile in the early 1930s. Is this a kind of geomancy, to read the ground of history? "It is undoubtedly useful to plan excavations methodically," writes Benjamin. "Yet no less indispensable is the cautious probing of the spade in the dark loam." I start digging in this medium, trawling and sifting through the past, without knowing really what to look for. Retrieving memories that aren't your own is a messy business full of traps. But perhaps it can elucidate the porosity of a place and how its past affects its present? So I begin at the most obvious point: here alone at the kitchen window, on the inside looking out.

I set myself the task of writing a portrait of the city. An impossible task perhaps, but the house seems somehow to suggest it. What follows concerns memory, the past and its retrieval, but it does not follow a single path, or proceed step by step. The memory of a place does not lie flat on a straight line of time; it is syncretic and simultaneous, layered in thin sediments of event and passage, inhabitation and mood. It is a compound of assimilated actions bound up in the material of streets and houses, or recorded in words and images that gather over time, or else it has no tangible form and must be felt out, reimagined.

When we found this house on the banks of the Landwehr Canal, I had thought of living on the water as a way to find a current. To write about the place in which I live could be a way to make an anchor and counteract the drift. Particularly if the things I write of are themselves the stuff of drift – flotsam of the past washed up on shores of consciousness. But this subject – this city – refuses neat containment. The writing has become sprawling and unruly, and so it begins to resemble the city itself, spread out wide without any discernible banks. Berlin.

Plan
von
BERLIN.

Gez. u. lith. in der Lith. Anstalt von
Hermann Delius

Verlag v. C. Grobe.

## · 1 ·

# Ditch

*There is an enduring appeal* to living on the water. Its surface suggests a depth otherwise unavailable in an urban landscape. A break in its concrete crust and relief from the relentless push of traffic, the flow of people, the upward thrust of buildings. Water simply lies there and offers back reflections – of sky, of trees, of passing birds, of the buildings lined up on its banks. An inverted image of the city through which it courses.

A canal is not a river, however; it doesn't *course* through anything. Its path is carved out and its waters contained by constructed concrete banks. Some days the canal outside my window seems to move in one direction, some days in the other. But mostly it is still and barely moves at all. A blue ribbon laid out on the map, from northeast to southwest across the city, with thirty-six bridges to hold it in place.

The Landwehr Canal is the first thing I see when I look out of the kitchen window. But it is not like the English canals I have known. The Manchester Ship Canal is narrow, deep and dirty, designed to serve the industries in the redbrick warehouses and factories alongside of which it skirts. The Bridgewater Canal, where my parents would take my brothers and me for weekend walks, runs straight and flat on raised embankments with single-file footpaths either side. The Regent's Canal I got to know in my early twenties in North London is just as narrow, carving its pass through the built-up inner city. My Berlin canal is generous: broad and tree-lined, as wide as the two-lane streets that flank it, as it glides through Berlin's residential districts. The two lanes of traffic on my side of the canal lead straight down into Kreuzberg, while the two lanes on the opposite bank head up through the Tiergarten district to Charlottenburg in the west. "Berlin was built from the barge," an old saying goes, and indeed, rather than serving smoky, dirty industries, this canal was used primarily to build the city's houses.

A pencil drawing from the early 1840s by Adolph Menzel, Berlin's foremost artist of the nineteenth century, shows the flooded Schafgraben, or sheep's ditch, as one stretch of the canal was known back then. A gnarled tree trunk bent over double is submerged in a still-standing pool of floodwater. A fence of wooden planks shores up the water on the right, while the flank of a house, its back turned away, is sketched out on the left.

The Landwehr Canal follows the path of the old Schafgraben, or Landwehrgraben, as it was more commonly known. This defensive boundary running east–west was laid out in the 1400s. *Landwehr*, or the defense of the land, was crucial in these early years, when the Hohenzollern prince-electors took hold of this small trading town – an unremarkable place save its position as a gateway between Hamburg, the Baltic and the East. Their determination to transform it into a formidable hub of politics, power and administration was backed up by an army of considerable size. From this point on Berlin's power grew, consolidated through a combination of rigid Prussian bureaucracy and brute militaristic force. When the Kingdom of Prussia was established in the early 1700s, with Berlin now its capital, the path of the Landwehr Ditch was formalized. It served to channel floods and high waters away from the grand architectures of the new city center, and towards the sleepy rural outskirts seen in Menzel's pencil sketch.

When I search for the Landwehr Canal online, two things come up immediately. The first is a reference to a gruesome song from the Weimar years about a corpse found floating in its waters. The second is a newspaper headline from January 4, 2009: "Twenty-one-year-old crashes car into the Landwehr Canal."

A photograph shows the rear end of a black compact car, ropes attached to its two back wheels, being hauled up out of the water. It is not the first car that ended up in the canal, the article tells us. In February 2002, a thirty-one-year-old missed a curve and too crashed into the water. That summer, a twenty-two-year-old woman drove into it, as did another, no age given, in December 2006. On November 3, 2007, a twenty-four-year-old woman drove her car into the canal, for no reason that could be discerned. That woman escaped to the car's roof as it sank into the water, and was rescued by police who brought her to shore at the corner of Tempelhofer Ufer by the Schöneberger Bridge. This corner is almost in front of my building. Would I have witnessed this accident had I lived here already? Would I have seen the woman, frantic and soaking, clambering onto the roof of her car, waving for help as it sank beneath the glassy surface? Would I have been the one to help? To call the police, and rush downstairs, to stand on the bridge and throw her the red and white life ring that hangs, ready and waiting for service, on the yellow-painted railings of the Schöneberger Bridge?

---

It was not until 1840 that plans were made to turn the Landwehr Ditch into a ship-worthy thoroughfare. These plans were drawn up by Peter Joseph Lenné, celebrated landscape architect turned city planner. Born in Bonn in 1789 to a family of gardeners, Lenné had arrived in Berlin, young and ambitious, in 1816. He began immediately in the service of Crown Prince Friedrich Wilhelm IV, and was set to the future king's estates and parks in Potsdam, relieving their stiff formal symmetry with a fluid archipelago of lakes and land, meandering bays and copses of trees. The "landscape garden," with its appearance of a nature left free to run its course, was Lenné's particular talent and, as he liked to say, *water* was his main material. His vision resonated with the aesthetically attuned crown prince, enamored of the trappings of pomp and ceremony, and Lenné was quickly elevated to the position of Chief Royal Gardener. By 1838 he was living in a newly built villa in Tiergarten, with his wife "Fritzchen," two old parrots and several generations of Newfoundland dogs. A year later the street on which his villa stood would be renamed Lennéstraße.

In 1833, Lenné had begun work on the redesign of the Tiergarten, Berlin's oldest park. Back in the fifteenth century, the Hohenzollern princes had turned its marshy forests into their private hunting grounds. Lenné had the Tiergarten in his sights as early as 1818 when, only two years into his job as gardener's assistant in Potsdam, he submitted a proposal to the Crown for its redesign. This faded drawing, which I find in a catalogue of his complete works, shows the Tiergarten's original radial axes embellished with an embroidery of watery pools, open meadows and finely looping paths. Such elements devise a perambulation not fixed on destination or the formal promenade, but rather on the sensual experience of walking from densely shaded woods onto broad sunny lawns, along grassy banks and over gently arching bridges. This precocious vision, unfettered by practicalities, was swiftly rejected at the time. But the modified version Lenné submitted in 1833, this time bearing the official stamp of the Royal Court and Garden Directorate, was embraced. "In the service of His Majesty the King, I am concerned to transform the Tiergarten of Berlin into a healthy and pleasant place for the relaxation of the residents of the capital city," declared Lenné in his successful proposal. His Tiergarten was to become Berlin's most public place, a *Volksgarten* as he put it – a Garden for the People – where all strands of civic society could gather, across the strata of class and income, for the first time in the city's history.

Lenné's concept was to extract a romantic, picturesque landscape from the existing raw and marshy terrain. He drained much of its forest areas to accommodate winding footpaths, which wove through clusters of trees and fragrant shrubbery, opening out onto broad green meadows traversed by streams and connected by bridleways. Serpentine lakes were dotted with little islands and crossed by countless bridges. Bodies of water and outlets of land intermingled until it was no longer clear which was island and which mainland. An infinitely spreading country landscape was conjured within the confines of the park. With few clear lines of sight, the Tiergarten was not to be a thoroughfare, but rather a destination in itself, a place to relax and indulge in the experience of simply passing time amongst the reviving elements of water and nature. Offering the privacy of shaded seclusion as well as open lawns on which to gather, observe and be observed, Lenné's vision marked the emergence of leisure within the urban landscape. It was a foil to the city's rapid growth and industrial development, which by this time was drawing ever more peasants in from the countryside to an urban working life.

When I arrived in Berlin in the summer of 2001 and moved into the apartment on Mauerstraße, I came to the Tiergarten to sit in the grass and work in the sun, amongst dog walkers, playing children and surprisingly naked sunbathers. I was tackling my first real writing job, composing hundred-word texts for a compendium on contemporary art. When I needed a break, I would ride my bike along the winding paths, invariably getting lost, my sense of direction befuddled by the fluid interchange of meadow, woods and water. Even now after all these years I still can't find my way. The park I get lost in is Lenné's *Volksgarten*, his Garden for the People.

This was also Walter Benjamin's park. He spent his early childhood years here and in the surrounding Tiergarten neighborhood. His family home as well as that of his grandmother were a short walk from the park, which to him exuded a mazelike influence. On the one hand, this place "unlike every other, seemed open to children," but it was nevertheless "distorted by difficulties and impracticalities," confusion, inaccessibility and dashed hopes. Benjamin's description in his book of reminiscences is thick with the haze of childhood perceptions. The Tiergarten park was unknowable, a place full of secret corners, heard of but never discovered.

Although Lenné authored the plans for the Tiergarten that still exists today, he did not oversee its final execution. Frustrated by small-minded Prussian civil servants who quibbled over paperwork, withheld payments and objected to even the slightest of deviations from procedures stated in the plans, he resigned in 1838. By this time in any case, his interest in landscape had expanded to take in urban planning of a socially orientated kind. A visit to England in 1822, which at that time was further along the one-way road to industrialization, convinced him that the pressures of city life must be alleviated through light, air and greenery. From then on, he designated himself a "garden engineer." As the population expanded, more than doubling between 1820 and 1848 to reach over 400,000, Lenné imagined a city designed to counteract these pressures. In 1840 he presented a grandly titled plan to the Interior Ministry: "Radial Geometry, Synthesis of City and Landscape, and Decorative Border Areas for the Royal Seat Berlin." This was his vision of a lush garden city that would accommodate and care for its ever-growing citizenry.

The central aspect of Lenné's grand plan was the canalization of the Landwehr Ditch. This would drain the marshlands in the southeast, alleviate the busiest part of the river Spree, and provide a comfortable means of transport for the city's expanding industries. The canal was to follow the meandering form of a natural riverbed, accompanied by avenues of trees and greenery. Once again, the waterways were the soul of Lenné's plan.

Running six and a half miles long, the Landwehr Canal was to be lined by a broad shaded boulevard with double rows of trees, 5,518 of which were to be planted along its length:

On Köpenicker Feld 888 lime trees, up to
Potsdamer Chaussee 1240 lime trees and 1240
elms, from Potsdamer Chaussee to Zoologischer
Garten 534 buckeye chestnuts and 534 oak trees,
up to Charlottenburger Chaussee 151 limes and
151 elms, and up to the opening into the Spree 390
silver poplars and 390 sweet chestnuts.

A sketch from 1846, creased and yellowing along its
folds, stamped with Lenné's official Royal Gardener
seal, shows two options for the planting along the westerly banks of the Tempelhofer Ufer, where my house
later would be built. In aerial view and cross-section,
rows of trees and borders of low shrubs are finely
drawn and shaded in pale washes of green and brown.
No tarmac surface or relentless traffic, just a soft dirt
track and peaceful shade beneath which to walk along
the water's edge.

The Landwehr Canal was opened to waterborne
traffic in September 1850. In less than a decade, the
tranquil waterlogged scene that Menzel had depicted
was replaced by the bustling and active waterways of a
city in the making.

In search of more of Menzel's drawings from this period of Berlin's development, I visit the library of the

Kupferstichkabinett, which holds the drawing collection of the Gemäldegalerie, the museum for paintings near to Potsdamer Platz. It is a short bike ride from my home: left up the canal, past two bridges and over the third, the Potsdamer Bridge, that leads to the Kulturforum. This cluster of museums was planned in the mid-1980s to house the portion of the city's art collection that had ended up in West Berlin's hands. It was only finished in the late 1990s, however, by which point the lay of the land had changed irreversibly. Unlike the stately steel and glass modernism of the Neue Nationalgalerie at the nearby canal corner, there is something oddly municipal about these brick buildings set back off the main street, huddling behind the car park that surrounds the nineteenth-century St. Matthäus Church. It is always surprising to find the phenomenal collection of Cranachs, Holbeins, Van Eycks and Rubens sequestered in their lower halls.

A man in a white lab coat behind the desk in the Drawings' Department Library informs me that they have Menzel's entire estate. Over 900 drawings in all. What is it that I want to see? I am looking for early works, from 1840 to 1860, but the lab-coated man tells me that the collection is arranged by subject, not chronology. It's hard to say what subjects I am looking for. Local landscapes? Buildings? Trees? Vague energetic undercurrents? There are four archive boxes of trees alone, the lab coat tells me as he looks up 'Landwehr Canal' in his computer database. One drawing appears with this tag, so he orders the box that this is in. I suggest some other themes – architecture, railways, interiors – and additional boxes are ordered. Ten minutes later, another white-lab-coated assistant wheels in a trolley laden with cardboard archive boxes, each containing a stack of drawings mounted on thick mats. He lifts the first box from the trolley and sets it on the desk in front of me. Number 167: the label reads *Leichen, Gefangene* – Corpses, Prisoners.

I unlatch the small brass hook and open the box. The very first drawing on the top of the stack shows a man kneeling on a flat barge, his clothes and moustaches pencilled in dark, hoisting a naked body up out of the water with what looks like a giant pair of forceps. Beside him another man, sketched in quick pencil lines, steadies the boat with a long wooden pole. Only the back of the corpse's head, covered in dark hair, and one of its shoulders, washed in watercolor pink, are visible above the water's surface. The drawing is titled, dated and signed: *Kanal, 1862, A.M.* Below this is a close-up sketch of the dead man. He lies on the shore amongst tufts of grass, his head turned to the side and eyes closed, as if enjoying a nap on the canal's green shore. The next drawing in the box shows the bargeman now on the canal banks, hauling the garish pink body beneath its outstretched arms, like a carcass of meat. Another page of rapid studies captures the two men's movements as they lift the dead weight of the third. At the top left corner, in a barely legible script, are notes scrawled by Menzel: "As soon as the corpse was brought to the shore, it stood upright, probably because of the current, stooping slightly with its head hanging forwards."

There is something enthralling about this forensic attention with its pre-photographic compulsion to bear witness. I imagine Adolph Menzel, an unusually short man, only four and a half feet tall, stout in his frock coat, walking along the canal on the outskirts of the city, with sketchbooks, pencils, watercolors stuffed into his pockets. (Did he add color to the sketched corpse then and there, I wonder, or touch it up afterwards when he got home?) Drawings in the other boxes, labelled *Landscapes* or *Places: B* describe his appetite for other low-key kinds of human drama, beyond the tragedy of a drowned man.

There may not be much photographic evidence of this time, but Menzel's early realist works are vivid visual documents. Beyond the depictions for which he is best known – of the court of King Wilhelm I, who succeeded his brother Friedrich Wilhelm IV in 1861 – there are countless incidental pieces that depict a city being made and how it is inhabited. In one of the boxes is a drawing from 1846 that shows St. Matthäus Church being built, the church that stands in the car park, that I passed on my way to the library. In Menzel's sketch, the blocky form of the church is supported by a sketched-in grid of wooden scaffolding. A great many pencil sketches show builders sleeping, lying with arms folded on scaffolding planks, napping in their breeches beside wooden handled buckets. As I sort through these stacks of thickly mounted drawings, enthralled by the particularity of Menzel's chosen vantage point, the bells of St. Matthäus Church strike midday, their chimes reverberating back through a century and a half.

A whole theater of incident can be found in the countless peripheral details that Menzel captures in his work. Laundry washing, iron rolling, train travel, beds, bicycles, musical instruments, the countryside beyond the city's walls. These pencil drawings, gouaches and sketches picture Menzel's daily journeys, which follow a meandering, diversionary logic to see what the streets and rural lanes could offer up by way of subject matter, in parts of the city still to be built. Backyards and alleyways, gates and fences that border on scrubby unkempt brushlands, areas that ambiguously straddle both urban and rural, where the city seems to lie in wait, gathering on the horizon, like a missive from the future.

———

"The population was swimming in the frenzy of progress and was almost only concerned with locomotives, steamships and other technical achievements," reads Peter Joseph Lenné's biography, written in 1937 by a fellow landscape architect. "Only a few men, of whom Lenné was one, understood and endeavored to counteract this development, and to preserve the citizens' most precious cultural assets, amongst them the German landscape. [..] He aimed to maintain the organic structure of the city, but he had underestimated the extreme pace of its rapid – and unhealthy – development."

Lenné's prioritization of landscape over practical efficiency fell foul again of the Prussian purse-string holders. He called for a higher water level in the Landwehr Canal, in part to prevent the Tiergarten's pools and lakes from stagnating and suffusing the *Volksgarten* with their foul stench, but also to protect its oldest trees, some eight-hundred-year-old oaks among them. His recommendations were disregarded, but despite this compromise, the Landwehr Canal is one of the few elements of Lenné's original city plan that was completed and remains visible and in use now, a century and a half later.

Journalist and writer Franz Hessel, close friend and colleague of Benjamin, devotes a chapter of his 1929 book *Walking in Berlin* to the Landwehr Canal. He begins with a picturesque image which follows the waterway as it "meanders through so much urban idyll that its name has a placid ring in our ears." Hessel, like Benjamin, spent his childhood in the late 1800s in the Tiergarten area, by which time the Landwehr Canal was known as the "green shore." It provided a liquid seam between the city's urban and rural aspects, and was crossed by bridges "as if they were crossing a garden stream."

> At the Cornelius Bridge, the park landscape of the garden banks transforms into a city landscape. And the atmosphere in this area, which combines a whiff of park, city and water, displays a subtle wealth of colors seldom found in Berlin's greyish contours. For anyone who spent their childhood in Berlin, no sunrise over the mountains or sunset at the lake can outshine the sweet dawns and dusks over the canal's spring and autumn foliage.

This wealth of colors, these sweet dawns and dusks, were what Lenné envisioned when he ordered 5,500 trees to be planted along the canal's banks. And now, more than ninety years after Hessel's homage, the whiff of park, city and water remains. From my front-facing windows, despite two lanes of traffic on each side of the water, I can see over a dozen different species of trees, each one a different shape, a different leaf, a different shade of green that turns a different gold or red once summer slowly fades. Are they lime trees? Elms? Or buckeye chestnuts? A surprising variety of insects gathers on the ledges of windows tilted open to catch a breeze. In the cooler months when the trees are bare, bright pairs of swans glide upstream. As it was for Hessel, this green shore is the backdrop to my sons' own childhood, but also to my daily working life. When we moved across the city, I gave up the little rented room in which I used to write, and returned to the conflicted discipline of working from home. The last of the four rooms that faces the canal, one wall of which is lined floor to ceiling with books, is where I write. A few months after moving in, I turned the table away from the window to face the bookshelves instead. The view was far too distracting. But by then it was too late; the view had become my subject.

## · 2 ·

# Witness

*The second summer* in the new apartment, the boys delivered to their father for his share of the holidays, I decide to walk the canal's banks. We are still adjusting to the disjointed format of our newly broken family, my anguish at being now only a part-time mother. It helps to have a clearly formed task, with well-defined start and endpoints, to give the day some shape. So on a warm July mid-morning, I leave the house, cross over the two lanes of traffic to reach the canal banks, and turn right along the Ufer. For the first stretch, road and water run parallel and are joined by the overhead U-Bahn train line, held up on welded iron struts. At the fifth bridge, now well into Kreuzberg, the road and train tracks veer to the left, while the canal path carries straight on, becoming quieter and more bucolic. Five minutes further and it widens out in front of the Urban Hospital, with grassy verges expanding into spacious slopes where people picnic, or couples sit at the water's edge, drinking beer from bottles. In the water, swans gather in extended family groups, chivvying and griping, or preening their feathers with singular dedication. Deeper into Kreuzberg, three arms of water meet in a node that opens into a triangular lake. This is the endpoint of the Landwehr Canal. Here I cross over the final bridge and return home along its eastern bank.

Three days later, I walk in the opposite direction: along the western bank, into the Tiergarten, cutting through the zoo itself, with sneak views into the pens of gazelles and aviaries of exotic birds, and on towards Charlottenburg. At the end, the canal joins the river Spree in another triangular node, and I cross over to return home along the opposite bank. These excursions are an attempt to bear witness, to plot a walked experience onto my poring over printed maps, sifting through online entries, or reading up on history. I take dozens of pictures with my phone, of iron bridges, graffiti-scrawled statues, memorial plaques, railway tracks, trees and grassy slopes, the swans gathered on the water's surface, the mute body of water itself, held within its tight concrete banks. But the experience turns out to be strangely flat. The canal and its pathways are just there, being used. The banks and bridges are simply integral parts of the city's terrain and traffic networks. My over-projection and desire for narrative or revelation, for some significant crossing of paths, are in vain. The most stirring moment comes when I pass an impressive old tree on the west banks, up near the Tiergarten. There aren't so many trees of this age and grandeur to be found in Berlin. Of the park's 200,000 trees, only 700 survived the devastation of the Second World War and its aftermath, when firewood was scarce. This one did: a two-hundred-year-old *Stieleiche*, or English oak, singled out with a sign that identifies it as a "Natural Memorial." An elderly German couple passing by joins me in my admiration. *"Oh, das ist ja ein Baum!"* declares the man to his walking partner. "Now that is a tree!"

A little farther up, just before the Liechtenstein Bridge where the canal weaves through the beginnings of the Tiergarten, I come across another sign. A bronze plaque of commemoration, marking not survival but disappearance. "The passionate socialist Rosa Luxemburg died as the victim of a treacherous political murder," read its blocky raised letters.

*Es schwimmt eine Leiche im Landwehrkanal,*
*Lang se mir mal her,*
*aber knautsch sie nich zu sehr*

"A corpse is swimming in the Landwehr Canal. Shove her over here, but mind you don't crush her." The corpse in this popular Weimar song is that of Rosa Luxemburg. On January 15, 1919, following the violent suppression of the Spartacist uprising, just two weeks after the formation of Germany's Communist Party, its leaders, Rosa Luxemburg and Karl Liebknecht, were arrested by members of the *Freikorps*, private right-wing militias that emerged following the First World War. They were brought to the Hotel Eden, one of the city's finest hotels, not far from the canal's Cornelius Bridge.

The bar at the Hotel Eden was one of the most elegant in the city, a celebrated meeting place for writers, actors and artists. "Chris, darling, you'll take me as far as the Eden, won't you?" asks Sally Bowles of Christopher Isherwood a decade later in *Goodbye to Berlin*. "Although we had only a few hundred yards to go, Sally insisted that we must take a taxi. It would never do, she explained, to arrive at the Eden on foot."

The Eden was also the headquarters of the Cavalry Guards Defense Division, a notorious unit of the *Freikorps*. These clandestine, thuggish networks, hoarding secret caches of weapons smuggled from the First World War, were "breeding grounds for an officer type steeled in discipline and obedience to the Kaiser," as Klaus Theweleit writes in his 1977 book *Male Fantasies*. Theweleit adopts the term "soldier males" to describe the *Freikorps* and their subsequent legacy of Nazi supporters. These "incurable militarists had always been acceptable to Weimar governments when it came to 'protecting' the 'republic' against the Left." The government, wary of surging Communist sympathy, became adept at the turning of a blind eye to a bullet in the head, or a lifeless body thrown into the canal in the dead of night.

After hours of interrogation and physical abuse in the Hotel Eden, Karl Liebknecht was driven to the Tiergarten and shot in the back near the banks of Lenné's Neuen See. Rosa Luxemburg was beaten unconscious with a rifle butt, shot in the head and thrown into the Landwehr Canal. Her body disappeared and was only discovered months later, on June 1, 1919, floating in the water. All the while that English oak looked on, a stoic witness on the banks.

What does it mean to be a witness, to see something firsthand, to look straight on and not turn away? "Witnessing," says the dictionary, is "the action of bearing witness or giving testimony." To give evidence, to be a spectator or auditor of something. "To see with one's own eyes." In German, the word for witness, *Zeuge*, or eyewitness, *Augenzeuge*, is related to *ziehen*, the verb "to pull." *Die vor Gericht gezogene Person* is the person brought before the law. The word suggests a legal demand, of testimony before an audience. But witnessing can also be a private act. The writer of a diary bears witness to the events, people, thoughts and feelings that coalesce to form a day. Menzel, Benjamin, Hessel and Isherwood all assume the role of witness, recording evidence of time and place for an unknown future audience. The incremental details that by then have disappeared. But it is harder to find the woman's view, the female testimony of the changing city. The words of the sisters that Menzel painted, or the wives of Hessel and Benjamin, who also witnessed the city firsthand as it rolled on through decades of industrialization, heading towards the chaos of war.

I cast myself in the role of the witness, giving testimony of this canal bank, this piece of history. I record things as evidence, to make sense of the visible, of this material, and witness what is there. But also to try to identify those weights and whispers whose presence cannot be seen with the eyes. To pin down the ambiguous forces that influence this place. "Berlin resists me," I find written in diary pages typed into my computer. "So hard to integrate into its flow. To even do anything. The city has no flow. Sinks into the sand and is forgotten. So many daily lives."

*"Es schwimmt eine Leiche im Landwehrkanal . . ."* I first came across this song, referred to as "that horrible old sing-song," in the wartime diaries of an "anonymous woman" in Berlin, written supposedly during the last days of the Second World War in April 1945. The woman has just heard from a Russian soldier, Anatol, whom she has befriended as a necessary protectorate (albeit at a price), that the battle's front lines have reached the canal.

> Anatol brings news that the front is now at the Landwehr Canal, and I can't help but think of that horrible old sing-song. Many more corpses will be lying in it now. Anatol reckons that 130 generals have surrendered in the last few days. He pulls a map of Berlin out of a cellophane bag, and shows us the front line on it. It is a very precise map, written in Russian. I have a strange feeling as now, on Anatol's request, I show him where our house is.

I recognize this strange feeling, as I place my finger on the map where my own house is now and was throughout these years: on the banks of the Landwehr Canal, at the front line of the war's final street battles. Intrigued by this chilling fact, I begin thumbing around on the internet, looking up more references. That's when I stumble across a mention of the flood. At the end of April

1945, the "North-South Tunnel," an S-Bahn train tunnel that runs beneath the canal, was purposefully flooded. An eyewitness, who lived on my very street, is quoted in the Wikipedia article.

> Witness "Frau R." lived on Tempelhofer Ufer. From there she saw corpses floating in the Landwehr Canal, at least a thousand altogether. A whirlpool had developed at the point of the explosion that pulled the corpses out of the tunnel and into the Landwehr Canal.

The chronology around this time is confusing. Above ground was the chaos of battle. Below ground thousands of residents crouched in bunkers or cellars for days on end. The Anhalter air raid shelter, a vast concrete block of a building on the other side of the canal from my house, was sheltering over 10,000 people. On April 25, 1945, the Red Army advanced along the Landwehr Canal's west bank, approaching Schöneberger Bridge from the south. The waters separated them from the governmental buildings on the other side. The following day, all of the bridges were blown up by German mobile forces, but two days later the Soviets found a way to cross, climbing the ruins of the elevated railway at Möckern Bridge. The Soviet soldiers would have marched straight past my house, which lies between the

Möckern and Schöneberger Bridges, as they searched for a means to traverse the water.

Some days later, around May 1 or 2, the ceiling of the North-South Tunnel beneath the canal was blown up, flooding its entire length. The details around this action remain vague and controversial. It has not been determined on whose command the tunnel was blown up, and if its consequences were known beforehand. For while ostensibly preventing the Red Army's access to the city center through these underground passage-ways, the subsidiary effect was to drown hundreds, if not thousands, of civilians seeking shelter from the street fighting and air raids overhead. The tunnels were the only safe way to reach the Anhalter air raid shelter from the water's west side. The thousand bodies float-ing in the Landwehr Canal that eyewitness Frau R. re-ported seeing were the bodies of these civilians.

The report comes from a book published in 1992 by the Kreuzberg District Authorities, which I track down and order immediately. In it, a grainy badly printed black-and-white photograph shows an enormous hunk of broken concrete erupting from the street surface, jutting up in a weird triangle above a gaping hole. The massive blast ripped the ground apart. The photo-graph's caption reads: "at the point of the explosion, the concrete roofs of the South Tunnel flew meters high up into the air, and when they fell back down they propped each other up." In the picture, the little figure of a man in a hat stands on top of this heap of blasted concrete. The point of the explosion, where the tunnels ran under the water, is only a few hundred meters downriver from my house, at the corner of the next side street.

Which house did Frau R. live in on the Tempelhofer Ufer? Was it upstream or downstream from mine? Or was it maybe mine? By that point one of only three buildings left standing on this block? In the online entry, another witness is quoted, on June 11, 1945: "such an unbearable stench is coming from the Landwehr Canal that anyone who passes has to cover his nose with a handkerchief."

# Plot

*The view that my window* frames is an extraction, but not exactly a slice through time. Rather it cuts across a different axis, to examine the continuity of place. If I were to flip it from the vertical to a horizontal plane, the rectangular field it pegs out could be an archaeological site of sorts, to dig into with the imagination, and sift its contents for nuggets of the past. For experiences that have disappeared and left no physical trace behind, except for atmospheric inklings that may linger around an edifice, pavement or park. Through what means can these remnants of the past be gleaned, to map out lost potential?

In our house on Tempelhofer Ufer, the third-floor kitchen window looks out over treetops that line the canal at a spread of urban architecture that recedes into the distance. You rarely see people on the street below, just a constant flow of cars, or summer tour boats on the water, marking their passage with a three-pitch chime, while birds cut paths through the sky. Most buildings in Berlin look onto line-ups of identical buildings directly across the street. But here the view is wide and open, intersected by individual architectures, each a remnant of a different era, laid out one behind another. The last is the Rote Rathaus, the redbrick city hall at Alexanderplatz in the east, a flag fluttering on its tiny spire, like the checkered flag at a finishing line.

It is a lush, sunny day at the end of May, after a whole string of days like this, when I make my way down the canal to the Land Registry Office. I am hoping to find a way into the actual story of our house and its surroundings, details that can't be found casually in internet entries or minor incidents of literature. A gentle breeze wafts along the water, bringing an unusual sense of movement. The Land Registry Office is nearby, on Möckernstraße, just across the Möckern Bridge over whose remains the Soviets clambered during the last days of the Second World War. Frau Lier, the registrar, has agreed to show me the building's files, as I am a partial owner of the property. When she asks why I want to see them, I tell her I'm a writer, which seems to be enough.

After retrieving the relevant files from the basement, Frau Lier hands over a pile of folders. A thin one
on the top with the most recent information, and two
thick folders, bulging with papers, their faded green
covers strapped together with grey woven cord. It is
thrilling to be handed a pile of papers like this, the
moment when the search begins. Will I find something
that rings a bell? A clue that opens up a pathway? This
search depends on vague currents of curiosity, on being
alert and extending the senses like tentacles, to per-
ceive, attach, interpret.

I take the stack of folders from Frau Lier and sit
down at the table opposite a window that looks into a
screen of dense green foliage on Möckernstraße. It is
jarring on opening the first folder to find my own name,
alongside that of my now ex-husband, in contracts of
sale and fat notarized documents. This isn't what I'm
after. I loosen the grey woven band holding together
the two other folders, removing it quickly. According
to Frau Lier, the papers date back to 1967, but a document right on the top is from 1943. It is signed by Bruno
Sala, the owner of the building at that time, proprietor
of A. Sala-Spiele, a luxury paper and printing company.
Dated January 22, 1943, it is his last will and testament. His wife Charlotte is to inherit it all. She and the
child they both adopted on July 31, 1942, an eight-year-
old daughter named Melitta. It has begun, I am here

already, thick into the past and a family history. The story of the house and a mysterious girl, adopted at the height of the Second World War.

A slim red folder underneath contains more loose documents which date back further, to the 1930s. One is a typed-out letter on a sheet of company letterhead. *A. Sala: Fabrik und Verlag der Sala-Spiele mit Rotsiegel*: "A. Sala: Factory and Publisher of Sala Games with the Red Seal," founded in 1845. Fitting for a high-end paper and printing company, the letterhead itself is elaborately designed and printed. Filling the top third of the page, alongside the details of the company's contact details in many different fonts, is a picture of the building on Tempelhofer Ufer, finely drawn and neatly printed. An aerial view from a sidelong perspective that shows the four-story street-front residential building, with a print-works beyond a courtyard planted with trees, a tall chimney piping out a trail of smoke. Trees line the street out front as well, while tiny people amble by in groups of twos or threes. A single figure beside two smaller ones stands by the entrance of the house, directly below the third-floor kitchen window. The window that I stand and look out of, now seen from the outside looking in.

There is little more to be found here about the building itself, however, and Frau Lier suggests I try the

Department of Buildings instead. So I make an appointment at the Chamber of Building Records and some weeks later I am settling at a table with two large box files and three additional folders, all related to our house, as Kreuzberg sun streams through the windows.

The first of the box files contains three further folders, the papers in them crisp and browned with time. As I leaf the first folder open, again I feel a thrill, not of the unknown this time, but the thrill of history. The inked cursive writing on the documents it contains dates back over a century and a half. The first mention of this plot of land on the Tempelhofer Ufer is a paper signed and dated *Zimmermann, Berlin, 27 June 1858*, a deed of ownership. A few months later, in November 1858, a request is submitted to build a three-floor residential building, centrally placed on the trapezoid plot. It is signed, again by Herr Zimmermann, whose occupation is noted as *Hofbäckermeister*, Master Baker to the Court. In another document, this one from 1860, Herr Zimmermann is seeking permission to build a stable for his horses. In 1862 comes a proposal for a workshop. By this time, he is no longer *Hofbäckermeister*, however, but rather *Holzhändler Zimmermann*, a dealer in wood. At some point in this four-year period, Herr Zimmermann made the transition from baker to wood dealer. During these years of rampant construction, wood was no doubt more lucrative than bread. Just think of all of Menzel's sketches, of bricklayers working on wooden scaffolds, with wooden buckets or wooden carts. Or the backyards with all their wooden fences and lines of fluttering laundry. Of Berlin being built by the barge.

That the first man to build on this plot of land was named *Zimmermann* seems uncannily apposite. A *Zimmermann* is a carpenter, but whereas the English word originates as a maker of cars, or chariots, its German equivalent means a maker of rooms, or *Zimmer*. "That's beautiful, isn't it?" remarks artist and poet Jimmie Durham, in a book about his own late-twentieth-century sojourn in Berlin. "This man is not making walls; they are only incidental. He is making the space within the walls." Herr Zimmermann, former Master Baker to the Court, has become, since his move to this oddly shaped plot of land, a maker of rooms in the most literal of senses. These rooms are made here on the banks of the Landwehr Canal, as all around them the city starts to grow.

In another folder in the archive, I find the original plans of the building that I live in now; drawings from 1869 that inked these rooms onto large, thin sheets of folded paper, before its bricks were laid. Submitted this time by the *Gebrüder Zimmermann* – the brothers Hermann August Emil and Carl Ferdinand Emil – the plans inscribe an architectural reconfiguration that reflects the changing cityscape. Their previous modest house, centrally placed on the generous plot, along with adjacent stable and workshop, are all razed to make way for a handsome four-story apartment building, set right on the property's front edge. Its style prefigures what came to be known as Berlin's *Gründerzeit*, or founding years. After 1871, as the capital of a newly unified Germany with a population increasing rapidly year on year, apartment buildings like this were appearing all over Berlin. Four floors high with a series of windows spread out across the front façade, and a side wing leading to a back courtyard, and often another courtyard beyond. The owners and more prosperous tenants would live in the brighter, generously proportioned front apartments, while the narrower, darker side wings surrounding the courtyard would be rented out to the lower classes, or used as factories and workshops for cottage industries. These were the notorious and much maligned *Berliner Mietskasernen*, Berlin's tenement barracks. Their very structure was designed to reinforce social stratification. But the city's rapidly expanding population had to be housed, and these imposing apartment buildings were adopted as the most efficient solution.

Judging by Zimmermann's plans, the house has changed little in the decades between then and now. In this building that has stood here on the canal banks since 1869, the sun begins each day shining brightly into the front rooms and by lunchtime it has circled around to glance diagonally into the room at the corner, before sidling into the side wing in the mid to late afternoon. The rooms, their layout, this pattern of illumination, all remain the same. But how did their inhabitation come to affect them over time? What kinds of experience rubbed off onto their unchanging geometries?

The corner room, the one that receives a brief angle of sun around midday, is called the *Berliner Zimmer*, or Berlin room. Typical of houses from this time, it forms the meeting point between the rooms at the front of the house, and the perpendicular side wing that looks onto the backyard. The *Berliner Zimmer* tends to be gloomy, with only a single window angled onto the central courtyard. A dim space for passing through. The *Berliner Zimmer* in Zimmermann's house was unusually impressive, however. Not just because of its large scale and lofty ceiling, over three meters high, but because it is an octagon. Settled on an angular plot of land, this building's side wing is not perpendicular, but turns in at an acute angle. The result is not only an eccentric octagonal centerpiece, but also other minor peculiarities that appear throughout the building. Hallways that end in strange tapering triangles, and lines of sight that appear symmetrical but do not in fact match up.

"We saw a new apartment yesterday," I find written in my diary notes. "It may be something. It's odd. It has potential. It is right on the canal and looks onto a crazy Berlin tapestry of different roofs and buildings. It's strange, perhaps a little spooky. A huge balcony looking out onto the street. It's exciting. We'll see."

Looking back now, I realize how naive I was, that day in November 2012 when we first came to see the apartment on Tempelhofer Ufer. The building was painted a garish orange back then, with the name *A. SALA* in capital letters above the arched entrance to the backyard. Apartments like this were hard to find: a spacious top floor flat in an *Altbau*, or old building, that was, most importantly, unrenovated. The photographs on the online real estate portal showed dull images of rooms with worn-out floorboards and oddly arranged pieces of furniture. I took the dinginess of these pictures to be a good sign. And it overlooked the canal, as the estate agent confirmed when I called him on the phone. We climbed the stairs to the third floor and the agent let us in. Four front-facing rooms, arranged in an impressive enfilade with interconnecting panelled wing doors, were all empty save piles of cardboard boxes stacked up in the center. Faded and musty but grandly proportioned, the rooms seemed full of potential. I gravitated immediately towards the windows and looked down at the water.

Cross-referencing the date of this first visit with diary entries from the time, I realize now with a dull thud that it came at an absolute low point in our home life, although we couldn't see it then. I was trying to finish a book. My husband was constantly travelling for work. Through these absences we lost sight of each other. Was this really family life? I had imagined the family as a delicate system of counterbalances, the buoyancy of one part requiring the fixity of the other, in a revolving state of mutual reciprocity. Instead, the divisions of responsibility that had found their place so naturally at the start had now hardened into fault lines. At some point, without realizing, I had lost my way. Like the women at the school gate that I read about once in a line from a poem that I never forgot but never found again – women sidelined in their own lives. A sequence of frustrations, disappointments and evasions had led to a pervasive silence that thickened and filled the space between us. And then we went to see the apartment.

A month later it came to a head. Between conversations about the new place – should we take it, or shouldn't we? – I broached the subject of our happiness. My husband's answer, remote and dulled, seemed dredged up from an ocean bed. *Ich bin nicht unzufrieden.* I am not unsatisfied. So many things were left unsaid.

Even at this point in time, in a society that has come so far, the difference Marguerite Duras delineated between a house and a home still remains the default. "The woman is the home," she writes, while as for men, "they can build houses but they can't make homes." Any alternative scenario requires concerted effort, attention, negotiation, reiteration. I – we – chose to avoid this effort and took the easy, off-the-shelf option. I looked after home and children, and the mass of loose ends that a family generates, squeezing my work in around the edges. He provided the stable income, was free to travel and grow his business. He built the house, so to speak, and sometimes did the shopping. As his buoyancy increased, so with it did my fixity. And locked in this state of imbalance, we drifted into a mutual dependency. Unhappy but not unsatisfied.

To me the new apartment seemed ridiculous, overdimensional, too much. But despite that, despite all of it, as if on a parallel track focused only on potential – of both house and home – we decided to go ahead. We bought the apartment, and it became our project. A surrogate through which to mask the void between us. Hours were spent pacing rooms, drawing up plans, consulting architects, making calculations. Months were devoted to the process, finishes sought, details agreed on, decisions upon decisions taken. Immaculate attention was paid to proportion, surface, appearance. It was just what we wanted. Wasn't it?

I put the apartment's eerie atmosphere down at first to its drabness. Its worn-out wood floors and greying paintwork. Or its lack of consistent inhabitation over the past few years. It was a superficial problem, a temporary setback that renovation would resolve. We opened up one wall and closed off another. Laid rough oak boards and poured concrete floors. The bathroom was fitted with rose-veined marble. Brass handles were attached to window frames, newly painted glossy white. The troubling undertone would disappear, I was sure, once all this work was finished, when we moved in and filled the rooms with life.

The apartment we finally moved into was certainly beautiful, but it was too brittle to support a family in crisis. The excessive care accorded its surfaces outbalanced the lack of attention to a relationship going under. Plus, it was far too big. According to the principles of feng shui, a house should be moderately sized: "neither too big nor too small. A small house with too many people living in it is not recommended. Neither is a large house with only few people." How could we, a family of four and two black cats, hope to fill up all these numerous and spacious rooms with life?

We moved in. I couldn't sleep. It felt uncomfortable. The side wing hallway that led to our bedroom seemed so interminably long. I christened it the Corridor of Misery. I kept coming up with new solutions to resolve what I thought were the apartment's problems. A curtain, a mirror, a built-in bookshelf. But within six months, precipitated by the pool of water on the kitchen floor, issues and undercurrents were forced into the open. Well-kept secrets rose up and made themselves apparent. Damp bruises of distrust and neglect became suddenly visible. Welled resentments burst their banks. The elegant new apartment played host to this domestic drama, providing backdrops for conventional arguments played out across the kitchen table, or late-night phone calls in the moonlit bedroom once the children were asleep. "Renovations cause more stress on a marriage than having a newborn child," I read in an online article. Twelve per cent of home renovations end, it says, in divorce.

———

It was the water damage that led me to consult Parvati, a feng shui master living in Berlin. By that point, six separate incidents had taken place, each in a different area of the apartment and each unrelated to the other. But I also just wanted some advice about domestic rearrangements, a second opinion to underscore the decisions I was now making on my own. Our initial attempt at living here had quickly run aground, and I was left rattling around the rooms of this oversized apartment, with two bewildered children and two indifferent pets. Perhaps a ritual would help, to mark a new beginning?

Parvati arrived on a Thursday morning, late, as she hadn't been able to find the house. She had walked straight past it twice, despite the fact that its number is displayed prominently on the façade. Indeed, the house is often overlooked; it seems to exist in a GPS black spot, as if it isn't even there. When I opened the door to Parvati, a bright-eyed German woman in her fifties dressed in loosely fitting clothes, with a halo of wispy brown hair and a breathy voice, I was expecting her to advise me on the correct placement of bedheads and angles of mirrors, or optimal areas for working and resting. But as we walked together through each room, her observations were not to do with arrangements of objects, but rather to do with atmospheres. How, primarily, the energy felt. She analyzed the symptoms as if the apartment were a body. It was clear to her that this body was sick.

The *Berliner Zimmer* most troubled Parvati. There wasn't much furniture in here – a saggy black sofa and leather armchairs on a Persian carpet in front of the TV, and a sideboard along one wall – but nonetheless it was hard to navigate. Your pace slowed down when passing through and a heaviness seemed to drag the legs. The air had a strange density as if clogged with some kind of subtle matter. Coagulated particles that gave the room a slight grey cast and occluded the view outside the window. Parvati's diagnosis had less to do with visual phenomena than some other ambiguous sensory territory that picked up on resistance and currents. Whether the symptoms were apparent or not depended on one's general sensitivity, and willingness to believe.

It was in the *Berliner Zimmer* that Parvati first mentioned the past. This heaviness, the denseness of the air, was because the rooms were already occupied. This was why it was hard for us to live here now. Unresolved historical incidents meant the apartment was still inhabited. Inhabitation is not the same as haunting, but it did mean that the space was not free. When I mentioned the water damage, she was not at all surprised. In feng shui terms, persistent leaking is a sign of trauma. Something that happened in the past has not been healed, it is as if the house is weeping.

## · 4 ·

# Watercourse

*The Chinese do not regard feng shui* as being super-
stitious but rather as a "science of observation," I read
in *Five Classics of Fengshui*, a translation into English of
five ancient Chinese texts. Its basis is always the site.
"There is no place where Man resides which is not a site.
When bad siting is stabilized, misfortune will cease just
like the effect of medicine on illness. Therefore siting is
the basis of human life." The discipline began with the
placement of graves in mountainous regions, and was
later applied to buildings. But whether graves for the
dead or buildings for the living, it all comes down to
"auspicious siting." Feng shui developed over time into
a macrogeography that reads the landscape like a book
and links the fortunes of humanity with the nature of

their environment. Both depend on fertility brought about by the interaction of moisture-laden wind (*feng*) with mountains to create water (*shui*) and topsoil. Meanwhile *qi*, or chi, meaning air or breath, is considered the origin of the universe. "The heavy and stable *qi* coagulated to become the earth. The light and unstable *qi* rose to create the sky. The *qi* of the earth and the sky met and became yin and yang." The painterly symmetry of this image appeals to me, but my real draw to feng shui lies in its practice of paying close attention.

The aim of this geomantic tradition is practical: to balance energy flows. Yin and yang, conflict and equilibrium, gain and loss, all involve cyclical movements of energy. "Spring and summer are yang, which thrusts upwards and outwards when energy is expended, and autumn and winter are yin, because the tendency of nature in these seasons is inwards and downwards, contracting and storing energy," writes British author Leslie Wilson, describing her encounters with feng shui when living in Hong Kong in the early 1980s. "Chi can be blown away or leak away, but a site must be sufficiently open for it to flow in." It is a question of fine-tuning: chi must be free to move, but should not disappear. "The ideal position for a house is on a well-drained but gentle slope, sheltered from high winds but open to breezes. A watercourse in front of the site is desirable, but only if the configuration is auspicious."

When we moved to this apartment, I had thought that living on the water would offer access to a current, but the watercourses around here are not known for their energetic flows. The river Spree, of which the Landwehr Canal is a man-made tributary, meanders in 400 kilometers of inconclusive curves from the eastern borders of Germany with Poland and the Czech Republic, to its outlet in Spandau in the west of Berlin. Unlike the rivers Thames, Hudson or Seine, there is no notion of being north or south of the river in Berlin, no left or right bank that defines the character of a neighborhood. When you cross one of the twenty-eight bridges along the length of the Spree, you barely register the body of water beneath you. "It doesn't connect, it doesn't separate; it is simply a watercourse which no one really thinks about," wrote Karl Scheffler, one of Berlin's foremost grumbling apologists, in his 1910 book *Berlin: Ein Stadtschicksal* [Berlin: The Fate of a City]. Its already very low average flow of only nine cubic meters per second along its entire length drops to a mere four cubic meters per second when it reaches the city. This slow-moving body of water is close to the point of stagnation. In 2003 in Köpenick, on the eastern edges of Berlin, the river Spree was reported to be flowing backwards.

In Berlin, the sluggardly flow of the river is countered only by the vicious thrust of the wind rushing in from the east, blowing unhindered across the flat land. Slopes, gentle or otherwise, are few and far between. In feng shui terms, this is a terrible place to plant a city. Scheffler considers this question of site: "If you trace the separate awkwardnesses of the City Plan back to their root causes, then the essential cause of all failures and ugliness can be found in the fact that Berlin did not grow organically like a plant, but like an artificially founded establishment. [...] That is why every lively feeling of beauty and nature is missing." The *Urstromtal*, or glacial valley, in which Berlin is sited, was carved out in the last Ice Age when outflowing meltwaters, trailing sand and gravel, left behind them a pockmarked landscape of lakes and water channels. "In Berlin, the underground water is the menace that is hard to control and hard to define as a watercourse," declared a speaker in an international feng shui conference held in Berlin in 2010. These marshlands, exposed and inhospitable, were settled by Slavs in the first centuries A.D. and remained a stable and prosperous Slavic stronghold until the twelfth century. By then, German Christians around the river Elbe and Catholic Poles who controlled the river Oder, were squeezing heathen Berlin in a pincer movement, until it finally fell in 1157 to a knight known as "Albert the Bear."

New York is built on solid bedrock. The moment you step out of your front door, you are swept into a fast-flowing current in which deals are made, opinions tested, decisions taken, ideas acted on, actions judged. If you cannot keep up with the speed of its rapids, you run the risk of going under. The pace of that city does not tolerate physical weakness. Here in Berlin, however, physical weakness is generously accommodated. Every year, as the seasons change and winter slowly bows an exit, a recognized phenomenon occurs: a shared drain on the population's energy levels that goes by the name of *Frühjahrsmüdigkeit*. As if the city's consolidated channels of energy are rerouted from its population and used instead to power the swelling buds appearing on the thousands of trees that line the streets and fill the parks. But even beyond such seasonal phenomena as "spring exhaustion," Berlin's relative stasis allows for a lethargic pace that both detracts and enables. Since the city is no longer a financial or trading capital, other paths may be followed than those determined by growth or success measured in economic terms alone. Berlin's lack of current allows for a slow motion *dérive*, an unfolding that follows the inconclusive weave of the river Spree, or the winding paths of Lenné's Tiergarten. It can be experienced at the unhurried speed of contemplation.

---

The Berliners, passionate as they can be about the correct minutiae of paperwork, have been less observant about other aspects of daily life that could foster general well-being or stabilize the possible misfortunes of a city's bad siting. "Elegance, auspiciousness, transformation and feeling," are the desired criteria for a good site, according to feng shui. A source of clear, fresh, meandering water should be found near a house and trees should be planted as windbreaks. Lenné's plans, with their abundance of trees and meandering waterways, as well as the drainage of the city's unusually high water table, would seem to adhere to these guidelines. So do his plans to furnish the city with straight, wide, tree-lined axes for the orderly flow of horse-drawn traffic, while an encircling green belt would gently enclose the residential developments. The integration of human needs with the natural environment that feng shui proposes would have found its place in Lenné's city, designed to enable work, health, pleasure and contact with nature in a unified field of experience. However, such concerns slipped down the list of priorities as the nineteenth century progressed and industrialization picked up its pace. Railways, iron mills and rapidly constructed housing took precedence over more nebulous qualities associated with well-being.

In the early 1860s, a new character appeared in the city-planning playbook, charged with developing a plan to house the ever-growing population. James Hobrecht, a thirty-three-year-old surveyor and civil engineer specialized in sewage systems, was inexperienced in matters of urban planning. Instead of Lenné's vision of greenery, health and leisure for all, in Hobrecht's *General Development Plan for Berlin* of 1862, rational sense and Prussian efficiency prevail. Hobrecht filled in the organic patchwork of fields, meadows and forest that lay beyond the built-up city's customs wall with a perpendicular cross-hatching of streets. He took his cues from Baron Haussmann's radically restructured Paris, which he had visited in 1860. But the rigid geometric street pattern Hobrecht contrived for Berlin made no provision for the elegant arterial axes of Haussmann's Paris plan, nor the generous greenery that was an integral part of his scheme. A grid of city blocks was laid out with which to solve the housing problem. The clear trajectories of Lenné's tree-lined avenues were either abandoned entirely or wrenched to skirt around railway yards. Decisions made at the draftsman's desk took in little account of the site itself.

The gaping plots of land sketched out by the new street plan were handed over to real estate developers and the largely unregulated building industry. With no overarching social vision or concern for the welfare of citizens, every square inch was built upon, maximizing living space, along with private profits. Over the ensuing decades until the early 1900s, *Mietskasernen*, or rental barracks, were constructed in the thousands, each with a series of receding and increasingly gloomy backyards, as many as the plot permitted. The sole planning stipulation was that a horse-drawn fire engine should be able to turn in the courtyard.

A two-tier social system was inscribed into the architecture of the *Mietskasernen*, offering the luxuries of light, space and elegance to those living in the front while the poor were crammed into dark, badly ventilated side wings and backyards, harboring squalor, sickness and crime. James Hobrecht defended the social discrepancy built into his plans in a much-quoted apologia, in which he naively imagines the benefits of rich and poor living in close proximity within one building. "Here a bowl of soup to strengthen the ill, there a hand-me-down piece of clothing, elsewhere the possibility of free help with schoolwork and everything which is the result of a comfortable relationship between such different social types." With a smooth inevitability, Hobrecht envisaged the ennobling influence of education and wealth elevating those suffering from bad living standards, overcrowding, dark and damp rooms, as if their environments and the everyday effects of such dismally disadvantageous sites would have no effect at all.

The reality could not have been more different. Good and healthy living conditions were available for those with the means, while the rigid social and economic hierarchies that held these divisions in place were norms not to be disturbed. Furious industrialization meant that already by 1870, Berlin had the highest urban density of any city in Europe. "By the turn of the century there were a staggering 1,000 people per hectare," writes Alexandra Richie in *Faust's Metropolis*, her inimitable chronicle of Berlin published in 1998. "Each room contained an average of five people but according to Berlin records, which were by their very nature incomplete, 27,000 had seven, 18,400 had eight, 10,700 had nine, and many had more than twenty per room." Auspiciousness came at a price. "Over 60,000 people 'officially' inhabited coal cellars," as Richie reports.

In the Chamber for Building Records, along with Herr Zimmermann's original plans from 1869 for the four-story house I now live in, with its octagonal *Berliner Zimmer* and sharp angled hallways, are countless other official documents spanning back over a century. The astonishing amount of paperwork that survives from these times, written in a jagged ink-pen scrawl, reveals the authorities' devotion to bureaucracy when it came to matters of planning, building and even plumbing.

As well as police orders demanding that Herr Zimmermann lay smooth cobblestones or asphalt on the
pavement in front of the plot, are the results of yearly
surveys that record the number of lavatories and bathrooms per inhabitant. Detailed documents itemize the
drainage systems, first implemented in 1888, listing
nine water closets and four bathrooms, five drainpipes
in the house, two in the cellar and four gullies, but no
water closet or pissoir in the backyard.

Amongst these official surveys is a letter typewrit-
ten in blue ink, dated December 5, 1899 and marked
"urgent." Addressed to Department II of the Royal Police Headquarters, it is from a Johann Tresp, a tenant
in one of the side wing apartments in the backyard. "My
apartment is so completely wet that all of my furniture
is starting to rot and we are all sick," he writes. "The
landlord refuses to have repairs made. My children are
small, and we cannot stay here much longer in these
conditions. I therefore request the most immediate
investigation. Your obedient servant! Johann Tresp."
Another letter follows a week later requesting that attention be most urgently paid to the matter: "particularly as the cold weather we are having at the moment
makes living in this side wing almost impossible." On
December 21, Herr Tresp, having received no reply to
the first two letters, writes again, exasperated: "I simply request confirmation whether or not my landlord is

obliged to take care of this matter, so that I know who to address my complaint to. As I have small children, this matter is terribly urgent, and I kindly request a prompt response." This is the last document in the file regarding Herr Tresp and his water problems. There is no more paperwork and no replies from the authorities to indicate whether the damp was fixed or not. Such everyday problems disappear between the cracks of history, barely recorded, and even less analyzed.

In 1899, thirty years after constructing the building, Herr Zimmermann's role as landlord saddled him with responsibilities of an awkwardly human kind – of his tenants and their environment, of rising damp, sickly children and rotting furniture – rather than the supply and demand logistics of lumber loaded onto barges tethered conveniently on the canal banks. A watercourse in front of the site is desirable, but only if the configuration is auspicious, and Berlin has always had problems with its water table.

## · 5 ·

# Swamp

*Things tend to disappear* in a city built on sand. On *Märkischer Sand*, as it's known in the region: a soft and porous medium that absorbs a good part of the energy that crosses over its surface. New York's bedrock is hard, certain ground from which its skyscrapers shoot up, across which the waters of the Hudson and East Rivers rush, and on which its millions of inhabitants hurry through their urgent, daily transactions. But Berlin's sandy floor, this soft and porous medium, exerts a constant, subtle downward pull. Does this explain the strange lethargy that sometimes hangs across the city? Its shared sense of inertia? I often feel a certain lack of momentum here, and in this I am not alone. The feeling that a portion of one's energy simply sinks down and disappears beneath the city's foundation, into that absorbent, accommodating sand. Is it accumulating somewhere in great hidden wells beneath the city's surface?

Berlin was not named after the bear it later adopted as its mascot, but after the Slavic name for swamp: *brlø*. This etymology is a two-fold source of shame: firstly, the admission of the city's Slavic roots, when all things east were considered uncivilized, and the dynastic claims of the Hohenzollern monarchs were emphasized instead. Secondly, the swamp, both geographically and metaphorically, is bad news. Stinking and heavy, a swamp conceals filth. To the upright Prussian mentality, obsessively concerned with the hygienic removal of bodily fluids, the swamp is the worst possible state. *Swamps, floods, morasses, mire, slime* and *pulp* were all anxiety producing substances that cast fear into the Prussians' erect, soldierly morals, according to Klaus Theweleit in *Male Fantasies*. "The swamp's attribute of leaving no traces of its activity, of closing up again after every action, invited the presence of hidden things, things from secret realms and from the domain of the dead. Someone was already lying in every morass or swamp you sank into." Theweleit links this fear of fluids to the dread and revulsion felt towards women by the *Freikorps* and their bands of "soldier males." Such proclivities fed the aggressive racism and authoritarianism that lead to the rise of fascism in Germany. "Harsh punishments were meted out if any of the wet substances in question turned up other than in its specifically designated place or situation" writes Theweleit, detailing the late Prussian "compulsion for mopping up"; a dangerous breeding ground of sexual repression and deep-rooted but well-concealed anxieties.

Berlin's swampy origins, "the veil of mist over the wet lowlands," is a fundamental but invisible aspect of the city. You cannot see it, so you don't often think about it. But sometimes you catch a whiff of subterranean swamp in the air. Smells that hint at the presence of hidden things. Things that belong to secret realms. Occasionally a disturbing odor like this appears in the bathroom at home. Musty, like rotting pumpkins. There is something shameful about it, though its exact point of emanation is difficult to determine. It is as if something that should have been discretely removed is returning unbidden but can't be seen.

Sometimes things that were supposed to disappear rise to the surface again and overflow into visibility. Like the body of Rosa Luxemburg, thrown into the Landwehr Canal, which reappeared five months later, floating down the water. Most things, however, sink without a trace. Does the swamp's capacity for swallowing evidence and *closing up again after every action* also have a role to play in Berlin's strangely amnesiac relation to its past?

It is ironic, I always think when accosted by these vile odors, that James Hobrecht, designer of the mainframe plan of Berlin's streets and buildings, which determined the city's footprint from then until now, was an engineer turned city planner with a passion for sewage disposal. Hobrecht may have had no experience in architecture, landscape, nor even the barest aesthetic sensibility, but when it came to organizing sewage, he was a pioneer. His *Radialsystem*, devised to manage the city's waste, left a less maligned and more exemplary legacy than his *General Development Plan*. To start with, it was not visible, fanning out in an orderly manner only beneath the city's streets. Implemented between 1873 and 1895, it divided the city into twelve radial systems, each with its own pumping station which collected wastewater and sewage, and transported it through pressurized pipes to the *Rieselfelder*, or sewage fields, in the surrounding countryside. Thanks to this concept, developed together with the socially minded scientist Rudolf Virchow, Berlin became one of the most hygienic cities in the world.

The first ever pumping station, *Radialsystem III*, designed by James Hobrecht himself, lies directly across the canal from my house. Incredibly, it survived the Allied bombing, tower and all, and is the only intact pre-war building I can see from my window. A Wilhelmine-era redbrick construction on the canal's east banks, its three-tiered redbrick chimney, adorned with recessed archways and carved sandstone crenellations, rises straight up in the air. It was constructed between 1873 and 1876 to serve the city center and Tiergarten areas, the most densely populated parts of Berlin at the time. 100,000 residents were served by over eighty kilometers of subterranean water canals, with almost a meter of pipes per person. *Radialsystem III*, a valiant totem for the correct disposal of unwanted fluids, forms the center point of my view.

When Parvati the feng shui master looked out of the window, she declared the redbrick tower of the *Radialsystem* pumping station to be a *Ruhepol*, a calming rod. A red pole can contain energy and prevent *qi* from escaping, she explained. Without this tower, the energy would dissipate, evaporating in the air or sinking down into the sandy ground. For those lucky enough to have views to the front, Hobrecht's chimney is a stabilizer, a counterbalance to the site's misfortunes. But those in the side wing are less well-placed.

Berlin's population grew and grew throughout the late 1800s, doubling in the ten years from 1864 to 1874 and reaching the million mark by 1877. By 1900, industrial workers made up almost sixty per cent of Berlin's population. Mostly immigrants, this rootless mass was not integrated socially or culturally. Appalling working conditions did their part to prevent such integrations: by the 1870s, the working day had risen from fourteen hours per day to as many as seventeen. The clothing industry was particularly bad, as Richie notes: "the women sewing and pressing in the Berlin sweat shops lived to an average age of twenty-six." The crime rate soared in accordance with these circumstances, and the deep recessive courtyards of Hobrecht's tenement buildings created labyrinths of well-concealed hiding places for a criminal underclass. The Prussian authorities were bent on control, and rather than laying the blame on poverty and dire living conditions, they attacked the working classes' moral standards instead. A split emerged between this "underclass" and the city authorities. The kaiser, the military and the new breed of industrialists rejected reforms out of hand and opted instead for even greater repression, leading the maltreated, dissatisfied teeming masses straight into the hands of the Social Democrats. The Socialist Labor Party formed in 1875 and began mobilizing immigrants and workers to vote. By 1890 the Social Democrats were Germany's largest party and "Red Berlin" (the "Red Menace" to some, including Reich Chancellor Bismarck) had come into being.

Hobrecht's ingenious engineering skills, impressive rationality and bureaucratic capacities had served him well when it came to devising an efficient, well-organized and economically feasible system for dealing with the city's shit. They fell short when it came to the more complex needs of its living population, however; an organism whose social and political well-being couldn't be simply flushed away and distributed to the outlying countryside. In fact, the problem was the opposite: the flow was coming into the city from the outlying areas, as growing industries attracted waves of workers from rural locations, west and east. This inflowing population was crammed into the dark, damp *Mietskasernen* and the buildings became notorious, blamed by some for the rising discontent of workers. Every day, the poor and homeless succumbed to cold and starvation but, as Rosa Luxemburg noted, "nobody notices them, particularly not the police reports." Like Johann Tresp in his damp apartment full of rotting furniture and sickly children. His letters go unanswered, but are dutifully stamped and correctly filed away for perusal a century later.

## · 6 ·

# Adrift

*On the wall beside my desk* is a map of Berlin, a facsimile of an original from 1896. There is no apparent direction to the irregular patchwork of city blocks it depicts, its web of streets laid out by Hobrecht. It is a "tidy mess, an arbitrariness exactly to plan, a purposeful-seeming aimlessness," wrote feuilletonist Joseph Roth in 1930. A result of "the wickedness, sheer cluelessness, and avarice of its rulers, builders, and protectors [who] draw up the plans, muddle them up again, and confusedly put them into practice." Writing half a century after Hobrecht's *General Development Plan* for Berlin was adopted, Roth laments what its residents have been left with: "a distressing agglomeration of squares, streets, blocks of tenements, churches, and palaces. Never was so much order thrown at disorder, so much lavishness at parsimony, so much method at madness."

Roth's impressions remain true now, ninety years later. The aimlessness of those responsible for shaping the city remains inscribed in its arbitrary urban landscape. A *Gleichgültigkeit,* or indifference, as urbanplanner Werner Hegemann has it in his famous 1930 lament *Das steinerne Berlin* [Stone Berlin]. Visitors and inhabitants alike are known to experience strange moments of disorientation, stranded on unpopulated street corners or at a vast open crossroads, with no sense in which direction to go.

"Streets are the space left over between buildings," writes Rebecca Solnit in *Wanderlust,* her treatise on travelling by foot. "A house alone is an island surrounded by a sea of open space, and the villages that preceded cities were no more than archipelagos in that same sea." In Berlin the reverse occurred and we ended up with what Benjamin called the *Häusermeer der Stadt,* the city's sea of houses. The best way to discover a place is on foot, but it is difficult to drift in a city conscientiously plotted out, but with little sense for how people move or inhabit the space around them.

"Moving on foot seems to make it easier to move in time," remarks Solnit, "the mind wanders from plans to recollections to observations." Besides the practical asset of getting from one place to another, particularly before horse, train or car intervened and upped the pace, walking is also a way to access cross-currents of cultural thinking and map out history, landscape, society, art or politics onto the streets themselves. For Solnit, it offers up "a secret history whose fragments can be found in a thousand unemphatic passages in books, as well as in songs, streets, and almost everyone's adventures."

There were purposeful cultural strollers in Berlin. Franz Hessel, champion of the canal's "green shore," describes "walking slowly down bustling streets" as a particular pleasure. "Awash in the haste of others, it's a dip in the surf." But many of the city's other walkers appear in literature's "unemphatic passages" and provide a surreptitious sidelong glance at the city and times through which they move.

One afternoon last December, I myself was wandering, awash in the haste of others, through Berlin's Mitte district. Not long ago, the streets here were shabby and potholed, but the area has been fully transformed in a handful of years into a seamless strip of high-end coffee shops and glossy clothes boutiques. Guided by hunger and a need for coffee, I ended up in one such café and picked up the *Berliner Zeitung* that was lying on the table. At the bottom of the page was an article about Theodor

Fontane, Berlin's most famous nineteenth-century author, commemorating the forthcoming bicentenary of his birth. The article was titled *"Sich treiben lassen"*: let yourself drift. "Fontane's way of thinking and writing did not follow a compulsive urge towards completion, regardless of how detailed one work or another may be. He believed far more in moods and coincidence than the need for comprehensiveness," wrote the journalist. Fontane, who had lived in Berlin, with short interruptions, from 1834 until he died in 1898, was an advocate of walking and published books about his journeys by foot in the nearby towns and countryside of Brandenburg. The wandering that occurs in his novels, meanwhile, transposes his own observations of a city in the making into real-time fictional narratives. These are the "unemphatic passages" that Solnit talks about. He sets his characters off to drift in the city's streets and social currents, leaving loose ends of unhappiness and disappointment hanging in works that resist the urge for tidy endings.

As Fontane's protagonists walk through the streets of late nineteenth-century Berlin, in novels characterized by acute observations of time and place, their journeys convey unexpected encounters or produce dramatic twists of plot. The title of his 1887 novel *Irrungen, Wirrungen* (which translates literally as *errors* and *tangles*, though the English version I have is called

*On Tangled Paths*) suggests the twists and turns such perambulations – or lives – can take. It begins with a precise topographical placement. A *siting*.

> At the point where the Kurfürstendamm inter-
> sects the Kurfürstenstrasse, diagonally across
> from the Zoological Gardens, there was still, in
> the mid-eighteen-seventies, a large market garden
> running back to the open fields behind.

Another map I have here, folded up on the bookshelf be-hind my desk, dates back to 1875. When I spread it out and peer to find this intersection, I notice words in tiny print: *Gärtnerei Dörr* – Dörr's Market Garden. Fontane's fictional version of Berlin has so fused with its real-life counterpart that Dörr, the name of his made-up mar-ket gardener, appears here on this historical document. On the map, a network of dotted lines traces over the expanse of green behind the market garden, plotting out the streets that had been planned by Hobrecht, but not yet built. *Bauerwartungsland*, the map's key calls it: land expecting buildings. The land in this expectant condition could only be used by gardeners.

In *On Tangled Paths*, Fontane not only drops a pin at this precise point on the map, he also establishes a fold in time. Although written and published in 1887, the novel is set in around 1875, so turns back the clock by a dozen years to Berlin's early *Gründerzeit* era. The novel, subtitled *An Everyday Berlin Story*, was initially serialized in the liberal newspaper *Vossische Zeitung*, at a time when the everyday Berlin it describes had already disappeared, swallowed up by the widely spreading, all engulfing *Häusermeer der Stadt*. The city and its inhabitants were being catapulted into an unknown urban future.

I follow Fontane's characters in *On Tangled Paths* out onto the everyday city streets, described with an astute eye for incidentals which anchor the story in its location. Here is Baron Botho von Rienäcker, a handsome, good-natured young aristocrat with a dwindling family fortune, strolling along Unter den Linden towards the Brandenburg Gate before he heads to The Club, for lobster and Chablis with his wealthy uncle. Later we find him crossing the meadows behind the Dörrs' market garden with Lene Nimptsch, the hard-working, open-hearted laundress's daughter who lives on the Dörrs' property, with whom he has fallen in love, and Frau Dörr as their chaperone. "Just listen to the frogs, Frau Dörr," exclaims Lene. "Oh, the puddocks," the latter agrees. "Some nights they croak so much you can't get no sleep. And do you know why? 'Cos it's really one big marsh round here, an' only looks like a meadow."

Lene and Botho are sweetly enamored, but society deems them incompatible. She is merely, as Frau Dörr puts it, "a tidy, hard-workin' girl, [who] can turn her hand to anythin', an' with a sense of what's right and proper." While Botho can declare loftily that "each station in life has its dignity, including a washerwoman's," in the end – inevitably – dignity isn't enough: he follows the path that his fate prescribes and marries a rich woman in order to shore up his family fortune. When Botho is asked for advice from a young soldier in a similar predicament late in the novel, despite his own unhappiness, he describes the pursuit of love beyond the class divide to be a hopeless dead end: if "you break with class, custom and tradition, then your life, even if you don't go to the dogs, will sooner or later become a torment and a burden to you."

After their marriage, Botho and his new wife move to Landgrafenstraße, a street running perpendicular to the Landwehr Canal, "not even a thousand paces" from the Dörrs' market garden. At that time, Fontane tells us, this street "was still only built up on one side" and the apartment balcony's westerly view looked "first over a small birch wood and the Zoological Gardens, and, beyond that, straight over open country as far as the northernmost point of the Grunewald." Here is an image of Berlin at the cusp of its transition from a wide-open terrain almost untouched by development. Here, "the most beautiful and most populous city in the world could have been built," laments Werner Hegemann in retrospect. But the city lacked a vision for its own future in the absence of "men capable of expediently guiding not only the national and economic powers, but also the Germans' artistic abilities." A brief glimpse of opportunity was quickly eclipsed by the rigid application of Hobrecht's plan and the subsequent spread of "disgraceful tenement buildings, which would doubtless take centuries to remove."

While reading Fontane's novel, I trace the streets he speaks of on the map on my wall; places fixed in literature through detailed observations. Not only are these my neighborhood streets, they were Theodor Fontane's too. Returning to Berlin in January 1859 after a stay in London, he set up temporary residence in the Hotel de Pologne just behind Potsdamer Platz. In the dozen years that followed, he moved house intermittently but always stayed within the triangular territory bordered by the Landwehr Canal in the south, Potsdamer Straße in the west, and Königratzer Straße (now Stresemannstraße) in the east. For almost a decade he lived in a house within this triangle, on a corner where, as he wrote to a friend, the "city wall stood nearby, and not far behind the tracks of the Stadtbahn ran." In 1872 his landlord sold up, the rent was raised dramatically, and he and his family were forced to move out. Real estate speculation, by those inclined to value the city purely in terms of price per square meter, was as endemic then as it is now, a century and a half later.

Fontane was in his early fifties when he moved with his wife Emilie to the apartment on Potsdamer Straße where he would stay for the rest of his life. There, in his study, he wrote seventeen works of fiction and two volumes of memoirs. Today a bronze plaque can be found hanging incongruously on the terra-cotta tiled wall of the Potsdamer Platz Arcade, a vast shopping center and office complex designed by Renzo Piano's Building Workshop and finished in 1997 as part of this area's hasty and erroneous post-unification rebuild. On this spot stood Fontane's apartment: third floor of the Johanniterhaus, as a quote on the plaque tells us, seventy-five steps up.

It would have been a short walk from Fontane's apartment at 134C Potsdamer Straße to the Landgrafenstraße, where Baron Botho lived out his unhappy marriage. A shorter walk still to the Königgrätzer Straße, home to Effi Briest, Fontane's most famous literary creation. Following her disgrace and divorce from her elderly, austere baron husband, we find her living in two rooms, "one front and one back, and a kitchen behind with a cubby-hole for the maid, all as plain and ordinary as one could imagine." The view from her apartment window describes a social divide that leaves her isolated and socially shunned. "Just look at all those different railway lines," exclaims a rare and kindly visitor, looking out of the window. "Three, no four of them, and look at the way trains constantly glide up and down them. [...] Really magnificent. And the way the sun is suffusing the white smoke!" The noise, the smell of those huge, soot-belching locomotives, clattering constantly up and down. Berlin is about to enter a new age of transformation, powered by the railways.

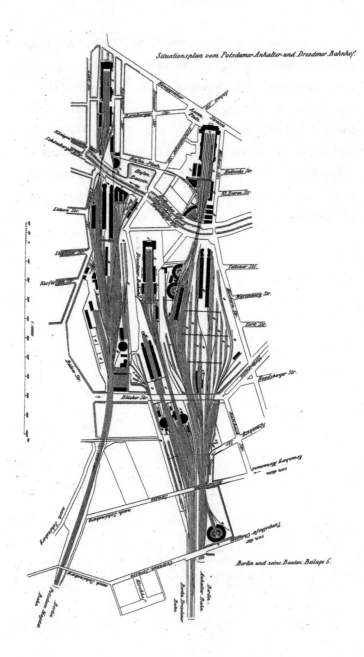

Situationsplan vom Potsdamer Anhalter und Dresdner Bahnhof.

Berlin und seine Bauten. Beilage 5.

· 7 ·

# Railway Time

*An early painting* by Adolph Menzel, *View over Anhalter Bahnhof by Moonlight*, looks out of a third-floor window, along the side flank of a neighboring house and down into the shadowy yard of the railway station. The rail yard and its heavy machinery are cast in darkness, while ghostly moonlight glances white on the tiled roofs and façade of the railway buildings center left. The rest of the picture is dark cloud-strewn sky, dimly illuminated by the small disc of a moon. When Menzel made this painting in 1846, the Anhalter Bahnhof was still a simple rectilinear structure, built just after the first railway lines had arrived triumphantly in Berlin. Anhalter Bahnhof and the nearby Potsdamer Bahnhof were the city's first railway stations. The Potsdamer

Bahnhof's tracks lead straight west towards the kaiser's residence in Potsdam, while those departing the Anhalter Bahnhof headed southwest to the Duchies of Anhalt.

Anhalt is the name of a territory but *anhalten*, the verb from which this word derives, means "to stop" or "pull up." An *Anhalt* is an indication. An *Anhaltspunkt* a clue. Something that stops you in your tracks. A stumbling block, an interruption, a sudden moment of clarity. The ruined remains of the Anhalter Bahnhof appear in the view from my kitchen window and seem to interrupt the present by inserting a leftover piece of the past. A jagged stretch of wall seen from the back, its four large brickwork roundels frame nothing but empty sky. This fragment of façade occupies the middle distance in my view, beyond Lenné's Landwehr Canal and Hobrecht's pumping station. Once part of the portico of Berlin's grandest railway station, this is all that is left of it now. A free-standing remnant that seems to exaggerate the uncanny lack of a building behind. The ruin of the Anhalter Bahnhof that appears in the view from my window is a cipher that speaks of intertwining histories. The violence of the aerial bombings and pitched street battles with which the Second World War came to an end, but also the vigorous railway industry that up until then had shaped the city. When the bombed-out remains of the station building were knocked down in the post-war years, this section was left standing. A memorial not only to a much-admired building, but also to the influence it exerted on the surrounding territory. The traces of this power are still there in non-sequiturs of built-up space: the unexplained absences and perplexing architectural crosshatch that make up this area's present-day fabric.

As the nineteenth century progressed, the primacy of the railway system in Berlin's expansion came to eclipse the clear and spacious vision that Peter Joseph Lenné had developed for Berlin. In his 1844 plans, Lenné had drawn a straight axis that began at Askanischer Platz in front of the Anhalter Bahnhof, and shot straight down across the canal, towards Wilmersdorf, in one clean southwesterly sweep. Another strong diagonal, the so-called *Generalszug*, or Generals' Procession, linked Südstern in Kreuzberg with Wittenbergplatz in Charlottenburg: a single tree-lined avenue named after the Prussian generals who lead Germany to victory in the Napoleonic Wars.

The aesthetic clarity of these elegant trajectories held little sway in the face of a voracious railway system, however, which devoured ever more land for engine houses and enormous freight depots. In 1857, Lenné met the minister of commerce and industry at the Potsdamer Bahnhof with an armful of newly drawn plans. He had come up with a compromise, to accommodate the railways while maintaining the key aesthetic qualities of his original design. But no agreement could be reached; again his plans were put on hold. When Lenné died in 1866, his principles were finally brushed aside, along with his concerns for the citizens' health and wellbeing. The smooth enablement of efficient transportation was now Berlin's top priority.

The flat mass of land that lies behind my house became a freight depot and goods yard for the Anhalter Bahnhof and the Potsdamer Bahnhof, its terrain sprawling brutishly across the routes of the arrow-straight boulevards that Lenné had envisaged. The only avenue that survived at all was the Generalszug, but its clean trajectory was forced into a series of awkward angles, bending around the goods yards' periphery. The Yorckstraße along their southernmost boundary suffered most acutely from these clumsy redirections, while being cast into gloomy shadow by six ironwork railway bridges crossing overhead.

This avenue's compromised angularity is something I experience often, now that my children's second home in their father's rented apartment is right at Südstern, the easterly starting point of the Generalszug. Having settled into the rhythmic comings and goings of a family split up and spread across two homes, we shuttle the children and their belongings along this axis every week or so. Each time I find myself driving down Yorckstraße, having picked up the boys and crammed my compact car full of school bags, skateboards, tennis rackets, electric guitars and sometimes the cats too, mewling unhappily in matching travel bags, I am dismayed when the road lurches suddenly to the left, instead of simply gliding straight ahead. I don't know why this diversion affects me so much, this loss of a clear path that had in fact never existed except for in Lenné's idealistic scheme. But I regret the loss of his clear vision, and the adoption of priorities skewed towards machinery, efficiency, pragmatism and the rational mind.

In the 1860s, the railways' growth was such that the Anhalter Bahnhof's modest two platforms that Menzel had painted fifteen years earlier could no longer accommodate the increasing numbers of passengers, engines, departures and arrivals. Expansion was called for, and not just in terms of scale. By 1871, it was clear that the new station building must not only be huge, but also of a grandeur fitting to the Prussian State Railway, the National Railway of the newly minted German Empire. Franz Schwechten, a freshly graduated thirty-year-old architect, was chosen for the job. He rose to the occasion, conjuring a train hall 170 meters long, where 40,000 people could gather beneath a vaulted, glassed-in, barrel roof. The entrance hall, thirty meters high and eighty-seven meters wide, comprised ticket and luggage counters, separate waiting rooms for four different classes of traveller, administrative offices and dedicated rooms for travelling members of Kaiser Wilhelm's Royal Court. By devoting so much space to the contingent activities of train travel, Schwechten orchestrated a smooth architectural transition from the accelerations of the railway journey into the bustle of the new metropolis. The station's neo-Renaissance portico, decorated with floral symmetries in terra-cotta and molded brick, was a theatrical threshold that marked the passage between these two facets of modern life. The whole was crowned with an enormous clock framed by two allegorical sculptures, representing Night and Day.

Schwechten's Anhalter Bahnhof, officially opened by Kaiser Wilhelm I and Reich Chancellor Otto von Bismarck in June 1880, was a conspicuous showpiece of the railway industry's success. By this point, over 18,000 kilometers of rail track crisscrossed the German Reich, with Berlin at its center. Whether heading west–east from Paris to Russia, or north–south from Scandinavia to Milan, passengers were forced to stop in Berlin. It was Europe's primary node of rail travel. The Reichsbahn belonged to the capital city, and its authorities were suitably proud.

A newfangled mechanical energy flowing constantly along these iron vectors came to override the swampy stasis underfoot as the railways became Berlin's life force. "The machine ensemble, consisting of wheel and rail, railroad and carriage, expanded into a unified railway system, which appeared as one great machine covering the land," writes Wolfgang Schivelbusch in his history of rail travel in the nineteenth century. As it spread across the new Prussian territories, connecting province to city, mountains to coastline, a unification of space came about that extended to the notion of time itself. Now that all these distant places were connected by machines, a unified system of timekeeping was needed for the engines' punctual scheduling. North German railways were regulated to "Berlin Time" in 1874, and by 1893 this "Railway Time" was officially recognized across the German Empire. The clock that crowned the grand portico of Schwechten's Anhalter Bahnhof was emblematic of the regulatory authority of "Railway Time." But now it is gone, as are the figures of Night and Day that framed it. All that remains is a cut-out roundel in the brickwork; an empty hole in an abandoned piece of scenery.

In the years that followed Menzel's first painting of the Anhalter Bahnhof in moonlight, he continued to document the railways' development. The train in his 1847 painting *Berlin-Potsdam Railway*, is little more than a streak of black trailed by a grey plume of smoke as it curves through a pastoral landscape, away from the shadowy architectures which form a horizon on the edge of the fields. In the following decades, Menzel's viewpoint moved incrementally closer until, in the 1892 gouache *Travelling through the Countryside*, he is right inside the upholstered interior of the train's carriage, experiencing all the commotion of the journey. Menzel's fellow passengers are in various states of animation: leaning out of the window transfixed by the engine's speed, standing ready with binoculars, reading, dozing or engaged in conversation. A scene of palpable excitement, it suggests all the thrill and social potential of this revolutionary form of transport.

Theodor Fontane brings us into a similar coach interior in *Cécile*, his 1886 novella which begins at a Berlin railway station. His protagonists have just boarded "one of the new carriages, with steps up to the door." A well-built man in his fifties and a younger woman, slim and dressed all in black, are settling in for their journey to the Harz Mountains in the Anhalt territories. "Thank goodness, Cécile," remarks the older gentleman. "Thank goodness we are alone." "Hopefully it will stay that way," replies his companion tersely. "With that the conversation ended."

As the train makes its way out of the city and the couple sits in silence, backyard scenes are sketched in fleeting details reminiscent of Menzel's drawings of peripheral, hidden spaces. In the backyards obscured from public view, bedroom windows stand open and side wings are black with soot, their high walls framing groups of acacia trees, folding tables and green-painted garden chairs. The Victory Column commemorating the several wars of unification in the 1800s appears, the golden winged figure astride its summit rising ghostly above the trees as the train leaves the city behind. For Fontane, train travel offers a conduit out of the constraints and anxieties of the city's social formalities, delivering his characters to the countryside with its promise of open space, convalescence and unconstrained opportunity.

In Fontane's novels, there is freedom in walking, or in views out of windows, but the interiors his protagonists inhabit are bound up into social strictures. Their maids and servants, heavy furnishings and ornaments, protocols and etiquettes, are all the cumbersome trappings of Wilhelmine decorum. Codes inscribed into interior spaces define behavior and social possibility. Out on the streets, however, the characters' meanderings reflect their inner moods. Wildness can exist out here amidst the unruly bustle of road works and traffic, railways, markets and the nervous energy of an expanding metropolis.

Cécile von St. Arnaud and her husband, referred to as "the Colonel," live in an apartment on Hafenplatz, a square that lies diagonally opposite my house on the other side of the Ufer. Now a pretty park full of blossoming trees, it used to be a harbor, where the canal's waters broadened out of their narrow path to form a large rectangular pool. Robert von Gordon, a handsome Scottish gentleman whom the couple meets on their trip to the Harz and the third point in Fontane's narrative triangle, lives on the nearby Lennéstrasse. On returning to Berlin, von Gordon sets off to visit Cécile at home. He walks around Potsdamer Platz, cordoned off for the installation of sewage pipes and traffic islands, passes through a vibrant street market, and turns left at the corner towards the St. Arnauds' apartment. His visit is in vain, they are not yet back from the country, but a subsequent trip is rewarded with an hour of Cécile's company. On taking his leave, von Gordon returns to the neighborhood streets and turns off the main road to take a quiet path beside the railway embankment, sidling along train tracks, goods yards and railway bridges, his head full of thoughts of Cécile.

Von Gordon's journey takes him past the corner of Schöneberger Bridge and Tempelhofer Ufer, at that time an empty plot directly opposite the harbor, a few hundred yards from the Zimmermanns' home. Five years after Fontane wrote this novella, construction

began on the neoclassical redbrick edifice, the length of
the entire block, that occupies this plot today. The most
striking features of the somber building are the red-
tiled pepper-pot turrets at its corners, which lend it an
authoritative fortlike appearance, while concealing its
unfortunate lack of right angles. Above the symmetrical entranceway, at the top of a short flight of steps, an
emblem carved in sandstone crowns the door. A wheel
seen in sidelong perspective, adorned with feathered
wings, from which lightning bolts emerge in all directions. The futuristic symbol of the Royal Railway Directorate: this building is its headquarters.

Alongside the rapid expansion of Berlin's railways,
an apparatus of baroque bureaucracy had evolved which
by then comprised eleven separate railway directorates
and seventy-five administrative departments. The new
building on the Ufer was designed to consolidate these,
accommodating all 600 employees under one roof
while manifesting the unmistakable authority of the
Royal Railway Directorate. The designated land, which
backed onto the rail goods yards, was already owned by
the railways and had proven unattractive to real estate
investors, given all of the tracks, yards, engines and
emissions in its immediate vicinity. But exactly these
factors, along with the prominent waterfront aspect,
made it the perfect location for the railways' administrative home. On the next block down, the site of the

Zimmermanns' house, once surrounded by water and greenery, was rapidly losing its appeal. Between canal barges and railway lines, the clamor of goods yards and trails of locomotive smoke, the tranquil tree-lined waterway that Lenné had devised was becoming increasingly compromised. Once enjoying the peaceful benefits of its peripheral location beyond the Customs Wall, it had since been thrust right into the midst of the city's central organ.

Construction began on the headquarters of the Royal Railway Directorate in 1891, but the high water table of the plot stalled its progress. The excavations into the swampy ground for the foundations of the substantial building grew deeper and deeper, reaching depths of four meters in places. This underground work absorbed more and more budget, reducing what was left for its visible features. When finally completed in 1895, the formal symmetry of the building's façade was duly impressive, but its cramped and lackluster interior, with low ceilings, sparse decoration and linoleum rather than wooden floors, was quickly dismissed in architectural circles as both parochial and oppressive.

On the map from 1896 that hangs on the wall beside my desk, the Royal Railway Directorate appears as a small black shape directly opposite the rectangular blue pool of the Hafenplatz. Built-up parts of central Berlin are colored in beige and threaded through with the pale red lines of the various railway tracks which clump here and there into knotty thromboses of stations, intersections or goods yards. The red lines and nodes appear like arteries and vital organs, circulating goods and people in and out and around the city, as if Berlin were a liverish corpus pumped into life by this vivid network. The site of my house is enclosed within a tiny beige triangle of streets, bordered on one side by the canal's blue ribbon, and on all of the others by a vicious red tangle. These are the train lines connecting the Anhalter Bahnhof and the Potsdamer Bahnhof across the canal with the vastly spreading railway yards behind. My house is locked within this energetic knot, like a foreign body lodged in a huge, bloody, beating heart.

Changes in local environment can enhance the desirability of a neighborhood, but the opposite can also occur. Unexpected developments can make a well-placed site seem unpleasant or even uninhabitable. In the living organism of the city, what was once peaceful can become a noisy hell, and the formerly peripheral can find itself right in the pulse of the action. In the early 1880s, when the wood merchant Zimmermann looks out of his window and across the canal, he sees the newly finished Anhalter Bahnhof, its 170 meters of glass roof gleaming in the morning sun. A decade later, he is witness to the ever-deeper hole being excavated at the next street corner. Meanwhile, the trains chug by left and right, belching out steam and blasting soot, just as wood gives way to iron as the desired construction material, and coal as the new combustible.

I attempt to flesh out the image of my building's former inhabitant and his daily life through scraps of information picked out of archives a century and a half later. An online ancestry portal feeds me the name of Carl Zimmermann's wife, Anna Wilhelmine Louise Koplin, seventeen years old when they married in 1865 and he was twenty-seven. She moved into the then still modest house, equipped with stables, gardens and workshop, on the trapezoid plot of land. Four years later they knocked this down to build the large apartment building that stands there today, and in four more years a daughter was born, Anna Elfriede Auguste Zimmermann.

When I try to imagine this young woman, perhaps the mistress of the very apartment I am living in now, I picture Fontane's Cécile, greeting von Gordon in her home on the nearby Hafenplatz: "Gordon followed the corridor to the so-called *Berliner Saal*, where Cécile was already standing on the threshold to greet him." She shows him to a room in the side wing, with a balcony overlooking the yard, apologizing for not receiving him in the *Glanzräumen*, as she calls the stately front-facing reception rooms. "We are still like guests in our own home and are limited to a few rooms in the back," she says. "Luckily we at least have a reasonably respectable garden balcony."

Von Gordon's own apartment on Lennéstraße is "quiet and free from traffic, as if it were a private road, with a gateway at each end." The only people he sees from his window are those walking in the Tiergarten opposite or sitting on its benches. "When I was in Berlin at the end of May," he reminisces, "the whole Tiergarten, especially around here, seemed all made up of red headdresses and blue and white baby carriages." These are the distinctive red-winged bonnets of the Sorbian wet nurses who came to Berlin in their dozens. Ever since Kaiser Wilhelm II had employed Sorbian nannies to nurse his seven children, they had become a desirable status symbol for middle- and upper-class families. The majority of the bourgeoisie had a least one maidservant at this time (a strikingly pretty young maid, or *Jungfer* as von Gordon calls her, opens the door when he visits Cécile.) For country girls or unmarried women, despite long working hours and meagre pay, a fixed domestic position in a middle-class household provided a sought-after stability. If space allowed, their sleeping quarters would be in the family house, often nothing more than a crawl space above the kitchen or bathroom, accessed by a fold-down ladder, like the "cubby-hole for the maid" we hear of in Effi Briest's apartment. The *Mädchenkammer*, or maid's chamber, in the Zimmermanns' apartment was comparatively spacious. In the side wing beyond the *Berliner Zimmer* was a room with a suspended ceiling, dividing it horizontally into two separate floors, each less than a meter and a half in height. The lower level was a pantry, the upper floor, with a flight of steps leading to a low doorway, was the servants' bedroom. When we first came to see the apartment, the *Mädchenkammer* was exactly as it had been in the Zimmermanns' time, a stuffy space for servants bent double, with two small windows on the upper level and two on the lower. We removed the steps and the dividing floor to turn it into a single room, but the four small windows remain, a class divide inscribed in architecture.

In Fontane's novella, the reader learns of Cécile's compromised past at the same time as von Gordon does, over his shoulder in a letter from his sister Klothilde. At the age of seventeen, Cécile's mother sent her off to live as "companion" to an elderly, wealthy nobleman. When St. Arnaud became engaged to Cécile years later, his own officer corps suggested to him that this union was not "acceptable." This in turn led to a duel with the eldest staff officer, who was killed by St. Arnaud before he married Cécile. For her part, Cécile had received no education. The daughter of a notable Silesian beauty, and a notable beauty herself, her purpose in life was simply to please, thus the less she knew the better.

No such letters exist to tell me of Anna Zimmermann's fate, though she was equally young when she married the wood merchant and moved to the house on the Ufer. The facts that remain of her existence are sparse. The documents in the digital ancestry archive record the men's professions, but all that we learn of the women are the dates and names that plot out the course of their lives. Dates of birth, marriage and death, maiden names and married names, and the names of children and dates of their birth. Even these few facts can incite a mystery, however. Following the trail of Anna Zimmermann's data, I discover that after the birth of her first child, a second was born in 1881, not in Berlin but in a small town in Hessen. The baby's name is also given as Anna, but no father's name is mentioned, and a death certificate reveals that the baby lived only a matter of months. It is little to go on, but these facts smack of tragedy, of an illicit love affair, an illegitimate child. A story tinged with the indelible stain of the "fallen woman," it seems to have all the makings of a Fontane novel. Of shame and secrecy and events not spoken of out loud.

———

According to the papers in the Chamber for Building Records, the house on the Ufer changed hands in 1907 when it was sold to Herrn Adolf Sala and his brother Fortunato. The Salas were the second generation in a family of printers of Italian origin whose company was founded in 1845. On arriving at the Ufer, the Sala brothers swiftly submitted plans for a factory, equipped with an electric lift, to be built in the courtyard in which to house their print-works. Hand-drawn blueprints of these buildings, on large, folded sheets of paper stamped in ink by the building authorities, detail their optimistic plans for expansion.

In 1882, Fortunato Sala had adapted the family business of luxury printed paper goods, by adding a branch named Sala-Spiele, which specialized in paper toys and games and had since become the company's mainstay. The Sala games were high-end products, employing fine color-lithography to conjure elaborate panoramas, miniature pop-up theaters or provide the illusion of motion through handheld gadgets that animated pictures printed in sequence on long paper strips. Most popular were the parlor games played by bourgeois Prussian families in *Glanzräumen* across the city: picture bingo and traditional card games like *Schwarzer Peter* or *Quartettspiele*. I played these games myself as a child, though in England we called them Old Maid and Happy Families. In Old Maid, pairs of cards were duly matched up, avoiding at all costs the dreaded unmatched spinster card. The "Happy Families," each defined by profession, were pictured in humorous caricatures: Mr. Bun the baker and Mrs. Bun the baker's wife, Mr. and Mrs. Bones the butchers, or Mr. Pot the painter and Mrs. Pot the painter's wife, each accompanied by a master and mistress of the same family name. Here the object of the game was to collect complete families in well-balanced four-cornered sets.

My fascination with the Sala family, beyond the appeal of their occupation, began with their name, which was emblazoned across the house in large capital letters when we first came to see it. It seems a perfect twist of fate that the successors of the Zimmermanns, who built the *Berliner Zimmer*, should be named for the Italian *sala*, the grand rooms or halls that their parlor games were made for. In the meantime, however, the Salas' three generations of brothers, with their confusingly recurrent first names, have cast an entangling spell on me. The first-generation brothers, Anton Vincenz and Alexander Fortunato, were succeeded by Aloys Fortunato and Vincenz Adolf. They in turn were followed by four more brothers, born to Fortunato between 1886 and 1891: Arthur Adolf, Bruno, Curt and Walter. It is a female Sala who irreversibly tightens the historical tangle of this family's knot, however. In 1888, Adolf, son of Fortunato, marries the daughter of his

Uncle Anton, his own first cousin, Marie. In 1889, Marie Sala, née Sala, gives birth to their daughter Annelise, the only girl of this generation.

When the Salas arrived in 1907, they brought with them not only industrious energy and the shine of good fortune caught up in their name, but also a band of youths. A new generation born into the smoke of the industrialized city, at one with the alternative anatomy of the great "machine ensemble," all circulation, hubs, limbs and directionals. An integral part of the forward motion that had seen the new century in. Four young male heirs and one young woman moved into the house on the Ufer.

· 8 ·

# Maiden

*I pass the former Royal Railway Directorate* often; the redbrick building with its pepper-pot turrets appears as impenetrable as ever. Flocks of black-hooded crows roost in the plane trees out front, and perch like ominous guardians on its sandstone ornamentation. Although the railway administration moved out many years ago, the winged wheel with its lightning bolts still crowns the front entranceway. I ride past this building every time I go to the Staatsbibliothek, the Berlin State Library that has been a personal refuge since we moved to this side of the city. The library provides an alternative to the domestic entanglements of home life. It removes me from the kitchen window and the stasis of gazing out. In the Zimmermanns' time, the kitchen was tucked away in the side wing beyond the *Mädchenkammer* in what is now the bathroom. The view out of that kitchen window is not so interesting and anyway, the servants would have had little time for looking out into the distance. We moved the kitchen to this front-facing room, bright and well-proportioned, with a view across the water.

The Berlin State Library is a short bike ride away: straight up the canal and across the Potsdamer Bridge, and there it is on the right, moored on Potsdamer Straße like a stately ocean liner. Locally known as the Stabi, it was designed by architect Hans Scharoun, as was the golden Philharmonie that lies diagonally opposite, set back off the street, in a glittering mystery of scooping curves and angled planes. Diagonally opposite to the left is Mies van der Rohe's Neue Nationalgalerie, the New National Gallery, a high modernist pavilion built of sheer glass perpendiculars. All three were part of an ambitious suite of buildings designed in the 1960s in a conspicuous West Berlin cultural triumvirate.

Unlike its near neighbors, the Stabi is unremarkable from the outside: several stacked horizontal modules and a pebbled flagstone forecourt full of armies of bicycles locked to stands. It is inside its interior that this building's distinction reveals itself. Not at all the shadowy, musty space a library is supposed to be, it is spacious and lofty, all pale shades of grey with marble surfaces and lichen-colored carpeting. Virtually the whole space is a reading room, spread over a series of hovering horizontal planes connected by little flights of stairs. Windows stretching across the building's whole breadth display a wide section of sky. There are no acute angles in the Stabi. All is orderly, open and right-angled here, designed for measured, settled, purposeful work. For me it is a place in which to escape domestic responsibility and become part of a silent productive community.

I am sitting in my usual place – on the second level up, facing the windows, the middle desk in the front row. I can see the New National Gallery to the left, and straight ahead the steeple of St. Matthäus Church. Tucked away behind it are the various museums and galleries of the Kulturforum, including the library where I viewed Menzel's drawings. The winged angel astride the Victory Column in the center of the Tiergarten glows small and golden in the distance. I have just found the Fontane section on the open bookshelves nearby, and am skimming through a stack of his novels, dipping into his liquid prose. But there is something about his female protagonists – Cécile, Effi, Lene – that I can't help but find irritating. Though Fontane guides them with compassionate omniscience through their narrow social and economic prospects, their youthful temperaments are invariably ringed with a note of doomed inevitability. The rigidities of Wilhelmine society prove inescapable, and their clear trajectories of hope and youthful promise are twisted out of shape by all kinds of obligatory compromise. Fontane offers them no way out and instead, with a sigh, the status quo remains regrettably upheld. As I sit here looking out of the library window at the angel on the distant horizon, I wonder how these literary scenarios would have played out had their author been a woman? Who were the female authors anyway to finesse such imagined emancipations? The artists and eyewitnesses who can show us Prussian life from a woman's lived perspective?

This loose end of thought leads me on a convoluted trail of research, one that ends with a thick bound volume on another of the library's open bookshelves: an encyclopedia of female artists, published in 1992 by the Berlin Society of Women Artists and Art Lovers. As I leaf through the columns of fine print in the dense compendium, a drawing of an apartment interior catches my eye. It pictures a solid wooden desk piled high with stacks of books and papers, a Biedermeier chair with curved wooden arms, a glassed-in cupboard full of books, a grandfather clock, a window framed with heavy drapes. It is Theodor Fontane's study, as the caption identifies, in his Potsdamer Straße apartment, a mere stone's throw from the library I am sitting in right now. It is a watercolor painted in 1898 by

Marie von Bunsen, an artist, writer and member of the Berlin Society of Women Artists and Art Lovers. I look her up immediately in the library's online catalogue and order two of her books: *Die Welt in der ich lebte: Erinnerungen aus glücklichen Jahren 1860–1912* [The World in Which I Lived: Memoirs of Happy Years 1860-1912] and *Die Frau und die Geselligkeit* [Women and Society]. A third, the intriguingly titled posthumous publication *Im Ruderboot durch Deutschland: Auf Flüssen und Kanälen in den Jahren 1905 bis 1915* [Through Germany in a Rowboat: On Rivers and Canals from 1905 to 1915], is sadly unavailable. Like many books in the library's collection, it didn't survive the war. A short while later, two small linen-bound hardbacks are delivered to my allotted shelf in the pick-up area. *Women and Society* is an early edition printed in Germanic "blackletter" script, with rows of violent spiky letters I struggle to decipher. But *Memoirs of Happy Years* is in modern type and transports me into Berlin's nineteenth century as seen through the eyes of a woman.

Born in London in 1860 to a Prussian politician and an English banker's daughter, Marie von Bunsen grew up in an enormous villa in the Tiergarten district. The house, commissioned by her father and built in the local neo-Gothic brick vernacular, was augmented with barns full of pigs and pigeons, several greenhouses, a separate apartment for the gardener, and a tennis court – the first one in Berlin, she tells us, apart from the English embassy. In von Bunsen's memoirs, we find her running along the neighborhood streets with her sisters to fetch the morning newspaper; learning to ride a bicycle in the early morning Tiergarten; meeting Adolph Menzel (*"der kleine Menzel"*) at a ball in 1883. The eldest daughter of a society family, she remained unmarried and didn't leave her parents' house until her mother died in 1899. Thereupon, she swiftly sold the house for half a million Reichsmarks in cash, split the fortune with her siblings, and moved, aged forty, into a first-floor garden apartment on the east bank of the Landwehr Canal. Here, a short way up the canal from the Potsdamer Bridge, not far from the homes of Fontane and Menzel, von Bunsen had her first taste of independence. "The best time of my life," she called it, "up until the war." Through an accumulation of peripheral details and the "unemphatic passages" that Rebecca Solnit speaks of, a portrait emerges of the city from a woman's viewpoint. A woman, certainly, with all the privileges that wealth and social connection confer, but still forbidden to go to grammar school. She trains to be a teacher, the only profession open to her, and spends her life teaching, socializing and travelling widely. According to von Bunsen, the difficulties experienced by unmarried women in Wilhelmine society are outdone only by the hypocrisies of married life.

During this period, when women were excluded from participating in the public male domain, their energies were squandered and their productive female force "trickled away in direct slave labor for men," as Klaus Theweleit notes in *Male Fantasies*. Women's productivity was rarely accounted for in literature, in which they were seen rather as vessels for male desire, and were put to use absorbing the productive force of men. Their routine exaltation "is coupled with a negation of women's carnal reality," writes Theweleit, reducing them to an image through which desire can simply flow, or "a force of absorption." Hence all of Fontane's doomed heroines, their vitality apparently sapped by sheer proximity to men. As the thick volume of female artists in the library testifies, the productive force of women was there, but lacking in visible outlets it simply trickled away unseen, seeping into the groundwater, leaving precious few lasting traces to access a century later.

Now as then, much of this female force is funnelled into the domestic realm. Like all forms of maintenance, the continuous work of keeping a home and family has little to show for it in the end. In fact, it only becomes visible when it is not being done, when the apartment is filthy, there is no food in the fridge and the children have grown out of all of their clothes. Working from home creates its own dilemma: clearly defined boundaries are hard to establish, and productivity can remain an open-ended question. When the kind of work being done at home is writing – a slow process, poorly recompensed, with little evidence beyond a string of words that take up space on a printed page – this ephemeral activity seems to dissolve into all the others. With this comes a creeping sense of inauthenticity. Caught up as I was in the attempt to combine my writing work with the incremental tasks of family life, it took me a while to realize that I had drifted into a form of dependence that had an uncomfortably nineteenth century feel to it.

While Marie von Bunsen had the rare good fortune of financial independence, in late-nineteenth-century Prussia there were over one and a half million unmarried women, and they were raised to be dependent. This is the tragic lesson of the one popular Wilhelmine novel written by a woman I finally track down. Written in 1895 by Gabriele Reuter and titled *From a Good Family*, it follows the fate of Agathe Heidling through a catalogue of female misfortune. There is the neurasthenic mother, depressed after the loss of several young infants. The maidservant who begs Agathe to help install a lock on the door of her sleeping quarters and prevent the unwanted advances of Agathe's older brother. The free-spirited friend Eugenie who marries this good-for-nothing brother and appears to have everything a

woman could ask for, but reveals herself to be superficial and selfish. Agathe herself can do nothing but
wait to be plucked from the rows of waiting maidens
by a prospective suitor. As the family's fortunes disappear into her brother's gambling debts, with them
goes Agathe's dowry and her marriageable status. The
years pass, disappointment follows disappointment, she
has no freedom to make decisions or even exercise her
mind. Suffering from the claustrophobia of dependence
and the inevitable bitterness of being left behind, she
has a nervous breakdown. Institutionalized, she is subject to electric shock therapy – and all this before she
reaches forty. She is relegated to the shameful status of
an *Alte Jungfer*. A dreaded old maid.

Though Reuter had been writing since her teenage
years, publishing articles while taking care of her sick
mother, *From a Good Family*, written when she was
thirty-two, was her breakthrough. "I wanted to reveal
what girls and women suffer in silence," wrote Reuter
in her memoirs. "But not the great pains and sufferings.
No, I wanted to reveal the silent tragedy of everyday
life." A bestseller, it established Reuter as the female
voice of her generation, and her subsequent publications continued to portray in compelling detail the various fates of women in German society at the turn of
the century. *Ellen von der Weiden* [Ellen of the Meadows]
addressed the institution of marriage and the shame of

divorce from a female perspective. *Das Tränenhaus* [The House of Tears], published in 1908, told the story of an unmarried young woman who becomes pregnant and is sent to a boardinghouse in the countryside to bear the child.

Reuter's readers didn't realize at the time that the author had close personal experience with the issue of illegitimacy. When she moved to Berlin from Weimar in 1899, forty years old and unmarried, she brought with her a two-year-old daughter, Lili, a fact known only to her closest friends, whose secrecy she could count on. Every year 180,000 illegitimate children were born in imperial Germany, but the phenomenon of the unmarried working mother was rarely granted visibility.

The new-found independence Marie von Bunsen experienced in 1900 – forty years old, her parents deceased, and finally living in her own garden apartment on the canal – was even rarer. She began to hold a "salon" on Sunday mornings, inviting writers, artists, philosophers and professors, as well as diplomats, close friends and members of court society, along with the occasional well-known personality who was passing through town. At this time, Berlin had by far the most salons of any city in the German-speaking realm. Internationally, it was second only to Paris. Von Bunsen's salon on the Ufer was amongst the city's most highly regarded. Handpicking her guests for their social and intellectual counterpoint, she was praised by contemporaries for the "exemplary composition of her gatherings." Given the lack of opportunities for self-expression for women at this time, the salon became a particular art form of a social kind: a tableau vivant of conversation.

The salons were one of the few areas in which women, mostly married (von Bunsen was one of the few unmarried examples), could exercise their intellectual and social independence. Crystallized around a woman in her home, the salon seemed to offer a dress rehearsal for emancipation. As a social art form, its binding together of individuals through thought and conversation was inextricable from the domestic interiors in which each one was held. A drawing by Adolph Menzel from 1875 depicts a salon evening at 73 Wilhelmstraße. The hostess, Marie, Countess von Schleinitz, reclines on a chaise, bare-shouldered in ruched finery, surrounded by aristocratic and artistic-looking company. The ladies are all seated, clad in similarly elaborate dresses, while whiskery men stand about, upright in tailcoats or uniforms with epaulettes, hands in pockets or clasped behind their backs. An elegant scene to be sure, but what was it they were talking about? Another salonist appears in a photograph several decades later: Marie von Olfers pictured in 1917 at the age of 91, stout in her well-upholstered living room. An author of poetry and children's books, she had hosted a literary salon in her apartment on the canal banks since 1843.

By nature, the salon was a profoundly ephemeral medium of expression. Though a handful of pictures exist, the social texture and conversational counterpoint that defined the success of its form can only be gleaned through snippets of contemporary correspondence, diaries or other fragments on the outermost peripheries of literature. Now, not only have the dozens of salons clustered around the streets of the Tiergarten district and the Landwehr Canal disappeared with barely a trace, but many of the buildings in which they took place are missing too. In fact, whole streets are gone, having been renamed, rerouted, or wiped away altogether in the violence of the intervening century.

The salons existed in a thoroughly bourgeois milieu, dependent on social privilege, economic stability and the kind of housing that went along with that. "For the propertied bourgeois woman," wrote Rosa Luxemburg in 1914, "her house is the world." When the Salas arrived in this neighborhood that had been home to Menzel and Fontane, as well as the grand apartments of the fictional Cécile or the real life Maries – von Bunsen, von Schleinitz and von Olfers – the streets around the Landwehr Canal were the center of Berlin's salon society, and its literary and publishing milieu. Things looked different for the workers in the dark and overcrowded rooms that were the province of the poor, however. "For the proletarian woman," said Luxemburg, "the whole *world* is her house, the world with its sorrow and its joy, with its cold cruelty and its brutal size." The shelter and financial security that the home represented was a bourgeois privilege that the lower classes could not count on.

Rosa Luxemburg herself had moved to Berlin from Zurich in 1898, and on arrival in the city had started right away to search for an apartment. "You have no inkling what it means, in Berlin, to search for a place to live," she wrote to her lover Leo Jogiches in May that year.

> The dimensions of things here are such that you spend hours on a couple of streets, especially because you have to run way up, many stories high, one building after another [...] and mostly it's in vain. The rooms are generally dreadfully expensive everywhere.

She describes Berlin's "depressing dimensions," "cold power" and "indifference" and the overpowering masculinity of the city, in which "officers are literally the dominant caste." When she finally finds an apartment to rent, it is in a garden house on a street bordering directly onto the Tiergarten "in the most aristocratic district, as you will see. The area is charming and quiet, there's no street traffic here, all around there's nothing but luxuriant greenery, and the air quality is excellent," she writes to Leo. "Buy yourself a map of Berlin without fail," she instructs him, "so you can see where I live."

Luxemburg writes to Leo Jogiches almost daily, addressing him with armfuls of endearments: *Golden Boy – Bobo – my only child – my Kukuchna – Dziodzi – Dziodziusiu – Dziudziuchna!* The letters are rich with details of her "extremely regular life," as she calls it: "eat and sleep at the right time, go for walks regularly, take care of my health and my clothes. All my affairs are in order. I read and clip the newspapers scrupulously every day, and I go to the library four times a week." But the city itself engenders a strange sense of disconnection:

> I feel as though something in me had died, I
> experience neither anxiety nor pain, not even
> loneliness, exactly like a corpse. It is as though I
> am an entirely different person from the one I was
> in Zurich. [...] Somehow I don't pay any attention
> to people [here], and I regard Berlin as not real. I
> long to be back in Silesia, in some village, and am
> already dreaming of when we will both be there.

Over the coming years, Luxemburg stays in Berlin, but she and Leo gradually drift apart and finally break up in 1907. Her subsequent letters are written to comrades, fellow activists and friends, including many addressed to Kostja Zetkin, who became Luxemburg's next lover, and even more to his mother, Luxemburg's close friend Clara Zetkin. Three years older than Marie von Bunsen, Zetkin was a radical socialist and fierce advocate of women's rights who, like her, had begun her career as a teacher. The editor of *Die Gleichheit*, the journal for women of the Social Democratic Party, from 1891 on, she believed that true female emancipation could only be achieved through a proletarian revolution.

Luxemburg's affectionate letters to dearest Klärchen are full of internal party wranglings, reports about congresses, complaints about politicians, and discussions of their work. "When are you going to write me that *big letter* about the women's movement?" she asks in 1903. On June 4, 1907, about to go "in the hole," as she calls her two-month prison sentence in the Women's Prison on Berlin's Barnimstraße, having been convicted of "incitement to acts of violence" in a public speech, she writes to Clara: "I'm very happy about it. It will do me good." In March 1916, just out from another spell in the Barnimstraße prison, she describes how women comrades welcomed her on her release: "more than a thousand in number, they gathered me up [from the prison] and then came in massive numbers to where I live, to shake my hand."

"Spring is coming, though very hesitantly," she writes a year later from the prison in Posen where she is now incarcerated, describing the "many tiny mice" that have come into her cell from the cold and "chewed a big hole in a silk dress in my closet." In November 1917 she is transferred to a prison in Breslau and describes all the gifts she has received which make "an entire winter garden in my cell," while noting: "I am now convinced that in the next few years a great upheaval in all of Europe is unavoidable."

From 1914 onwards, Luxemburg's letters are seeded with references to the First World War and commiserations for the deaths of sons and husbands, friends and comrades who have lost their lives on the battlefields. The German strategy of attrition and their rigid policy of "No Retreat" leads to calamitous suffering on all sides, as death enters the homes of families across Europe, across the German Empire, and across the city of Berlin. In May 1916 in the house on the Ufer, Walter Sala, the youngest son of Fortunato, dies aged twenty-four. His battalion, the 52nd Infantry Division of the Imperial German Army, is one of the many that fought at the Battle of Verdun, the longest and most bloody battle of the war. Over half of the 300,000 French and German soldiers who lose their lives in this battle remain unidentified. Walter Sala is brought back wounded, and dies later in Berlin. One of the Sala brothers is gone and only three are left.

"If the men kill then it is up to us women to fight for the preservation of peace," writes Clara Zetkin in an appeal titled "To the Socialist Women of All Countries." "If the men are silent then it is the duty of us women, imbued with our ideals, to raise our voice." When Rosa Luxemburg is finally released from Breslau in November 1918, after a decade in and out of prison, she returns to Berlin and begins to consolidate plans for the Spartacus League. This is formed by Luxemburg, Karl Liebknecht and Zetkin, who is invited to edit a women's supplement to the Spartacist publication, *Die Rote Fahne*. "You should be the one to put it together," writes Luxemburg to Zetkin on November 29. "Go about that as you see fit."

# Triangulation

*Plotting my present-day movements* onto the 1896 map hanging on the wall, I am drawn to, obsessed, even, by the location of our house and the small beige triangle of streets it inhabits. This triangle is like a foreign object within the clotted red mass of railway lines and freight depots all around. A triangular-shaped house or a triangular lot is inauspicious, I read in my online trawlings. In it, energy is pulled in all three directions. "There is no rest or nourishment within the triangle's dynamics," advise the feng shui masters. "The best shapes for a lot or house are square or rectangular, because these allow feng shui energy to settle." Our apartment is full of awkward triangles, its corridors tapering into tight, inescapable corners. Then there is the domestic triangle in which we live, my two sons and I, as three points within our reconfigured home, having abandoned the four-cornered stability of the two-parents-two-kids "Happy Family."

Triangles may be difficult, spewing out energy in all directions, or getting stuck in tricky angularities, but corners also offer shelter. Every corner in a house, every angle in a room is a "symbol of solitude for the imagination; that is to say, it is the germ of a room, or of a house," writes Gaston Bachelard, that fine parser of lived-in spaces. To begin with "the corner is a haven that ensures us one of the things we prize most highly – immobility." A corner offers the opposite of the unboundedness of heath or moor or open land. "The unbounded is abhorrent," states poet Anne Carson in a talk called "On Corners." "It is nothing but beginning, or infinitely unravelling rope ends." Train lines make sense of the unbounded by connecting A to B to C, rendering all that lies beneath them territory to be traversed. But triangles themselves are immobile, inward looking, self-absorbed. Creating ricochets of energy that induce a state of permanent depletion; another sinking drain. In German, the term for "blind spot" is a *toter Winkel*, a dead corner.

———

"I affirm the triangular railway junction. It is an emblem and a focus, a living organism and the fantastic product of a futuristic force," declared Joseph Roth in 1924, in his regular newspaper column for the *Frankfurter Zeitung*. "It is a center," he continued:

> All the vital energies of its locus begin and end here, in the same way that the heart is both the point of departure and the destination of the blood as it flows through the body's veins and arteries. It's the heart of a world whose life is belt drive and clockwork, piston rhythm and siren scream. It is the heart of the world, which spins on its axis a thousand times faster than the alternation of day and night would have us believe.

This essay appears in *What I Saw*, a collection of Roth's texts about Berlin written between 1920 and 1933 that was given to me by a close friend from New York shortly after I moved here in 2001. I remember reading Roth's acrid descriptions of Berlin in the 1920s – with its heavy traffic and building sites, its café society patrons, displaced persons, pleasure industry and "very large department stores" – while riding the U-Bahn from our home in Prenzlauer Berg in former East Berlin to the more familiar hub of consumer civilization over in the West. By that time, I was pregnant and travelled this line for monthly visits to an English-speaking gynecologist, feeling heavier on each journey as the months progressed. Roth's writing about the "triangular railroad junction" struck a particular chord, as my train passed through this triangle. The Gleisdreieck is literally a *triangle of tracks*, three corners of rails, where two separate lines of the U-Bahn meet. For Roth, the Gleisdreieck was emblematic of Berlin's drive for speed and connectivity. "Grey, dusty grasses will sprout shyly between the metal tracks," he prophesied. "The 'landscape' will acquire a mask of iron."

As the train traversed the elevated rail lines, I would look down onto the spread of sandy terrain below. All the vital energies that Roth had described were gone. Trains would crisscross intermittently above, but nothing seemed to happen down there. No activity and barely any vegetation: just a sprawl of dried-out earth with occasional puddles. Once home to the goods yards and freight depots of the Railway Directorate, it had been a "triangular tangle of veins, polygons, polyhedrons, made from the tracks of life," as Roth puts it, in which "the great, shining iron rails flow into one another, draw electricity and take on energy for their long journeys and into the world beyond." Now it just created dead ends. Local streets ended abruptly when they met the high fence that surrounded these

wastelands. Its inaccessibility made them seem somehow sinister: so much empty space in the center of the
city. Both abandoned and fortressed. A physical blind
spot this time, a *toter Winkel* of spreading sand and
rusting tracks.

When we moved to the Ufer in 2014 the Gleisdreieck
lay right behind our house, and I came to know it at
close quarters. By this time, its sprawling wastelands
had been converted into a surprisingly successful and
well-used urban park. Wide lawns and children's playgrounds border on areas left in their wilderness state,
where self-seeded birch forests and bramble bushes
sprout between rusted rails, leading straight and purposefully into nothing. These days my sons come here
to play soccer and skateboard, or meet friends in the
shadow of the overhead U-Bahn lines. I cross the park
on my bike on my way to the nearby shops on Potsdamer
Straße. This once abandoned expanse now embraces
a hundred forms of human activity, across all ages,
races and social strata. Dog walkers, joggers, pension-
ers shuffling along its footpaths, toddlers shovelling
sand in the playgrounds. Tight circles of pot-smoking
teens, picnics for extended families, buff aerobic fitness
freaks. Above these hubs of vivid social action, trains

head in and out of the station in regular yellow arrows on the elevated tracks.

The Gleisdreieck U-Bahn station occupies one point of the beige triangle of streets around my house. An artist friend who lives a few blocks farther down the canal and collects historical printed ephemera, gave me a postcard he had found of the Gleisdreieck U-Bahn station that dated back to 1908. It pictures a scene of devastation: a train has derailed while crossing the raised railway bridge and one of its carriages has crashed through the barriers down onto the street where it lies, its body mangled and crushed. A crowd is huddled at street level around the fallen railway coach, while up on the bridge tiny figures stand in groups, surveying the wreckage below. The postcard's caption reads: "The terrible catastrophe on the raised railway in Berlin on 26 September 1908. The scene of the disaster." On that day, the signals had failed, and two trains collided on the triangle of tracks, killing eighteen people and injuring twenty others. It seems strange that such a gruesome image should be printed on a greetings postcard. But before photographs were printed in newspapers, these postcards satisfied the public's desire for evidence of disaster, spreading news of train crashes or terrible fires, witnessed secondhand. This postcard is addressed in a looping ink script, now brown with time, to *Professor Berger, Oberbahnassistent*, a senior railway administrator. I screw up my eyes and try to decipher the tiny, neatly inscribed words that the sender had appended to this tragic scene, but can only make out its signature, *Maria*.

Did Adolf and Fortunato Sala, optimistic new owners of the house around the corner, witness the aftermath of this catastrophe that occurred just months after their arrival? Did their wives and children hear the screeching wheels, the crunch of iron, the screams of passengers as the trains collided on the triangle of tracks, crashed into the railings and hit the ground? Was this not an inauspicious start to a new chapter on the Tempelhofer Ufer?

That same year in 1908, the Hotel Excelsior opened at Askanischer Platz, in front of the Anhalter Bahnhof. It was the largest and most modern hotel in Europe: a six-story neoclassical edifice complete with crenelated columns and pediment, connected via subterranean tunnel to the station's main entrance hall. Opening with 200 rooms for guests, the hotel had doubled this number by 1912 and expanded again to 600 rooms in the 1920s. Though the Hotel Esplanade, at nearby Postdamer Platz, was considered to be finer, the Excelsior offered something different. This hotel was *modern*, conceived with the new breed of business travellers in mind who were delivered daily into the city by train lines spanning the whole German Reich. Both the Excelsior and the Esplanade were owned by the same hotelier, a restauranteur's son named Curt Elschner who had begun his career as a waiter in Leipzig, and came to exemplify the dynamic entrepreneurial spirit of cosmopolitan Berlin. The Excelsior was his masterpiece. Elschner modernized and enlarged it constantly. He replaced its coal heating with gas in the 1920s, and installed electric kitchens in all of the dozen gastronomic establishments. It had its own dedicated power station and waterworks in the backyard, and seats for 5,000 guests who drank over a million litres of beer per year in its various restaurants and bars.

It was in the Hotel Excelsior, on November 11, 1918, that Rosa Luxemburg and Karl Liebknecht officially founded the Spartacus League. They produced their newspaper, the *Rote Fahne*, in its rooms. "If only you knew what life is like for me here," wrote Luxemburg to Clara Zetkin on November 29, 1918. "It's like being in a witch's cauldron. Last night I didn't get home until midnight, and then only because we were both – Karl and I – thrown out of the only hotel in this district!"

In December, the Spartacus League renamed itself the Communist Party of Germany, but a month later it was brutally crushed in the Spartacist Uprising. On January 11, 1919, Luxemburg wrote to Clara Zetkin, describing the daily chaos:

> It is impossible to describe the way of life that I – and all of us – have been living for weeks, the tumult and turmoil, the constant changing of living quarters, the never-ending reports filled with alarm, and in between, the tense strain of work, conferences, etc., etc. [...] I've only seen my own place now and then for a couple of hours at night."

When it comes to the Communist Party, she is more optimistic: "On the whole our movement is developing splendidly, and throughout all of Germany at that." Though, she admits, "at this moment in Berlin the battles are continuing. Many of our brave lads have fallen." This letter to Zetkin turned out to be Luxemburg's last. Four days later, she and Liebknecht were tracked down by members of the *Freikorps* and taken to the Hotel Eden, from which they would never return. On April 8, 1919, Clara Zetkin writes a letter to "Esteemed, dear friend and comrade Lenin" and apologizes for not having replied earlier.

The murder of Karl and especially Rosa was a terrible blow. It hit me with equal cruelty as a militant as it did as a human being. Almost immediately afterwards came the death of my friend [Franz] Mehring and then soon after the murder of Leo [Jogiches]. This came hardly 24 hours after I left Berlin. [...] Of the four who first protested against the world war and fought for the revolution I am now the only one alive, and in Germany I personally feel completely orphaned. For me, with Leo they killed Rosa a second time.

A rippling surface of water moves into a horizontal rush of lines, increasing in velocity, and cutting suddenly to an approaching steam locomotive. A tight crop of carriage windows passes by in a blur. Tracks, pistons, wheels: the rush of train travel brings us into the city from the outlying countryside. Past the industrial outskirts and overhead electricity cables, signal boxes, couplings; into the urban conurbation, through a mass of railway lines, yards and hoardings, until finally pulling into the great arched hallway of the Anhalter Bahnhof. Wheels and pistons slow, expressing bursts of steam. It is five o'clock in the morning. A sign, full screen, announces our destination. Here we are: BERLIN.

This montage begins Walter Ruttmann's 1927 film *Berlin: Symphony of a Metropolis*. The film's next sequence scans the sleeping city, first aerial shots of its densely packed buildings, four-sided sentries around hidden central courtyards. Then down to the street level, shop windows shuttered, few signs of life save pigeons and the odd stray cat. The only person out is a solitary dog walker. But in the following scenes, the city's inhabitants start to arrive: a liquid mass of people pours off trains, floods down station steps, rushes along sidewalks and across bridges. Cut to the factories and their relentless mechanical choreographies – whirring cogs and turning pistons, regular, symmetrical, ceaseless rhythms – all the "belt drive and clockwork, piston rhythm and siren scream" that Joseph Roth wrote of.

The point of view in Ruttmann's film is constantly roaming. Through editing sleight and well-observed detail, he constructs a vision of a city on the move. There are smoke-exhaling factory towers and the non-stop action of mechanized production lines. Shops and their delivery boys, maidservants with shopping baskets, offices full of typists, printing, telephoning, in constant communications. Building sites, window displays, trains, traffic, advertisements. Passengers on busy platforms getting on and off the trains, loading up trunks and suitcases. Double-decker buses and failed attempts to cross the road. This is *Großstadtwahn*: big city madness. Tempo, mobility, production and exchange. Above all the simultaneity of all these experiences. It is clear to see in Ruttmann's film that the railways are the driving force.

By the 1920s, Potsdamer Platz is the most trafficked crossroads in Europe: five major roads lead into it and twenty-five trams converge here, along with automobiles, buses, horse-drawn carts, bicycles and pushcarts. An average of 2,753 vehicles per hour traverse it, according to an official count in 1928. Disaster is always imminent. Thus, in its center, a steel beam and concrete tower is erected: the city's first traffic light. Not, to Joseph Roth's disappointment, something "soaring and magnificent," but rather "a little grey metal stump of a tower, with large, and at that stage, still-closed round eyes at its top edge." Potsdamer Platz, despite looking like "a suppurating wound," as Roth had it, where "day after day, night after night, workmen scrabble around," became a booming attraction at the center of the new metropolis, drawing residents and visitors into its maelstrom.

Ruttmann's film captures the height of the Weimar Republic. Established on November 9, 1918, two days before Luxemburg and Liebknecht officially founded the

Spartacus League, its catalyst was mutiny: mass movements in the streets and workplace that called for an
end to the First World War and for the abdication of the
kaiser. This act of revolution in itself broke through the
conventions of acceptable behavior, overthrowing the
stuffy, rigid, authoritarian society of imperial Germany
dominated by royalty, nobility and the military, and a
constrained and hypocritical sexual morality. The new
constitution, adopted on July 31, 1919, granted universal
suffrage for all those over twenty. It was a leap into democracy and the modern world, but unlike the all-out
Russian Revolution which completely overturned the
old order, the new Weimar government tried to find a
middle ground from which to govern. Its political leaders agreed to compromises with army officers, high-
level bureaucrats and industrialists in return for their
cooperation. They believed this pragmatic approach
would help steer Germany out of the chaos of defeat
and revolution towards democracy and economic re-
vival, but these concessions, along with their signing of
the widely despised Treaty of Versailles, undermined
its integrity from the start.

Berlin was the heart of the Weimar Republic and
the Hotel Excelsior was at the heart of Berlin, host to
the broad cast of characters that came to define the city
in the 1920s. It was the model for Viennese born Vicky

Baum's hit novel *Grand Hotel*, published in 1929 following its newspaper serialization. The novel was adapted for the stage, playing to rave reviews at the Theater am Nollendorfplatz, and translated into English, selling 95,000 copies in the US in the first six months after publication. By 1932 it had been turned into an MGM movie starring Greta Garbo and Joan Crawford, and won an Oscar for Best Picture. This breathless trajectory to fame and glamour itself seemed to replicate the pace and vivacity of both the novel and the city in which it was set.

In *Grand Hotel*, the bookkeeper Otto Kringelein has left his provincial hometown, having being diagnosed with a life-threatening illness, and comes to the big city to live out his remaining days in style. After several false starts, he moves into Room 70 at the Grand Hotel, intending to luxuriate in its mahogany furniture, silk upholstery and lace curtains, but is chronically inhibited by his sense of not belonging. A narrative of big city life unfolds, set within the confines of this hotel's imposing structure, and against the vivid backdrop of the fast-paced metropolis. Industrialists, starlets, ageing ballerinas, good-looking cads, fashionable copyists, and disfigured veterans of the First World War populate Baum's *Grand Hotel*. Love affairs begin and deals are brokered. "Sugar got more expensive; silk stockings, cheaper; coal became scarce – these and a thousand other contingencies depended on the issue of battles fought out in the conference chamber of the Grand Hotel." The atmosphere of the city spools out in medleys that smell like gasoline and are full of the noise of traffic. Street-sweeping machines and buses sail along the streets like ships, illuminated by giant electric advertising signs. Otto Kringelein, incredulous, looks out of the window of his hotel room:

> There was even a tree that spread its branches not far from the hotel, but its branches were very different from those in Fredersdorf. This Berlin tree occupied a little island of soil in the midst of the asphalt and around the plot of soil there was a railing as though it needed some protection against the city.

Baum's lively narrative follows the fortunes of her cast of protagonists, while bridging passages articulate the pulse of the city, a character in its own right. Technology, movement, speed, traffic, fashion. The energy of it all! The city's momentum is as relentless as its inhabitants' fates are interconnected. Meanwhile the Grand Hotel, impassively accommodating, contains them all with stoic resolve. Even at the novel's end, the momentum doesn't stop. "The revolving door turns and turns and turns," reads its final line.

The whiff of Weimar-era decadence is still deeply en-meshed in Berlin's identity, but little of that era re-mains in the neighborhoods around my house. There is the magnificent Shell-Haus on the Landwehr Canal, up towards the Tiergarten, built as the Weimar pe-riod was waning. A sequence of seven elements rising progressively from six to ten stories, it stands there still, its façade flowing in an ever-futuristic wave. But other landmark buildings, such as Erich Mendelsohn's Columbushaus on Potsdamer Platz, have disappeared completely, replaced by the anonymous boxes of twenty-first-century mall architecture. The Weimar spirit was dispersed rather amongst the friction of bodies in cafés or crowds on the streets, in the frantic energy pictured in Ruttmann's film, the cultural outpourings of music, theater, dancing, mass media, in liberated sexuality and loose, suggestive clothing. But the backdrop to the new-found freedoms of the "Golden Twenties" was do-mestic violence, foreign intransigence, steep inflation and the splintering of political support amongst many disparate parties.

The Weimar Republic's democracy was built on contradiction. Lucrative mergers of huge industrial concerns versus long hours and poor working conditions in the factories. The cultural and artistic blossomings of figures such as Bertolt Brecht, Thomas Mann and George Grosz were seeded in precarity and disillusion. In the 1920s, as Hannah Höch was fashioning new-fangled Dada anatomies from images snipped from the pages of the illustrated magazines, Käthe Kollwitz was sketching in charcoal a black-cloaked pregnant woman, poised on the banks of a body of water, hand grasping her mouth in horror (*Pregnant Woman Drowning Herself,* ca. 1926). Sexual reform was in the air, but more widespread were conditions defined as "marital misery" and "the crisis of the family." By 1933, the birth rate was half that of 1900. More than thirty-five per cent of married couples that year were childless, while a million women had illegal abortions, with accompanying health complications and a high death toll to show for it. In the years before, Kollwitz designed posters in support of social causes and to promote the issues of unwanted pregnancies, housing shortages, domestic violence and alcoholism. *Nieder mit den Abtreibungs Paragraphen!* – "Down with the abortion laws!" declares the script beside the image of a pregnant woman clasping a small baby, her face pinched and her eye bruised black. *Herausgegeben von der KPD* is printed on the poster's top right corner: "Published by the Communist Party of Germany."

Kollwitz, born in 1867, had come to Berlin aged thirty to study art and was one of three women amongst the sixty-five founding members of the Berlin Secession. Höch, born in 1889, also came to Berlin to pursue her artistic interests, arriving in the city in 1912 and enrolling in Kunstgewerbeschule Charlottenburg, the School of Applied Arts. She was the same generation as Kollwitz's two sons, the youngest of whom, Peter, was killed in the First World War. As a woman, Höch was spared the fate of the men her age who were sent to the front and never returned. In 1916, her father cut her off financially, refusing to support her continued art studies, and she began working three days a week for Ullstein Verlag, Berlin's publishing giant. Here, with easy access to illustrated magazines and publications, she started to make her first collages and photo montages. The social critique of Kollwitz's figurative drawings took another direction in these early works by Höch, which juxtapose the hardware of war and a fragmenting militarism with the burgeoning mechanization and capitalism of twentieth-century city life. In *The Beautiful Girl* (1920) women sporting contemporary hairstyles and skimpy clothing fuse with fragments of machinery. An electric lightbulb stands in for a face.

Höch became involved in the Dada movement crystallizing around George Grosz, John Heartfield and Raoul Hausmann and was the only woman included in "The First International Dada Messe," held in Otto Burchard's gallery on Lützow Ufer in 1920. She had been in a turbulent relationship with Hausmann for five years by then, though he was married. Hausmann professed his disdain for the patriarchal structure of family and believed in a sexual revolution, but he still refused to leave his wife. For her part, Höch wanted children but not with a married man. According to the biography in the back of a catalogue I have – from the 2007 exhibition *Aller Anfang ist DADA!* [Everything Starts with DADA!] at the Berlinische Galerie – she had two abortions during the time of their relationship, and her health suffered as a result. Höch satirized her situation in a short story called "The Painter" written in 1920, which portrays a modern couple that embraces gender equality in their relationship – a novel and shocking concept for the time – but the male artist protagonist is thrown into crisis when "at least four times in four years he was forced to wash the dishes – the kitchen dishes." The painter feels that his wife is thwarting "the boundless flight of his genius," he feels degraded "as a man and as a painter," he suffers nightmares. As a modern person, "in theory he had to agree with the equality of the sexes," but still, "in your own house – her demand seemed to him comparable to an enslavement of his soul." Höch and Hausmann broke up not long after and a few years later she met the Dutch writer Mathilda (Til) Brugman. Embracing the fluid opportunities available during that era, they embarked on a relationship, spending ten years living together happily, first in the Hague and then in Berlin.

In the years following the First World War, the constraints on women were beginning to loosen and opportunities were starting to grow. Though the first grammar schools for girls had been established in the 1890s and access to higher education had been pledged by the Prussian State in 1908, it was only after the First World War that this became generally available. International Women's Day was founded by Clara Zetkin and first celebrated in 1911, and in 1918 women in Germany received the right to vote. There were more opportunities for women to work and for female writers to have their work published. Crop-haired, clad in short, loose-fitting flapper styles, smoking, dancing, frequenting cafés and going out alone, the "new woman" was emblematic of the Weimar period. The subject of bitter discussions and divergent opinions, she was depicted satirically by Otto Dix and George Grosz, or more sympathetically by Berlin artists Jeanne Mammen or Lotte Laserstein. According to Weimar scholar Eric Weitz, the "new woman" was "the most visible, most talked about, most conflicted symbol of the moral and sexual revolution of the 1920s."

Despite the centrality of these modern active women, it is still not easy to find out who they were. Peter Gay's 1968 book *Weimar Culture: The Outsider as Insider* is a touchstone for this period in Berlin, but in its seven page, double-columned index, there are only eleven female names, amongst them Kaiserin Auguste Victoria (noted in passing as Kaiser Wilhelm II's "Empress") and Marlene Dietrich (or rather her legs, listed as an embodiment of Weimar spirit, along with Gropius's buildings and Kandinsky's abstractions). Vicky Baum is dismissed as a "facile mediocrity," although Gay does go on to quote at length her appraisal of Berlin's liberal publishing world of the time. The names and achievements of those women listed in the Berlin Society of Women Artists' publication are by and large forgotten, though some are slowly being recuperated now, nearly a century later. Judging by those who did get a mention in Gay's index, you were far more likely to be remembered as an actress or singer than a writer or artist. The Weimar period may have celebrated the outsider, but women were still being sidelined. How am I to track down these disappeared voices? Finding myself at another dead end, I return to the streets themselves.

· 10 ·

# Signs

*Ever since I began* this research, I've felt my attention snagging on details as I walk or bike around the city. Drawn to things that appear to be missing or don't quite seem to fit, I start reading every sign I pass. I am amazed to discover, for instance, that there used to be a public swimming pool right behind the Gleisdreieck. This information is on a sign in a little patch of parkland which another sign tells me is called Nelly-Sachs-Park. I look up this name online and discover Nelly Sachs to be a Nobel-prize winning German-Swedish poet and playwright, born in 1891 to a Jewish family in this neighborhood. Through the combination of street sign and internet, I can darn her back into a historical fabric holed with disappearance, obliteration and active misremembering.

Rosa Luxemburg has long had a street named after her, as has Karl Liebknecht. Both, not surprisingly, in the former Communist East. There is a Lennéstraße and a Hobrechtstraße, a Walter-Benjamin-Platz, a Menzel-Straße, a Fontanestraße and a Fontanepromenade. In the former East, Clara-Zetkin-Straße used to run straight through Mitte, parallel to the River Spree. But in 1995, post-unification, Zetkin's Bolshevik connections made her undesirable and it returned to its original name from 1822, Dorotheenstraße, after local aristocrat Dorothea von Brandenburg.

In 2011 Berlin's city government adopted a formal policy to name all new streets after women, in an attempt to redress the gender imbalance: ninety per cent of streets at that time were named after men. Now of the city's 10,000 streets, around 500 have women's names. Given that the main thoroughfares are already dedicated to the Wilhelms, Friedrichs, Bismarcks, or Generals Gneisenau, Yorck, Bülow and Kleist, these female streets are invariably to be found in odd new parts of the city. In former dead zones sacrificed to rash post-unification redevelopment or real estate sell-offs of the early 2000s that aimed to fill up the city's depleted coffers. Banks of bland apartment blocks or anonymous office developments can be found on streets named after remarkable, often radical women, whose achievements in politics, literature, art or music are most probably little-known today.

The areas across the canal and upstream from my house, around the Berlin State Library and Potsdamer Platz, are just these kinds of strange, new-build neighborhoods. The territory here was uniformly flattened in the Second World War and severed by the Berlin Wall that crossed it in the Cold War era. In the early 2000s it quickly became host to countless flashy building projects that turned a blind eye to its trauma and scars. On one of my regular journeys, from my house to the local gym, I ride my bike up the canal and cross the second bridge, turning left at the corner of Hafenplatz, where Cécile and the Colonel lived over a century ago. I take the next right and come to the gym, in a brand-new door-manned apartment building named, with typical misplaced aspiration, The Charleston. This journey became increasingly frequent as the months progressed and the steady unhappiness of a dying relationship was replaced by the sharp pain of the break itself. The development of physical strength offered a counterbalance to the slow process of emotional repair. In the center of the street that the gym is on is a long mound tilted at an angle and completely grassed over, creating an asymmetrical green form the length of the whole block. It was several months before I realized that this strange landscape feature conceals the tracks of what used to be the Potsdamer Bahnhof. It is an unwitting funerary mound for a now deceased railway station; a fact not mentioned or recorded in any way at the place itself. After this discovery I finally registered the street name: Gabriele-Tergit-Promenade. Who is this Gabriele and why is this weird street named after her?

Gabriele Tergit, I discover, was the pseudonym of journalist and writer Elise Hirschmann. Born in 1894 to a Jewish industrialist family, she grew up on Corneliusstraße, close to the borders of the Tiergarten on the most picturesque stretch of the Landwehr Canal. Her first article, about vocational training for women, was published in 1915 when she was twenty-one, in the magazine supplement of the *Berliner Tageblatt*. When Tergit arrived at the newspaper's offices to collect her fee, the editor was horrified to discover she was so young, and declared that he would never have taken the article had he known. "A young woman from a good family was not supposed to write for the newspapers," remarked Tergit in her memoirs many years later. "I was the subject of general scorn." Undeterred, she continued to write while studying, bringing out articles in both the liberal *Berliner Tageblatt* and the older, respectable *Vossischen Zeitung*. In 1924, she began to write a regular column for the *Tageblatt*, specializing in reportage from the criminal courts in Moabit. Court hearings, as Tergit observed, reveal much about the social make-up of a time:

> Better than the work of poets and historians, is the original source – the letter, the diary, the recorded conversation – for giving the essence of an era. The files of a criminal case, as formal recordings of these original sources, are insights into the typical feelings of an epoch.

As a working woman in the city, Tergit's place was not the salon but the *Stammtisch*, the table for regulars in the local pub or restaurant. Hers was at the Capri, an Italian trattoria beside the Hotel Excelsior. Once a week a group of journalists would meet here for an Italian lunch, washed down with a glass or two of Chianti and a grappa chaser: "our symbol of camaraderie." At the Capri *Stammtisch*, Tergit was a journalist amongst other journalists, editors, regulars and visitors, almost all exclusively men.

Tergit's weekly reportages capture the daily breath of the city in short, blocky observations. Focusing on its small-scale players and everyday dramas, they display a grudging affection for this place, typical of those born and bred in Berlin. *Schnauze mit Herz*, it is called: surly but heartfelt. Her concise texts journey through the city as if across a map, delineating the social caesura that had occurred in the wake of the First World War. With a close eye finely tuned for telling details, she describes the city's buildings, shops, bus routes, and inhabitants. The young men sent off to war who write weekly letters to their mothers, thanking them for sending the parcels of sausages; men whose correspondence stops abruptly, who never come home again. *"Kompliziert ist unser Dasein,"* she concludes one text, with characteristic understatement. "Our existence is complicated."

Gabriele Tergit's text *"Eingewöhnen in Berlin"* [Settling into Berlin] sees her returning to the city in the early 1920s from a sojourn in the south. Arriving at Anhalter Bahnhof after such a trip, she writes, is "one of the most dreadful moments of existence." She describes the city's meagre forests, its poor pine trees struggling in terrain hijacked by the railway ensemble. "Down there lies Berlin – Berlin? The main square is taken over by railways, tracks, sheds, cottages, greenery, iron scaffolds." The city itself, its houses, its citizens, lie in the dead zones in between. Meanwhile the elegant streets bordering the Tiergarten, where Tergit herself grew up, appear like an anomaly from a bygone time in the calamitous aftermath of the First World War: "streets of pleasure and exclusive villas for pre-war existences," is how she puts it. Tergit's mournful sensitivity extends as much to the city as to its inhabitants, as if it were a living organism; one which, for two hundred years already, "had been an object of exploitation for the Prussian kings, its freedoms limited, its expansion hindered, deprived of its green lungs."

The establishment of the Weimar Republic had upturned the status quo but the lack of political consensus meant the coalition government remained fragile and precarious. When Christopher Isherwood came to lodge in the overcrowded attic apartment of the Nowak family near Hallesches Tor in Kreuzberg, Frau Nowak was an imperialist who longed for the return of the kaiser, her youngest son Otto wanted a Communist revolution, and Lothar, her eldest, had already joined the Nazis.

In Berlin, young couples and families like the Nowaks suffered from the lack of affordable housing while the vast apartments of the Wilhelmine era appeared suddenly unwieldy to those realigning themselves to a modern way of life. Elderly impoverished widows rented out the many rooms of their grandscaled *Gründerzeit* apartments to Slavic refugees or out-of-pocket students. When they were eventually forced to leave, their outmoded, oversized furniture was simply left on the street: "What was formerly representative and comfortable is now dreary and burdensome," Tergit wryly observes.

Her text *"Die Dame aus den 80er Jahren"* [The Lady from the 80s] paints a vivid picture of an ageing *salonistin*: "She talks a lot about the past," remarks Tergit. "She is charitable and good to 'the people,' but she hasn't the faintest idea what work is." Meanwhile, in another article, Tergit overhears female neighbors complaining about how *demanding* younger women have become, hankering after silk stockings or permed hair. Tergit sides with the demanding young women and swiftly counters that while they may desire such small luxuries, they have no need for big apartments, heavy furniture, glass, silver, figurines and bronze – all the cumbersome trappings of the bourgeois Prussian wife. Independence is what they are after, and they are ready to work for it. Silk stockings and curled hair have become "weapons in their daily battle," writes Tergit. The girl that her neighbor deems *demanding* is evidence of a post-war social realignment. She is:

> a particularly brave fighter in the struggle for life,
> and some of those who walk around like a doll
> with a head full of curls, support an old mother at
> home and an unemployed brother's family.

Gabriele Tergit – direct, compassionate, witty and sharp – is the eyewitness I have been looking for. The female eye fixed on the city's streets, buildings and people, parsing generation shifts and social strata. But social emancipation was just one side of the volatile Weimar years. There were the politically motivated murders of the 1920s, the assassinations undertaken by the *Schwarze Reichswehr* known as the *Feme* murders. Tergit sat in the criminal courts of Moabit during the trials of these crimes, noting down the criminals' dispassionate confessions: how one lets a man fall – "splash" – into the water, and another speaks of a "little bullet in the back of the head." The *Feme* murders, as Peter Gay has it, "belong to the most atrocious crimes in a century filled with atrocities: unemployed fanatics and unemployable ex-officers clubbed men to death and strangled women often on the mere suspicion of 'unpatriotic activities.'" Unlike their socialist counterparts who were vigorously punished, these right-wing murderers, later feted as the first soldiers of Hitler's Third Reich, were rarely tried, or went largely unpunished in courts stuffed with judges whose allegiances lay with the old order of the empire. Tergit records the terror of an eyewitness to one of these criminal acts who rescinds his testimony. *"Er schwieg,"* she writes – he holds his tongue. The word for silence – *Schweigen* – is also a verb, as she dryly notes.

## · 11 ·

# Collision Course

*I am grasped* by a grim sensation when I think about this period in Berlin. A forceful downward pull. Like a negative maelstrom that senses disaster beneath the increasingly frantic pace taking hold of this metropolis. By the time Irmgard Keun's bestselling novel *The Artificial Silk Girl* is published in 1932, the energy of the city is undercut by a hard seam of ruthlessness, one that affects the fortunes of its young protagonist, Doris, a wide-eyed newcomer to Berlin. Doris has left her home in the Rhineland and come to the city to seek her fortune. *"Ich werde ein Glanz,"* she declares repeatedly, "I will be a star." Her narration is breathless as her eyes gulp in the sights of the *Großstadt*:

I walk and walk through Friedrichstraße and
walk and see shiny cars and people, and my heart
blooms heavily. [...] I walk evenings and mornings – it is a full city with so many flowers and
shops and lights and pubs, with doors and felt
curtains behind them – I paint myself a picture
of how it is inside, and sometimes I go in and look
around as if looking for someone who isn't there –
and then I leave. [...] I love Berlin until my knees
are weak and I don't know what to eat tomorrow
but I don't care, I sit in Josty on Potsdamer Platz
and there are marble columns and so much space.

For Doris, Berlin is a place to see and be seen; the practicalities of making a living are decidedly secondary.
When she befriends a neighbor, Herr Brenner, who lost
his sight in the First World War, she becomes his surrogate eyewitness. "I look at all the streets and pubs
and people and lampposts. And then I notice my seeing
and I bring it to him." [...] "What did you see, what else?"
asks Brenner, unable to see the new Berlin for himself.
"I unpack my eyes for him," Doris says.

By 1932, the glittering promise of lights and commerce at Potsdamer Platz, Friedrichstraße or Kurfürstendamm have begun to seem illusory. The real heart
of Berlin, writes Isherwood, is "a small damp black
wood – the Tiergarten." In the winter, "the cold begins

to drive the peasant boys out of their tiny, unprotected villages into the city, to look for food, and work. But the city, which glowed so brightly and invitingly in the night sky above the plains, is cold and cruel and dead. Its warmth is an illusion, a mirage of the winter desert."

Keun's novel follows Doris through three seasons as her luck and optimism slowly dwindle: she loses her job, steals a fur coat, shacks up with a man, and gets thrown out. In the third and final part, titled "A Lot of Winter and a Waiting Room," we find her disorientated and homeless: "I walk around with my suitcase and don't know what I want or where to go. I am in the waiting room at Zoo Station a lot. Why is it that waiters are so scornful when you happen to have no money?" Though the circumstances for women would appear to have improved, this novel is as much a catalogue of female misfortune as Gabriele Reuter's *From a Good Family* was in 1895. The female desire for independence may have started to blossom, but the necessary social structures to allow it to flourish were still few and far between.

As the 1930s progress, the latent aggression of the *Freikorps* and the increasingly organized National Socialist German Workers Party lie beneath the city's surface like a deadly undercurrent. A chilling shift is about to take place that will switch the city's track from a vibrant liberal intellectualism and socially-orientated politics to the blunt and reactionary brutality of Hitler, Goebbels, Göring and their brown-shirted armies. It is almost unbearable, observing this in retrospect, as a slow-motion horror begins to unfold.

The summer of 1932 is blighted with clashes between the Communists and the Nazis' storm troopers. There are hundreds of street battles in the run-up to the July elections, as well as constant intimidation and politically motivated murders. On election day alone, nine people are murdered. The election result is a massive victory for the Nazis, who win 230 parliamentary seats, though with only 37.3 per cent of the vote it is far from a clear majority. But with opposition splintered across Communist and Social Democratic parties, the government is thrown into disarray.

"The presidential cabinet bears a great burden of guilt," proclaims Clara Zetkin, now seventy-five years old. "It is fully responsible for the murders of the last few weeks, through its abolishing the ban on uniforms for the National Socialist storm troopers and by its open patronage of Fascist civil-war troops." It is August 30, 1932 and Zetkin is giving the opening address to the Reichstag, an honor bestowed on her as its oldest member. She has held a parliamentary seat for the Communist Party since 1920. In the audience, the newly elected

NSDAP members of parliament take up half of the room. Despite having suffered a heart attack the previous year from which she is still convalescing, Zetkin mounts a visceral assault:

> The task of the hour is to establish the united front of all working people in order to repel fascism, in order thereby to preserve the power and strength of the organizations of the enslaved and exploited, and even to save their very lives.

Zetkin attacks the institution from within its own walls, disparaging the "rotten soil of the bourgeois social order" that allows for a cabinet stuffed with barons and military officers. Laying the blame squarely at the feet of those at the top of this governmental institution, she contrasts them with the disenfranchised and "trampled upon." Among which are the "millions of women who are still subject to the chains of gender-slavery, and thereby the harshest class slavery" and who, therefore, "must not be absent from the united front of working people that is also being formed in Germany."

A few months later, in winter 1932, Gabriele Tergit meets her colleagues at the Capri one last time. They meet outside the restaurant, which in the meantime has become a hangout for local Nazi storm troopers.

"We were driven out before we were driven out," she grimly observes.

As the Weimar Republic wavers and resignations abound, a fateful deal is made by the same presidential cabinet that Zetkin disparages in her speech. On January 30, 1933 Reich president von Hindenburg appoints Adolf Hitler as chancellor of the German Reich, the idea being that Vice Chancellor von Papen and other conservative cabinet members will keep him in check. They believe that they can use the Nazis for their own ends, to overthrow the Weimar Republic and re-establish an authoritarian, militaristic governmental system. Instead, the entire democratic institution is quite literally torched. On February 27, a fire breaks out in the Reichstag. Hitler blames the Communists and Hindenburg signs an emergency decree. Arrests can now be made without charge. Storm troopers and police comb Berlin's housing estates for evidence of resistance, rounding up Communist Party members, Social Democrats, left-wingers and trade unionists, abusing them and throwing them in jail. There are pages and pages of horrific, brutal, sadistic incidents in Richie's *Faust's Metropolis*. On March 5 federal elections are held. The NSDAP win 43.9 per cent of the vote, still not an outright majority. But on

March 24, Hitler's "Enabling Act" is passed, giving the cabinet the power to enact laws without the consent of parliament. In July 1933, a new law bans all remaining parties. The takeover is complete.

On the night before the March elections, storm troopers visit Gabriele Tergit's Tiergarten apartment, hammering at the door at 3:00 a.m. and yelling for her to open up. Fortunately, having received a tip-off a few weeks earlier, her husband has fitted their door with an iron bar. The storm troopers don't get in. Early the next morning Tergit packs her suitcase and leaves Berlin with her son for Czechoslovakia. Shortly after, they meet her husband in Palestine, where the family lives for several years before emigrating to the UK in 1938. Tergit remains in the UK, living the rest of her life in exile. By 1935, Irmgard Keun has left Berlin too, initially for France, with fellow exile Joseph Roth who has become her lover. After several years of precarity, moving from hotel to hotel and drinking heavily, Roth dies in Paris in 1939. Keun returns to Germany in 1940, living incognito in her hometown of Cologne. Vicky Baum, who has been living in Los Angeles, where she moved in 1931 to write the screenplay for *Grand Hotel*, stays there until her death in 1960. Walter Benjamin is also gone by the early 1930s, and is working on his Berlin childhood reminiscences in Ibiza and Italy. They remain unpublished, however, and in 1940 after his plans to emigrate to the United States are thwarted, Benjamin commits suicide. His friend Franz Hessel, who was Jewish by birth, leaves Berlin for Paris in 1938, and dies in exile in 1941. Werner Hegemann, author of *Stone Berlin*, flees too, moving to New York in November 1933 where he teaches urban planning until his death in 1936.

There is always a certain amount of replacement in a city. The comings and goings of individual lives, washed over by waves of new inhabitants, generation after generation. Berlin had long been characterized by such a fluid population, seeping in and out. During this period, however, the disappearances are sudden: stark and brutal interruptions in ordinary people's lives. The Jewish, Communist, literary and intellectual threads in the city's weave are systematically plucked out. On May 10, 1933, books by a list of over 150 authors are extracted by students from libraries across the city and brought to the square in front of the Staatsoper. Over 20,000 books are burnt in a ceremonial pyre to the triumphant pronouncement of Joseph Goebbels, the newly elected minister of propaganda: "Fellow students, German men and women. The age of extreme Jewish intellectualism has now ended." Works by Hegemann, Benjamin, Roth, Luxemburg, Keun, Baum and Tergit are amongst those fed into the flames. "The future German man will not just be a man of books," proclaims Goebbels, "but a man of character."

Over on the Tempelhofer Ufer, the Salas' business expansion has continued throughout the Weimar era. The Battleship boardgames that sold well during the First World War have been augmented in the 1920s with a new *Quartettspiel* featuring color pictures of movie stars. In May 1929 they are able to build a garage for the company's new motor car, according to plans in the Chamber for Building Records. Besides this there is little evidence to flesh out their lives during this period. I need a new resource. Berlin's historical phone and address books have all been digitized and are available online, so I begin to comb through them from my desk, searching year by year for clues about the Sala family. The three remaining brothers are all listed as living here, in the house of the Ufer. But in 1936 Arthur Sala, the eldest, appears to have moved to Wilmersdorf. Returning to the building records I realize that around this time, Arthur is no longer listed as an owner of the business, which seems strange, his being the eldest and presumably the heir. Has there been a falling out? A family feud of some kind? In 1936, within a month of each other, the bachelors Bruno and Curt marry, both, oddly, to women named Charlotte. Bruno and Curt, both in their mid forties, act as witness on each other's marriage documents. The Charlottes are both in their thirties. Nazi Germany, with its emphasis on wifely duties and child-rearing, was no place for age-ing single women.

With nothing to go on beyond this handful of sparse facts, I am left in the realm of speculation, but one influenced by the dark shadow of the times. These volatile years of political extremism led to many disagreements within families, businesses, and communities. Not everyone could endure the violence and persecution that underpinned the Nazis' rule. The brothers' mother's maiden name is nagging in the back of my mind. Amanda Bertha Goldmann. Although the Salas are registered Protestant, this name seems to flag up Jewish ancestry. The Nuremberg Laws had been passed the year before, forbidding marriage or sexual contact between Jews and Germans and declaring only those of German blood to be Reich citizens, denying rights to all others. Did this play a role in the brothers' falling out?

As I trawl crosswise through archives and online sources, a new version of Sala-Spiele's *Quartettspiel* turns up and provides unsettling evidence of the Third Reich's influence on the Sala family business. I find it in the online database of the German Historical Museum, who hold a copy in their collection. It is titled the *Führer-Quartett*. Determined to see this chilling artifact firsthand, I get in touch with the museum. Dr. Sabine Witt, in charge of the Museum's Collection of Everyday Culture, invites me out to Spandau where the

museum's collection is stored in four vast hangars behind double rows of high metal fencing. Here shelf upon
shelf of obscure and often ordinary historical objects
are wrapped, packed and awaiting deployment in the
museum's exhibitions. Dr. Witt invites me in and offers
me a pair of white cotton gloves.

At a high table, gloved and ready, I am handed a small
glassine bag containing the pack of *Führer-Quartett*
cards. Dr. Witt helps me sort them out into groups of four
under various categories, each illustrated with a sepia
toned photograph and captioned in blackletter script.
There are several groups of "Leaders" (portraits of Hindenburg, Hitler, Heß, Göring, Goebbels, Himmler and the
rest). Other groups plot Hitler's rise to power, or "The
Führer's Background," "The Führer's Path of Suffering"
and "The Führer's Path to Joy." The propaganda images
that illustrate these narratives are stomach-churning,
but none as much as those in the group called "The Führer
as Role Model" which picture Hitler cuddling children
and dogs or striding in the mountains to prove that he is
an "Animal Lover" and a "Nature Lover." As "Art Lover"
he is shown at the ceremonial opening of the newly built
Haus der Kunst in Munich. There are cards picturing
the "Youth of the Third Reich," "Guardians of the Third
Reich," "Germany's Defense," "Flags and Banners." In all
of these cards, sixty in total, no women appear, besides
a little girl in traditional dress whom Hitler holds by the

hand in the card titled "A Friend to Children." Otherwise, it is all uniformed men, parades, flags, weaponry. These picture cards lay out the Führer cult in the guise of a pleasant parlor game. So much for Happy Families.

I feel deeply disappointed that the Salas have produced this in their print-works, in our building. Responding to the times is one thing, but to make something so grotesque? Would they have freely chosen to make it? Dr. Witt analyzes the content of the cards – the particular ministers portrayed, the 1937 opening of the Haus der Kunst – and deduces that the game was most likely produced in 1938. By this point, the Nazis' power was so thoroughly consolidated that the production of the *Führer-Quartett* would have been recommended, if not all out demanded, by the party, she suggests. The images themselves, clearly stock propaganda shots, would have been supplied by Goebbels's Ministry of Public Enlightenment and Propaganda. Perhaps the Salas had little choice. During these years, printers and publishers who did not toe the party line simply had their paper supplies cut off.

The Sala-Spiele's *Führer-Quartett* describes the kind of moral dilemma that filtered through all aspects of society and commerce during the Nazis' twelve-year rule. Where did the Sala brothers' responsibilities lie? To their ancestors? To their family? Their business? Their community? Their city? The party? Each family, each individual was forced to define their priorities in the face of a regime which allowed for no weighing up of personal ethics or differentiation. The fear of being watched, reported and denounced by neighbors was constant. Desire for resistance was checked. Compromises were made. Survival instincts prevailed. No one wanted to stand out. Difference was sublimated into the mass formations, parades, and militaristic rituals pictured in the *Führer-Quartett*, in which the individual "felt privileged by being a stream himself, one small part of an enormous tamed flood; for that moment he was lifted out of every double bind," as Theweleit writes. Women were firmly excluded from the public arena and realms of male production, responsible solely for the silent, continual work of home maintenance and child-rearing, all behind closed doors. *Die Deutsche Frau schminkt sich nicht*, declared the regime. The German woman does not wear make-up. She is rendered all but invisible.

By 1936, when membership of *Hitlerjugend* became compulsory for boys over fourteen and girls were expected to join the *BDM* or *Bund Deutscher Mädel* – League of German Girls – even children were forced into uniforms. In the winter of 1939, after the Nazis' invasion of Poland and the Allies' declaration of war, Goebbels announced that every Nazi child should look forward to finding a package of tin Wehrmacht soldiers wrapped up beneath the Christmas tree.

# Transport

*If I leave my house*, turn right and follow the canal down for a block and a half, I come to a building on the corner with a façade of glass and steel which backs onto the new park at Gleisdreieck: The City Museum for Science and Technology. It opened its doors in 1983, initially in one of the abandoned engine sheds of the Anhalter Bahnhof depot in which, beyond this modern street-front foyer, many of its exhibitions are still housed. A history of the German railway industry is plotted out here, through a collection of engines, carriages and railway paraphernalia from all different eras, some still caked in soot. There is a replica of Berlin industrialist August Borsig's first German-designed locomotive from 1844. There are plushly upholstered railway carriages from the 1880s like those we find in Menzel and Fontane. Here too are the original allegorical sculptures of Night and Day that used to frame the clock on top of the Anhalter Bahnhof, salvaged from its ruins. But as I follow the collection through this historical timeline, I sense again that sinking sensation, the insistent downward pull. What will I find once we reach the 1940s? Will this exhibition elide the war years, as so many official histories seem to do? I fear that instead of attempting to find a way to address an historical moment that is somehow beyond language, the choice will have been made for elision. Better to say nothing. *Schweigen.*

But I am wrong. Amongst the other carriages and engines is a wooden-slatted wagon made for transporting cattle. A deportation wagon, used to carry the Jewish people from Berlin's railway stations to extermination camps in the east. Here it is, in all its dumb materiality.

Documentary film maker Claude Lanzmann's *Shoah* begins with steam locomotives, like those that left from Berlin's stations, including the Anhalter Bahnhof, pulling behind them a convoy of livestock wagons crammed with people. They clatter along overgrown tracks through the countryside, weeds and grasses poking up between the slats. Muddy roads with potholes. Slim silver birches reaching their skinny branches up. The dun-colored countryside is familiar to me from the dry pine forests around Berlin. Lanzmann's extraordinary nine-and-a-half-hour documentary about the Holocaust was released in 1985 after eleven years of research, interviewing and filming. With the apartment to myself for a week, the children with their father, I decide to watch the entire thing. I close the curtains in the *Berliner Zimmer* and press play.

Lanzmann's camera films the bare ground of one of the Nazis' first concentration camps at Chełmno, the memorial of huge granite shards at Treblinka, and the museum-like preservation of Auschwitz. Of the mass graves and burnt bodies, nothing remains, there is no evidence. "The proof is not the corpses," says Lanzmann in an interview when asked about the Holocaust. "The proof is the absence of corpses." All that is left is word of mouth: eyewitness accounts of the scant survivors.

Lanzmann lays the eyewitness accounts of the past onto images of the present, to track the missing evidence. Only now, immersed in this filmic document, does the sheer scale of the horror, and the blank-faced detail involved in its production, finally become clear to me. The exact intention of the "Final Solution to the Jewish Question" was never clearly stated by Heinrich Himmler, who was responsible for its draft. The fact itself was circled around, left to be inferred – or not – by the bureaucrat responsible for its operation. A strategy of evasion that proved chillingly effective when it came to avoiding personal responsibility. "No one ever spoke of killing," remarks a former SS *Unterscharführer* from Treblinka, caught on a hidden camera. "The Führer ordered a resettlement program." The language used is warped and euphemistic. There is talk of "circumstances," the Jews were "processed," they are referred to as "pieces," a "load" to be calculated per square meter, or "merchandise onboard." The transport of the Jews, in train wagons designed for cattle, was cloaked in lies and the bureaucratic language of the railway system. At least thirty to fifty wagons a day would arrive in Treblinka, shunted in from the village train station, ten to fifteen wagons at a time, along a narrow-gauge railway that led to "the ramp," their final destination. The ramp led straight up to the gas chambers. These trains each carrying three, four, five thousand passengers, arrived three at a time, every two days, when Treblinka was running at "full capacity." In two hours, it was all over. A whole trainload of passengers reduced to ashes. In Sobibor, a Polish eyewitness who lived in the local village remembered the first trainload, forty wagons long, arriving. And then, the day after, utter silence. "A really total silence [...] Forty cars had arrived and then nothing [...] It was the silence that tipped them off."

Treblinka was "primitive" compared to Auschwitz, asserts the *Unterscharführer*, as if he were talking about a factory. Auschwitz was a "murder machine," its capacity ramped up in 1944 in a production-line designed for destruction in an orderly fashion. Its unimpeded progress was oiled by the lies told to the "newcomers" who mustn't be allowed to panic. After all, one doesn't want to "lose time" – railway time according to which the whole process functioned. Lanzmann interviews Walter Stier, ex-Nazi and former head of Department 33 of the Railroads of the Reich. He worked day and night, at his desk, and "never saw a train" he asserts. Department 33 was in charge of "special trains," the *Sonderzüge*, as they were called. Stier's task was timetables: "coordinating the movements of 'special' trains with regular trains." "Resettlement trains" is how he refers to them, losing himself in the technicalities of procedure, chain of command, who issued the orders and who was to implement them. Just one of hundreds of bureaucrats, like those at their desks in the administrative building of the Reich's Railway Directorate on the Ufer, correctly filing paperwork but never looking beyond their task or thinking to join the dots. When Lanzmann asks Stier if he knew that Treblinka and Auschwitz, the end points of the special trains, were used for extermination, he replies "How could we know? I never went to Treblinka. I stayed in

Kraków, in Warsaw, glued to my desk." Treblinka or Auschwitz was "a destination. That's all." Trains arrived at these destinations from all over Europe, after journeys sometimes three weeks long. On arrival, all 5,000 passengers were delivered straight to the gas chambers. Meanwhile the head of Department 33 of the Reichsbahn "never saw a train."

"The Reichsbahn was ready to ship any cargo in return for payment," remarks historian Raul Hilberg, a pre-eminent scholar of the Holocaust. He cross-examines the fine print of paperwork documenting these railway movements, searching for clues about the nuts and bolts of the processes that lead to mass extermination. The entire procedure was organized through the Central European Travel Agency, which organized the billing and ticketing of Jews' journeys to Auschwitz as if it were the most regular thing in the world.

Throughout Lanzmann's monumental film, steam trains clatter across the screen, whistles blowing as they chug through misty green landscapes, past pine forests, and small-town Polish railway stations with gravely familiar names.

A memorial plaque stands beside the ruins of the Anhalter Bahnhof today. On it is a list of convoys that left from the station with the date of departure and the number of deportees for each. Beginning on June 2, 1942 and lasting until March 1945, deportation trains left at least every couple of days. The only significant break was from December 17, 1942 to January 12, 1943, for the Nazis to celebrate Christmas.

From the Anhalter Bahnhof, the back of whose ruined façade I can see from my kitchen window, a total of 9,600 Jews were deported to ghettos and extermination camps in the German-occupied territories of Eastern Europe. The departures of these trains were scheduled alongside the regular early morning commuter traffic. Nothing distinguished the passengers waiting on the designated platform, except for the yellow star they wore on their sleeve, and the fact that they were surrounded by guards. This was the only inner-city passenger station used for the deportations of the Jews. A total of 116 convoys, with between 50 and 100 persons each, left from here and only a handful survived. Who bore witness to these Berliners' final departure? Over sixty-five years later, in 2008, these minutely organized excisions of the city's population, these departures, disappearances, were marked by a plaque erected beside the station's ruins.

The ruin of the Anhalter Bahnhof is itself a constant reminder. A phantom limb of the city's lost energy, the amputation of the *machine ensemble*, once this city's beating heart. But it is also a memorial to the corruption of the railway mechanism, bent to serve such murderous ends. And to the thousands of citizens loaded into wagons there, whose journeys ended at the ramps. Now it is nothing more than an elaborate pigeon roost made of molded terra-cotta. But it remains.

· 13 ·

# Free-Fall

*What can I do* with these facts? How can I lay my life's petty derailments and coincidental geographies alongside a violation of this scale? My confrontation with these historical events results in another total loss of axis. My disorientation in the face of this knowledge seems to echo the loss of the city's own moral compass. How can these experiences be pictured, when so much evidence was erased, and the witnesses turned away? The peaceful view outside my window appears to be deceptive.

Agitated and anxious to get a closer understanding of those grim years of the Second World War, I return to the library and find another stack of books. Eyewitness accounts of the last days of the war and Berlin's downfall – *Der Untergang* – in 1945. I scour them for references to the Landwehr Canal and the Anhalter Bahnhof, seeking out the possibility of picturing these last days. Embedded in the chaos of warfare in the inner city, they reveal another chink in the dense fabric of my present-day city view. A flap unfolds and I enter. It leads me into darkness.

On April 25, 1945, the *Panzer-Division Müncheberg* has retreated from the River Oder near the Polish border back towards Berlin. A German officer describes in his diary the new battle lines at Schöneberg Town Hall, Belle-Alliance Platz and Hallesches Tor. Hallesches Tor is only four bridges south along the canal from our house. His diary records heavy street fighting, fallen civilians and dying animals. "Unforgettable scenes" in which women flee from cellar to cellar while deserters are hanged and shot.

By this point in the war, the German army has run out of recruits to send to the front. A female diarist, out searching for coal along the S-Bahn tracks, is shocked to notice the new ranks of soldiers: "soft-faced children under huge steel helmets . . . so tiny and thin in uniforms far too large for them." Some are as young as thirteen, the age my own soft-faced youngest son is now.

Following heavy artillery fire, the German troops retreat farther to the Anhalter Bahnhof, and a defensive line is established at Askanischer Platz. Bombs rain down constantly. By this point, one of the largest refuges in Berlin is the bunker at the Anhalter Bahnhof: a huge rectangular mass of concrete behind the main station, three stories above ground and two below, with walls up to four and a half meters thick. Here 12,000 people are crammed in under appalling conditions to escape the horror outside. The bunker is linked directly to the U-Bahn tunnels so residents can reach it underground, without being exposed to the dangers above.

The "anonymous woman" is recording events in her diary, hiding in the cellar with her neighbors as the Red Army approaches her district. Unable to protect herself from the soldiers prowling the streets and bombed-out buildings, looking for watches to steal and women to rape, she seeks out a high-ranking Russian officer who can act as her protector, a Ukrainian *Oberleutnant* named Anatol. He brings her schnapps and a round loaf of dark bread and tells her that the front is now at the Landwehr Canal.

At the Anhalter Bahnhof, the platforms and ticket offices are now an army camp. In the underground train tunnels, women and children are crowded in niches and corners, others sit on folding chairs, listening to the noise of fighting on the streets above. Explosions shake the tunnel ceiling and chunks of concrete crash down. Then, as the German officer's diary reports:

Suddenly, unexpectedly, water splashes into our
command post. Screams, cries, curses. People
fight over the ladders that lead up to the air ducts
and through them to the surface. Gurgling water
floods through the shafts. The crowds stumble
over the thresholds, leaving children and the
wounded behind. People are trampled. The water
seems to reach for them. It rises a meter and still
more, until slowly it begins to disperse. Terrible
panic for many hours. Many people drown.

The bulkheads of the Landwehr Canal between Schöneberger and Möckern Bridges have just been blown up by
the Nazis. The tunnels are flooded to prevent the enemy
from advancing underground. The fact that thousands
of civilians are sheltering in them has been utterly disregarded. *Es schwimmt eine Leiche in Landwehrkanal* . . .

As evening falls on April 27, 1945, a full moon rises
over the city, illuminating these other-worldly scenes of
destruction. Not many would notice its glow, from their
shelters in underground cellars, bunkers or tunnels.
Hitler himself has been hiding in the Reich Chancellery
bunker beyond Potsdamer Platz since mid-January.

By now, Potsdamer Platz itself is a field of debris full
of smashed up vehicles. There are dead bodies all over
the place, many of which have been driven over by tanks
or trucks and are horribly mutilated. The Tiergarten

district, an elongated ellipse eight kilometers long and two wide, is all that remains of the Third Reich. "An island surrounded by a sea of flames, which was shrinking inexorably." Soviet officer General Chuikov's 8th Guards Army are marching up the Landwehr Canal, attacking northwards into Tiergarten amid rolling tanks, billowing smoke and sheets of fire. The assault on the Reichstag is planned for dawn the next day. That morning, Adolf Hitler and Eva Braun, whom he married a few hours before, commit suicide. Their corpses are burnt immediately, all evidence is destroyed, and all present are sworn to secrecy. By the end of the day, the area around the Anhalter Bahnhof is a graveyard of burnt-out tanks. On May 1 in the early hours of the morning Chief of the Army General Staff Hans Krebs meets Chuikov to request a ceasefire. Stalin refuses and demands total capitulation instead. The following day the Germans surrender. The suicides begin.

In following the Nazis' nihilistic agenda to its inexorable self-destruction, the Second World War had become a suicidal enterprise. After Hitler's suicide, which had been predicted by many, Joseph Goebbels and his wife killed themselves in the Reich Chancellery bunker, murdering their six children who were there with them. Heinrich Himmler, in captivity in

Lüneburg, did the same, as did many other high-ranking Nazi and SS officers across the Reich. Ordinary people followed suit, so many that the rash of suicides came to be seen as an epidemic. In Berlin, 3,881 people killed themselves in April alone, numbers which peaked at the climax of the battle. "For the mass of Germans, life had been restructured to promote an eventually suicidal campaign of war," writes Christian Goeschel in his book *Suicide in Nazi Germany*, "and when this failed, killing oneself became culturally and socially acceptable in a culture of suicide in defeat." In the party's line of propaganda, a violent death was considered a distinctly masculine way to die; suicide was a "heroic self-sacrifice" rather than cowardly surrender. The total number of suicides in Berlin in 1945 was 7,057. The causes of death noted on police reports were clouded in euphemism, declared as "the Russians," "the current situation," or "the war."

"Again and again these days I notice that my feeling, the feeling of all women towards men is changing," writes the anonymous woman in her diary.

We feel sorry for them, they seem so puny and powerless. The weaker sex. A kind of collective disappointment is gathering beneath the surface with the women. The male-dominated Nazi world, and its glorification of the strongman,

teeters – and with it the myth of Man. [...] At the
end of this war, amongst many other defeats, is
the defeat of the male sex.

And then? Silence. Dust rises over scenes of wholesale
devastation. People emerge, ragged and creeping, from
their underground shafts, tunnels, bunkers, cellars.
"This fearful hidden underworld of the great city," the
anonymous woman calls it. "The life spent crawling in
its depths, split into tiny cells that know nothing of each
other's existence."

An eyewitness, a child at the time, describes the scene
that greets him when, on Wednesday May 9, he finally
comes out of the cellar where he had been hiding with
his family for weeks. His mother has heard that there
is food in the cooling halls at Gleisdreieck, a large brick
building, several stories high, whose roof I can see
through the back window of my *Berliner Zimmer*. The
child and his mother head through Schöneberg in this
direction, traversing the goods yards of Gleisdreieck.

Soon we reached the Landwehr Canal. Möckern
Bridge lay with its spine broken in the canal.
Debris was everywhere. We followed Tempelhofer
Ufer, to get to the cooling halls at Gleisdreieck. [...]

There were dead bodies, weapons and equipment
lying everywhere. The adults kept calling me to go
on. They were not as keen as I was to look closely
at everything. [...] At the corner of Hafenplatz,
the Russians had set up a roadside check. [...] We
reached Askanischer Platz at the Anhalter Bahnhof. Heavy fighting had raged here, there was rubble everywhere. The houses were destroyed, the
station a ruin. In the middle of the chaos stood a
destroyed tank with a red cross. There were no
other tanks or cannons, but bazookas and rifles
all over the place. The adults were stunned by the
sight of unimaginable destruction.

And then? Standstill. Nothing. They called this moment
*Die Stunde Null.* The Zero Hour. As if the clock could
simply be wound back to the start, and the entire Third
Reich era annulled.

## · 14 ·

# An Interlude

*I've reached the so-called Zero Hour.* Standstill. The
moment of Berlin's collapse. Not only its physical breakdown but also a moral evacuation and psychological
shutdown. In many ways it is a relief to reach this point
and have the war behind me, but what am I to do now
that the narrative of the city has brought me to this terrible, traumatized wasteland? This desperate moment
in history. Where can I go from here? The view I see
from the window remains obdurate. What would the
Salas have seen back then, witness to street scenes of
increasing devastation?

The documents in the Land Registry Office give me
a smattering of facts about the war years. In January
1942, a fire was reported in the Sala building. Then, on

July 31, of the same year, Bruno and his wife Charlotte adopt a daughter, Melitta Sala, born Richter. On January 22, 1943, Bruno writes his last will and testament.

Jumping to dramatic conclusions that fit the narrative thrust of wartime, I construe that the fire must be the result of bomb damage, and that Melitta's adoption is in some way related. In fact, the carpet bombings on Berlin did not begin until 1943. There is no obvious reason for these events to be connected. So who was this girl, eight years old at the time of her adoption? What had happened to her parents? Were they sent to the front lines? Or worse? Was she related to the Salas? An illegitimate daughter of a family member? Did her existence play a role in the family split of 1936? Unlike the case of Anna Zimmermann, where documents in the online ancestry portal help me sketch out speculative details, there is no information to be found about the young girl Melitta.

What I do know is that as of 1943, the Allied bombing campaigns in the immediate vicinity of Tempelhofer Ufer were relentless. One of their main targets was the railways, with which the house was surrounded. An air raid in December 1943 caused extensive damage and later, in February 1945, bombs fell so densely here that fires raged for four days after. Dozens more air raids followed, day and night, over the next few months. Were the Sala presses still turning? And if so, who was running them, now that most fit working men had been sent off to the front lines to fight the losing battle? Were they manned by *Zwangsarbeiter*, the forced laborers brought in to keep factories going, whether local Jews who had escaped deportation, or the thousands brought in from the eastern territories, many of whom were women? There were over 600 camps for forced laborers in Kreuzberg, Tiergarten and Mitte, and all are well-documented. *Zwangsarbeiter* were employed by the *Telefunken* communications company across the canal at Hallesches Ufer, and hundreds worked the Gleisdreieck rail yards, loading and unloading freight trains, or oiling the cars. The name Sala-Spiele does not appear on any of the lists, however.

No records exist that can tell me if Melitta and Charlotte left the city, and so I picture them here, at the window, witnessing the incremental destruction of their neighborhood. My imagination inserts them into the wartime narrative that unfolds in the anonymous woman's diary. Of days and nights spent crouching with neighbors in dark cellars. Endless queues for food. Water, gas and electricity supplies interrupted or cut off entirely. Frantic dashes across open courtyards to avoid the shells and bombs. The fear and real danger of sexual violence from the Red Army troops, bent on revenge for German soldiers' abuse of their countrywomen.

Did Melitta, Charlotte and Bruno hide in the basement on the Tempelhofer Ufer? Or were they amongst the ten thousand huddled for days on end in the Anhalter air raid shelter across the canal? The bunker is still there, set back in a yard behind Schöneberger Straße, towards the station's ruin. It is a museum now, or two in fact. Upstairs is the "Berlin Dungeon," a horror show contrived to scare its tourist audience with generic frighteners, taking no account of the actual horrors that occurred right here only decades ago. In the two underground levels, the "Berlin Story Bunker" is similarly flat-footed: a half-hearted exhibition in these chilly subterranean rooms which gives a rough potted history of Berlin but little information about this particular bunker, or bunkers in general, or even about the Second World War, beyond the most well-rehearsed points. But the bunker itself is fact enough. As is the graffiti on its exterior walls, daubed in huge black capital letters – *WER BUNKER BAUT WIRFT BOMBEN* – those who build bunkers drop bombs.

A thousand bunkers were built in Berlin during the war years. Anhalter is one of the hundred or so that remain. Giant marooned hulks, so undifferentiated in form and surface that they do not even seem like buildings, but rather a hybrid matter, much closer to material in its raw state. They are indestructible, these bunkers, they cannot be got rid of. They remain, merging with their surroundings, all sharing the same strange feature of being practically invisible despite their enormous size. I realize that the Anhalter air raid shelter, this immense grey mass, is there in the view from my window. But its dull, uninflected concrete surface, partially camouflaged by undergrowth, is almost impossible to distinguish. The bunker is another blind spot.

"The scandal of the bunker" is how French philosopher Paul Virilio describes it. "These solid masses in the hollows of urban spaces, next to the local schoolhouse or bar, shed new light on what 'contemporary' has come to mean," he writes. Indeed, right in front of the Anhalter air raid shelter is the local primary school. But the normalcy that this suggests is shattered by the grim experience of the bunker's interior. "Slowed down in his physical activity but attentive, anxious over the catastrophic probabilities of his environment, the visitor in this perilous place is beset with a singular heaviness, in fact he is already in the grips of that cadaverous rigidity from which the shelter was designed to protect him," writes Virilio. These abandoned objects carry the weight not only of their own purpose, but also of the contingent bomb-dropping of their governmental architects. Not only *Abwehr* – defense – but also *Angriff* – attack. I am thoroughly disoriented when I emerge into the August sun after my one visit to the Berlin Story Bunker. "I felt sick when I was leaving," I find jotted down in my notes. "Sick and dizzy. The weight of it all."

The deeper I get into the fabric of this place, this view, the less sure I am about my relation to it. Why is it I am here again? And who am I to tell this story? My view exposes an inherent dilemma of history, and raises the question of where responsibilities lie. Do I have a responsibility to this past? A past that belongs to the house in which I happened to choose to live? Can such a sense of responsibility traverse eras and knit us together in the present, in a self-made community of remembrance? Is this in fact the shared responsibility that comes with the territory of Berlin? To look and then look again?

"He was not stupid," writes Hannah Arendt after sitting through the trial of Adolf Eichmann in Jerusalem in 1961. "It was sheer thoughtlessness – something by no means identical with stupidity – that predisposed him to become one of the greatest criminals of that period." Bureaucracy, says Arendt, is the "rule of Nobody." It is the essence of totalitarian governments, and perhaps of bureaucracy itself "to make functionaries and mere cogs in the administrative machinery out of men, and thus to dehumanize them." Arendt's choice was to witness the trial and report it back, defining "the banality of evil" in an essay published in the *New Yorker* magazine in February 1963, amongst advertisements for ladies' shoes and refrigerators. "Every government assumes political responsibility for the deeds and misdeeds of its predecessor and every nation for the deeds and misdeeds of the past." Does the same thing go for inhabitation? Is this my responsibility?

When I came to Berlin aged thirty, following a gut instinct and looking for change, at no point did I think about the war. In fact, the Second World War had played very little part in my understanding of the past, beyond history lessons at grammar school. Both of my parents were born in the war years, but as my mother was in Scotland and my father near Pittsburgh, it never felt so close at hand. But now, eighteen years after my arrival in Berlin, here I am, standing at my apartment window scrutinizing the view, trying to pick apart the facts it presents as if they were clues. As I said, the building itself, this view from the window, seemed to suggest it.

When my marriage broke down and my anchor to this place was dislodged, my instinct told me to grab the kids and get out of here. To abandon the scenery of this apartment and start somewhere else, somewhere smaller, more manageable, less freighted with the past. To turn my back on this view. But for practical reasons I stayed. And now this place is mine. And here I am, looking out of the window and into the aftermath.

Sometimes this whole process feels like a blind grasping, as if guided by a flashlight in the dark. All I can do is assess what is revealed to me piece by piece, and lay these pieces out like patchwork. I am less a historian and more of a seamstress, stitching together scraps of evidence, loose threads and patches of meaning. I have a vague sense that it will form a whole, that it will lead to a conclusion of some kind, but I don't yet know what that will be. Its frame is a window on this cut-out piece of land. It offers itself as subject matter for a task-like kind of writing. A way to counteract the drift.

"My ideal method of writing a travel book, I realize, would be to stay at home with the phone off the hook, the doorbell disconnected and the blinds drawn," writes British author Jenny Diski in *Strangers on a Train*, a book which documents her railway journey across the United States. Solitude is essential for the writing state of mind. Like Diski's ideal travel book, written from home with the blinds drawn, my book about a city is more a roaming through a pattern of thoughts or excerpts of written history than a striding through its present-day streets.

In another piece of Diski's writing, we find her at home on her own for three weeks; her daughter is away with her ex-husband, and her live-in lover has just moved out. Finally she is free to indulge in the pleasures of solitude, uninterrupted, for days on end.

> I do nothing. I get on with the new novel. Smoke. Drink coffee. Smoke. Write. Stare at ceiling. Smoke. Write. Lie on the sofa. Drink coffee. Write. It is a kind of heaven. This is what I was made for doing. It is doing nothing. A fraud is being perpetrated: writing is not work, it's doing nothing.

In this staring at the ceiling and doing nothing – much like standing at the window and looking at the view – the interior of the room and the interiority of the inhabitant become interchangeable. The body is separated from the thoughts. For Diski, this particularly alert frame of mind "follows the activities slightly up and to the left of one's physical body." The inside is cut off from the outside. For me, the window marks the cut.

The window suggests a moment of truce. I look out while waiting for the kettle to boil at various points throughout the working day. The kettle is strategically positioned on the marble worktop between the sink and kitchen window. The cups, tea leaves, coffee grounds and filters are all in the drawers below. I can prepare my cup of tea or coffee and organize my interlude without moving more than a pace or two away from the window. The local crows cut arcs across the sky and the willow on the banks dips its fronds into the water. It is an incidental domestic stage, one set up for rumination. The breaks, the cups of tea or coffee, the looking out the window, become habitual motions, a refrain that interrupts the rhythm of working. But the more I look out of the window, waiting for the kettle to boil, the more I realize that this view does not just form a pause. It is also material. A riddle looking for an answer. A point of intersection. An incentive. The place in which I find myself has insinuated itself so deeply into my thoughts that it has become my subject matter. And so, here we are. Standstill.

On a spring day in 1845, exactly a century before the full moon rose to illuminate a devastated city, Adolph Menzel made a painting of his room. Pale spring light breathes through thin muslin curtains which frame the open window and billow gently into the room. The light lies in a bright shaft of reflection on the polished parquet floor in the foreground, and shimmers on the back of a mahogany chair, placed at an angle to the open window. A matching chair, back-to-back, is also angled, like a mirror image reflected on an invisible diagonal plane.

On the wall behind the chairs is an actual mirror, tall with a carved mahogany frame, reflecting a gold-framed picture on the opposite wall, shown at another oblique angle. The motion in this painting is all diagonal, and all of its action occurs on the right. On the left is just a spread of parquet floor, a corner of red carpet, and a bare expanse of wall. Hovering on this wall is an ambiguous patch of white. A painted void, as if unfinished.

Menzel was thirty years old when he painted this intimate picture of his own interior. It was here in this room that he made the contemporaneous work, *View over Anhalter Bahnhof by Moonlight*, looking out of his own window onto the shadowy railway building. His house must have stood right where the primary school stands now, backing onto the Anhalter air raid shelter. If it were still standing, I would see it from my window. This titbit of proximity thrills me, even more so when, after searching through volumes of his collected letters and biographical notes, I find out Menzel's exact address: 18 Schöneberger Straße. The interior painting, titled *Balcony Room*, is one of Menzel's "private pictures," a small number of modestly-scaled works made early on in his career and kept in his studio for most of his life. They were only made public in 1905, a few years before he died. This one was bought by the city and hangs today in the Alte Nationalgalerie on Berlin's Museum Island.

I am so excited to discover that Menzel was practically my neighbor when he made this painting, living
right by the canal and the railway station, that I want
to see it right away. I dash out, jump on my bike and
ride straight across the Schöneberger Bridge, past the
school where his house once stood, past the ruined Anhalter Bahnhof, and along the wide straight Leipziger
Straße eastwards towards the river Spree. In the Old
National Gallery on the Museum Island, the guard di-
rects me to the Menzel wing where I find the *Balcony
Room*, a small painting prominently displayed opposite
the room's entrance. It is full of ambiguity, less a painting of a room and more of the light that floods in and
the breeze that seems to animate it. The space within
the walls, rather than the walls themselves. In fact, it
seems to be about *nothing*. About doing nothing, and observing yourself doing nothing. The ambiguous mark on
the wall is a flourish of self-reflexivity. That the work's
central focus is this patch of paint suggests that paint is
being employed literally – tautologically – to replicate
its own material state.


Returning home after seeing Menzel's *Balcony Room*
up close, my mind leads me, somnambulant, to a short
story by Virginia Woolf, written in 1917 and titled "The
Mark on the Wall." Ten pages long, its paragraphs track

the agile movements of the writer's mind as she sits in a chair by the fire, having noticed a mark on the living-room wall. The writing moves around and beyond her own domestic interior, swooping from visual incident to tangential thought, from the present to the past, to people, ideas, minor mysteries, life and even death. More than any of the subjects it touches on, it becomes a vivid portrait of the act of thinking.

> The tree outside the window taps very gently on the pane ... I want to think quietly, calmly, spaciously, never to be interrupted, never to have to rise from my chair, to slip easily from one thing to another, without any sense of hostility, or obstacle. I want to sink deeper and deeper, away from the surface, with its hard separate facts.

Woolf's text cultivates an ambiguity of speculative thought, the same type of drift that Diski evokes. It indulges in not knowing, in distancing itself from the hard reality of observation, as a means of accessing other patterns of knowledge or perception. Just as Diski's writerly attention floats "up and to the left," Woolf's attention seems to attach to the ambiguous mark on the wall, as if it is an external eye through which to observe the state of things. To adopt a consciously different viewpoint through which to question rules and generalizations. To circumvent what Woolf defines as "the masculine point of view which governs our lives, which sets the standard."

Menzel paints the paint on the wall and Woolf is writing about writing, but both tap into something that precedes either: thought itself and how it originates, in being still, doing nothing and, most importantly, being alone. Woolf's lucid train of thought is interrupted, however, when her husband enters the room: "Everything's moving, falling, slipping, vanishing . . . There is a vast upheaval of matter. Someone is standing over me and saying: 'I'm going out to buy a newspaper.'" Not only that, on his way out, he identifies the mark on the wall, reducing its imaginative potential down to a hard separate fact: "Ah, the mark on the wall! It was a snail." In the shared space of the living room, Woolf's isolation is not enough to spare her unwelcome interruptions. Menzel finds solitude in his balcony room, in the apartment on Schöneberger Straße he shares with his mother and sisters. He describes it in a letter to a friend on March 1, 1845: "I am moving out at the end of this month, and moving in front of the Anhaltsche Tor in Schöneberger Straße, number 18, two flights up, where I will have more space and a dedicated room to paint." Finally alone in a room of his own, the artist can indulge in interiority. This painting, made a century before the city's rapid rise and equally rapid fall, depicts a

calm before the storm. It remains filled with the breath
of potential.

The house in which Menzel lived and worked is no longer there and the Anhalter Bahnhof, once the pride of
the German Reich, is now a portico leading to nothing.
An elaborate pigeon roost looking onto a gaping wasteland. I have a printed-out image of it stuck on the wall
behind my desk: it pictures utter desolation. In the
foreground is an abandoned upholstered leather seat,
which perhaps once belonged inside a train carriage.
Beside it a hunk of rock that could have been part of the
station wall and a hinterland of scrubby undergrowth
and gatherings of detritus. The jagged fragment of the
station's portico is like a piece of theatrical scenery. A
huge rectangular block of a building looms in the background, the Excelsiorhaus.

The Hotel Excelsior, site of Vicky Baum's *Grand
Hotel*, was taken over in the late 1930s by the *NS-
Volkswohlfahrt*, the Nazis' social welfare organization.
The hotel's owner, Curt Elschner, had initially refused
to serve Nazis and was blacklisted as a result. Like so
many others, he eventually fled. When Elschner returned to Berlin after the war, he found his beloved
hotel badly damaged by fire. Despite his hopes of its
salvation, its remains were torn down in 1954. Between

1966 and 1968, the Excelsiorhaus was built in its place: seventeen stories high, with 500 apartments, each one small and functional, a real machine for living. The building's best-known feature is its metal windows which pivot on central axes, so that both inside and outside can be cleaned without leaving the apartment. There are fifty close-spaced windows per floor and seventeen rows from top to bottom.

In the photo on my wall, SASKATCHEWAN is spelt out in huge block letters on the façade's top left corner. This exotic sounding name was given to the bar on the top floor of the building. Its panoramic view looked over what was once the city center, now an awkward periphery on West Berlin's easternmost edge. The building sits squarely in the view from my kitchen window, beyond the empty portals of the Anhalter Bahnhof. In 2013, the Excelsiorhaus façade was painted with a pattern of pixellated squares in shades of blue and white that reads from a distance as a cloud-strewn sky.

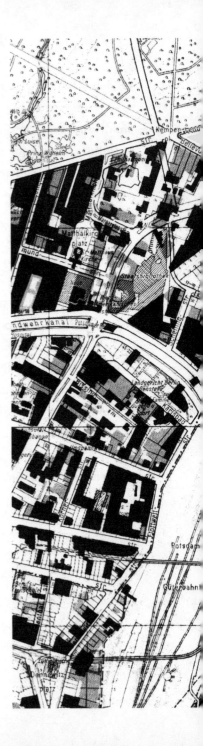

Destroyed Buildings

Damaged Buildings

# 15

# Standstill

*The sun rises early* in May in Berlin. By six a.m. the whole city is illuminated. On the morning of May 8, 1945, the first day after Germany's capitulation, the view from the window is static and grey. Standstill. On this stretch of the Ufer, only my house, the one next door and the last one on the corner remain. There are craters where buildings once stood. Rectilinear edifices are now cascading inclines and rolling hills of debris. Façades are peeled away, and entire floors stripped open to the elements. In the place of a cityscape is raw material in incremental degrees of collapse. 600,000 apartments have been destroyed. Of the Tiergarten's 200,000 trees, only 700 have survived. Instead of willow branches, the twisted steel entrails of bridges hang down into the canal. The water itself is thick with dust and wreckage. The smell of smoke hangs in the air. Above all there is silence. "No living sound from people or animals, from cars, radios or trams," writes the anonymous woman in her diary. "Only a heavy silence in which we hear our steps."

I repeatedly attempt to plot this vision onto the neighborhood in which I live: to lay it over the view that I see from my window, like the transparent sheets used in animation films. But the difference is too extreme. Not only the landscape itself, but also the dissolute cast of Red Army soldiers, Allied troops, surrendered Germans and exhausted women and children. Horses are slain on pavements and carved up with butter knives, hunks of meat extracted while the animal's flesh still shudders and its eyes are rolling in its head. Tens of thousands of women are raped – according to some estimates as many as 100,000 – mainly, though not exclusively, by the occupying Red Army. Such nightmare scenarios become a malignant obsession, repeating in my mind on an endless loop. This moment – standstill – drags me down with it, preventing onward progress.

I recognize the same loss of orientation and stagnant sense of time in a book of black-and-white photographs by Michael Schmidt titled *Berlin nach 45* [Berlin after 45]. The images, more incremental greys than clear-cut blacks and whites, picture aftermath.

Bare exposed walls, dark stretches of tarmac, hulks of buildings irregular and solitary on featureless horizons. Foregrounds full of unchecked weeds take up half or two-thirds of the picture. Devoid of presence, commerce or movement, with not a person to be seen, the streets are inhospitable. No inhabitation registers.

The camera's eye scrutinizes this desolate territory. Each direction faces blankness: a wall, a wasteland, a ruin. The anonymity of the pictures' relentless greyscale lets up only gradually as certain features make themselves known, reappearing from different angles in different images. The ragged outline of the Anhalter Bahnhof's ruins. The looming Excelsiorhaus. The desolate bulk of the Anhalter bunker. A long, exposed firewall, uneven in height, the length of a whole block. Such windowless walls were not built to be seen. They usually backed onto the firewalls of other houses and are only exposed now by the disappearance of their neighbors. Despite the repetition of would-be landmarks, and sometimes even street signs – Stresemannstraße, Hafenplatz, Schöneberger Straße – I can't quite place these pictures' vantage points, adrift in an infinite scale of grey.

The title of Schmidt's book, *Berlin after 45*, is at once accurate and misleading. The fifty-five photographs in it depict a mere fragment of Berlin and were all taken in 1980. This aftermath has gone on for decades. They were shot in the streets around the Anhalter Bahnhof, an area of Kreuzberg bordered to the west and south by Potsdamerstraße and the Landwehr Canal, to the north and east by Zimmerstraße and Prinzenstraße. This area, known as "Southern Friedrichstadt," was laid out in the eighteenth century during the reign of King Friedrich Wilhelm I as an extension to the medieval city center. This is the section of land that I see from my kitchen window.

In his introductory essay to Schmidt's book, Janos Frecot, a curator, archivist and specialist in photography, recalls bicycling around these streets as a boy: "Before the war, the buildings had crowded in on one another but in the 50s, looking off into the distance, I could make out the buildings individually, as solitary entities, a view that had not been possible for decades." No longer the "sea of houses" that Walter Benjamin wrote of, now the buildings are single ships on a flat and open ocean. The topographic absences, empty passages and undeveloped gaps in street frontages describe an archaeology of the uncovered city, opened up and stripped of its vital organs, with "not an inkling of urban life." Most remarkable, however, given the year of the photographs' making, is the lack of cohesive postwar development. This area, once the energetic heart of the city, is now an abandoned periphery on the borders of divided territory. "A slag heap of urban development of oppressive proportions," Frecot calls it. Instead of renewal is the paralysis of grief.

Schmidt's pictures are not sequential, they do not propose a narrative trajectory of discovery; no hopeful horizon implies a future of something other than this. Instead, they plot out an ambivalent territory stuck in time that refuses to be known. In these border areas in the decades after the war, it was not peacetime that prevailed, but *Waffenruhe* – ceasefire. Following twelve years of barbaric totalitarianism, Berlin had become the front line of the Cold War. The precarious mental state that grips the city is written in its landscape. In Schmidt's pictures, this terrain describes an ongoing state of suspension – of urban development, but also of social, political and emotional progress – and the functional void of ceasefire.

Michael Schmidt, born in Kreuzberg in October 1945, was conceived in the last futile months of the war. (Infant mortality was extraordinarily high in that year: dysentery alone killed sixty-five per cent of Berlin's newborns in 1945, notes historian Alexandra Richie.) The pictures in *Berlin after 45*, taken when Schmidt was thirty-five years old, walking in solitary circular paths through streets he knew inside out, are also autobiography. For him, this is *Heimat*. "His photographs do not speak of history," writes Frecot, "instead, history has become a visual form within them, and the pictures seem to be completely saturated with its weight." Twenty-five more years passed before Schmidt published the pictures as a book in 2005, as if the distance of a quarter century was needed to even look at them. By now, another fifteen years later, their silence is still eerily palpable. These photographs, according to Frecot, offer us "a singular view of the city as a catastrophe turned to stone."

British archaeologist turned paranormal researcher T. C. Lethbridge claimed that past events are stored in the "energy fields" of objects and can theoretically be accessed and listened to like tape recordings, a belief sometimes known as "Stone Tape Theory." Lethbridge's 1961 book *Ghost and Ghoul* is a personal investigation filled with vivid accounts of his own brushes with the paranormal. He examines the facts of each case like a detective searching for clues as to whether there was indeed "something of its past story locked up in every ancient object which simply awaited the correct treatment to bring it to light." Events with an extreme energetic release can burn into the very rock of a place, he believed. Fragments from traumatic experiences such as death, betrayal, heartbreak, suicide or war can recur again and again over time as residual hauntings or vague atmospheric reverberations. Are stony echoes audible across Berlin's cityscape, through decades past and into the present? Can we hear them, read them, decode them? Is this what I am attempting here?

The hypothesis of morphic resonance and the collective unconscious was proposed in the early 1980s by another renegade British scientist, Rupert Sheldrake, a Cambridge and Harvard educated biologist, who, like Lethbridge, "turned" and became a researcher into paranormal phenomena. According to Sheldrake, "morphic fields" are like collective memory banks that store shared experience. "They enable memories to pass across both space and time from the past," he says. "They help to explain habits, memories, instincts, telepathy and the sense of direction. [...] They have an inherent memory." Sheldrake's research into the immaterial in the 1980s led to his effective banishment from the scientific establishment but in the meantime, the study of epigenetics has become generally accepted. Investigating the transgenerational influence of past experiences and inheritance of acquired characteristics, epigenetics examines how behavior and environment can imprint genetic material and affect "gene expression." For Sheldrake, unorthodox methods in the hands of well-qualified scientists can lead to unexpected breakthroughs. Parvati, the feng shui master, agrees. "Memory fields are all around us," she said when she first visited my apartment. "Every event is stored in morphic fields, which are like a hard drive. They remain there and continue to have an effect as long as they are not released."

"What is past is not dead; it is not even past. We cut ourselves off from it; we pretend to be strangers," begins Christa Wolf's memoir, *Patterns of Childhood*, published in 1976. Wolf was a child during the Nazi era and lived in a village in former East Prussia, now a part of Poland. Every morning she walked through the village, turning into Hermann-Göring Straße to reach the girls' primary school on Adolf-Hitler Gasse. Most towns and cities had streets with these names. In Berlin, Königgratzer Straße, where Theodor Fontane's Effi Briest had lived, was called Göringstraße from 1935 until 1947 when it was renamed Stresemannstraße. In January 1945, when Christa Wolf was fifteen years old, she and her family fled her village in a truck to escape the Red Army approaching from the east. They became refugees, another handful amongst the seven million who had left their homes to flee westwards.

Wolf's memoir recounts a visit to the village of her childhood as a grown woman, along with her husband, brother and teenage daughter. Through the tentative retelling of this journey and the forgotten scenes it reawakens, snapshot remembrances emerge of fleeting looks or broken phrases, which Wolf holds up to the light of experience to reconsider in retrospect. Flickering glimpses of brutality and discrimination reveal unanswered childhood questions. Growing up in a village where the streets were named after Hitler and his men, where membership in the Hitler Youth was compulsory, and a portrait of the Führer hung on the living-room wall at home, was to be saturated with totalitarian ideology. Even in the disastrous first months of 1945, Wolf recalls, a child could not believe that the Second World War would ever be lost.

In Wolf's interrogation of the past, memory becomes a character in its own right, derailing the narrative trajectory with unasked-for interjections. It "probably has its reason for projecting unexpected scenes when prompted by a certain word," Wolf writes. For her, the act of remembering is not only a journey into the past but also an ethical undertaking. "An unused memory gets lost, ceases to exist, dissolves into nothing – an alarming thought," she asserts. "The faculty to preserve, to remember, must be developed. Before your inner eye, ghostly arms emerge, groping about in a dense fog, aimlessly."

In revisiting the village of her childhood, and asking her own daughter to bear witness, Christa Wolf attempts to break open the concealed chambers of her memory and release their musty contents. Reflecting on the relative innocence of her own position as a child, Wolf notes parenthetically, "You can't get around the fact that in this country innocence is almost infallibly measured by age." Plastered over by the post-war mantra, *uns geht es doch gut* – we're doing just fine – the suppression of painful memories, guilt and shame was subconscious work undertaken by the generations that lived through the war. "You have to ask yourself how many encapsulated vaults a memory can accommodate before it must cease to function," Wolf writes. "How much energy and what kind of energy is it continually expending in order to seal and to reseal the capsules whose walls may in time rot and crumble?"

Shame is an awkward subject. You cannot point an accusatory finger at someone else's shame without considering what might be lurking in your own swampy depths. But being averse to openness, shame does not want to be revealed, never mind examined or discussed. It is rarely recognized as a shared ordeal, even when it affects a whole society. Instead, it festers away unseen and hardens into something that seems stubbornly individual.

In writings about Germany's twentieth-century past, shame is a recurrent theme, as are its companions, guilt and repression. German writer W. G. Sebald, born in Bavaria during the war, had lived in England for almost thirty years when he published an essay in 1999 that addresses the complexities of Germany's past. "The quasi-natural reflex," he writes of the Germans after the war, "was to keep quiet and look the other way."

> The stream of psychic energy that has not dried up to this day, and which has its source in the well-kept secret of the corpses built into the foundations of our state, a secret that bound all Germans together in the post-war years, and indeed still binds them, more closely than any positive goals such as the realization of democracy ever could.

My endeavor here to address this period of German history and poke around in a past that does not belong to me elicits shameful feelings of my own, of the *"Who does she think she is?"* variety. We English have our own style of repression, buttoned-up and stiff-upper-lipped. In England, the common causes of national shame have to do with its imperial past and colonial transgressions or, more lately, with the decision to leave the European Union. We have plenty of shame concerning our bodies, far more so than in Germany. It is not generally acceptable, for instance, to take your clothes off on an English beach. But a great deal of English shame is rooted in

class structure. Relative positions in the social peck-
ing order are finely calibrated through voice and expression and immediately discernible to any English
listener. An involuntary mental calculation takes place
that determines a relative positioning within the fixed
hierarchy of class. Depending on the context, one is by
comparison either too low down or too high up, both of
which can result in shame.

Shame cleaves to cultural norms and the perceived
reactions of others, and as such, it needs a witness in
order to be effective. To address your own shame is to
attempt connection with the witness: looking up and
ahead rather than down at the ground. Catching another's eye on the street. Letting your guard down for once.
When Sebald's essay was published in Germany, it was
criticized for considering the trauma that the Germans
suffered. Could the perpetrators of the Second World
War also be seen as its victims? In a foreword, Sebald
wrote that when it comes to the years from 1930 to 1950,
"we are always looking and looking away at the same
time." This unspoken group dynamic soon hardened into
a cultural norm: "the population decided – out of sheer
panic at first – to carry on as if nothing had happened."

Moral failure, maladjustment, loss. All of the individual sufferings during this period of defeat in Germany,

where new power relations were being inscribed daily on the city's occupied territory, have a ready counterpoint. The rape of Berlin's women by occupying armies is held up against the rape and atrocities committed by Nazi soldiers on the Eastern Front in the early years of the war. There are risks of false equivalence when the trauma of homeless civilians, refugees, prisoners of war, or those who lived through carpet bombings, are pitted against the grim monolith of the Holocaust. Instead of a binary arrangement, with a clear divide between doers and done-tos, is a wide zone of incremental greys, where qualifiers face qualifiers. The Berliners who survived the war years were trapped in a victim–perpetrator quandary where innocence was sucked down into the muddy waters of complicity and ankles were bound by implication.

In Berlin, where whole families perished in bombed-out homes, many losses remained unacknowledged and seeped into the water, the soil, the stones of the remaining buildings and the roots of the Tiergarten's 700 remaining trees. The empty plots of land all over became the city's scars. Scrappy patches of unused territory, fenced-off and breeding ragged assortments of weeds, became an integral part of the cityscape. In their semi-permanent state of abandonment, they seemed to express obliquely the traumatic events of the recent past. The many wastelands spoke to both wartime losses and the appalling events that had caused them. Their dereliction was both memorial and warning.

Unlike the confession, which absolves its bearer of guilt, the therapy for shame is not a redemptive act of expression, but rather a broader attitude of openness towards life itself. Shame is charged with self-loathing and goes right to one's basic sense of self. Being tightly intertwined with and reinforced by fear, it is as difficult to admit to as it is to get rid of. Rather than risk the danger of discovery and of possible rejection, habitual patterns of evasion and repression take over: attack, defense, retreat. An attitude of openness is the hardest thing of all.

Such openness towards life itself found its inverted image in the attitudes of those who survived the war in Germany and emerged, startled and blinking, in the silent city as the sun rose over a ruined landscape. A massive effort of repression, one already cemented in the repressive patterns of Prussian society, was required to simply survive. Forgetting was a necessary tool. This group phenomenon had far-reaching consequences. Neurobiologist Gerald Hüther, a specialist in "the biology of fear," describes how a traumatized population can "lose their openness, curiosity and trust, and thereby the capability to admit something new." In the face of external catastrophe, equilibrium was restored through actions and gestures. Those that remained once the war was over, mainly women and children, set about clearing the rubble on the streets, bringing order to the chaos of the ruins, straightening out the city. They did not want to talk about it.

In the days immediately following my encounter with the leaking pool of water on my kitchen floor, I believed that what was being revealed to me had to do with the state of my marriage. On some level I felt grateful to the house for precipitating this crisis; for insisting that I look closely at and recognize the situation that I was in. It took longer to realize the full scope of that invitation, to look beyond myself and towards this place, its present and its past.

I felt ashamed in those days of my new status as a single woman. Ashamed to have a broken family, to have failed to hold its parts together. But I was also angry at the ruthlessness with which my former husband accepted this change of status, his readiness to turn the page, abandoning our intact family life. He simply extracted himself, leaving the home and its contents otherwise undiminished, as if his absence made no difference. A character silently exiting stage left. Silence was not a new response for either of us; this was simply its latest manifestation. We both knew how to operate in an emotionally reduced state: stay busy, build your life, construct an attractive environment as a strategic defense against unhappiness.

My memories from those first disorientated months are vague and sporadic, but in one of the most insistent, I am sitting with my youngest son on his bedroom floor, sorting out Lego bricks by color. I don't know what compelled me towards this futile activity, while my son sat patiently beside me, quietly helping and not questioning the logic of the task. The temporary arrangement of Lego, color-coded into separate plastic boxes, was something we could accomplish. It did make me feel better, at least momentarily. It was an avoidance strategy. My only other vivid memory from this washed-out period of time is of the three of us, my two sons and I, sleeping huddled together in my big bed every night. It was a choice we made instinctually and never talked about, but it continued until we had each found our equilibrium in our new three-cornered constellation.


Bewilderment and disorientation met those who returned to Berlin from exile once the war was over. Gabriele Tergit's memoirs describe her return to her birthplace, from England in 1948. She walks alone through its bombed-out landscape. The "Old West" is now a ruined desert growing green.

> All that remained of the house at the Landwehr
> Canal, where my parents had lived and where,
> from 1908 to 1928, I had been a child, a teenager,
> lived through the war and inflation, were the two
> sides with the bay windows. In the middle, like a
> petrified waterfall, was the collapsed stairwell.

Assessing what is left of its architecture, Tergit folds her memories of how it was before into the desolate vision that greets her. She records it all with incredulity: the landscape, the ruin, the casual unrepentant Nazis. She meets an old friend who tells her of "the terrible drowning of 12,000 Berliners by Hitler, who gave the order to flood the subway, full of refugees. As usual, the Nazis rescued themselves and left the population to their fate."

Finding herself lost, unable to recognize the streets she grew up on, Tergit asks a woman the way and is yelled at in response:

> "Why are you asking me? I don't belong here!" A
> refugee, a displaced person who had forgotten
> how to deal with other people. All the things that
> could have contributed to this: being brought
> up by Hitler, the loss of husband and children,

girlhood in the Hitler Youth, the company of other
German women.

The compassion that Tergit expresses so naturally
was just what was absent in much of Berlin's post-war
population – a population that was increasing by 20,000
a day following the expulsion of millions of Germans
from the east. The culture of lies with which the Nazi
propaganda system had constructed their image of a
superior Germany meant that the population had lost
their ability to trust their own senses. The straggling
citizenry that remained was rewired for bare survival.

Arriving at Potsdamer Platz, "the entrance to old
Berlin, its center for decades," Tergit finds nothing
but a "heap of rubble: The stations are destroyed, the
beautiful Potsdam Station, the Anhalter Bahnhof by
Schwechten where I would pick up uncles and aunts
from southern Germany, and from which I would travel
to my grandparents." For years after the war, the site
of this heap of rubble, the former Potsdamer Bahnhof,
was a flat and barren wasteland, truncated at one end
by the Berlin Wall and in the late 1980s, host to the wild,
open air *Polenmarkt*, the "Polish market." In 1998, in the
throes of post-unification urban renewal, it was turfed
over and turned into a "promenade," though barely anyone cares to walk there. The grassy mound is like a long
green carpet under which the atrocities of the Second

World War were swept, rail tracks, rubble, bones and all. An anti-memorial that does not remember the disappeared station, but simply covers it over. It was given Gabriele Tergit's name.

Hannah Arendt's observations on her own return to Germany in 1950 remain the most perspicacious. She recognizes that German survivors, conditioned by a decade of totalitarian rule, are gravely ill-equipped to come to terms with the devastation in which they found themselves. "Totalitarianism kills the roots," she writes. The experience of Nazi rule had "robbed [them] of all spontaneous speech and comprehension, so that now, having no official line to guide them, they are, as it were, speechless, incapable of articulating thoughts and adequately expressing their feelings." There was a profound helplessness, not just amongst the military men who had literally lost the war, but also amongst the civilians who had lost their framework for existence.

> If you see how the Germans stumble through the
> ruins of their thousand-year history and simply
> shrug their shoulders at the ruined landmarks,
> or how they complain if you remind them of
> the terrible events which still hold the rest of
> the world in a tight grip, then you realize that

keeping busy has become their main weapon of defense against reality.

Unable to face the destruction – the visible evidence of their ethical failure – many looked away. They were suddenly vulnerable, like the firewalls exposed after years of safe concealment behind the backs of other buildings. Standstill, this ongoing state of paralysis, holds such exposure at bay. Work like Arendt's or Tergit's reportage, or Christa Wolf's conscious retrieval of memories, can lead to revelation, while memory's subconscious interjections also do their part. All are asking for the same thing: a breakthrough into visibility.

As I am reading around, trying to picture this moment of the past and understand the quandary of the post-war German state of mind, the name Mitscherlich keeps coming up. Alexander and Margarete Mitscherlich, both psychoanalysts, were authors of a groundbreaking book published in 1967 that applied the tools of psychoanalysis to the widespread emotional and social problems of post-war West Germany. Titled *Die Unfähigkeit zu trauern* [*The Inability to Mourn*], it identified a rerouting of mental energy that had taken place in the West German post-war psyche. Many bridges to the immediate past were broken and only certain parts were allowed to be remembered. Avoidance strategies were devised and maintained that constructed a superficial friendliness. Economic industry became the common goal, covering open wounds with work, prosperity, and smothering administrative routines. The *Ich-Ideal* that had been constructed through Nazi ideology, was so fundamentally destroyed, wrote the Mitscherlichs, that each individual experienced a central debasement and psychological impoverishment. Subconscious mechanisms of self-preservation were necessary to survive the psychological emergency that the end of the war brought with it, and to avoid collapsing into all-pervasive melancholy. Psychic energy was channelled into the work of denial rather than remembering, which lead to immobility and emotional rigidity: an *Ich-Entleerung* – the draining away of the ego. The Mitscherlichs' book touched on many long-nourished taboos, hoping to interrupt the vicious circle of repression and break through the reduced perception of reality that had left its traces in the population. The collective mental state that this passionate book plots out is like the standstill that pervades Michael Schmidt's photographs of *Berlin after 45*.

Despite the determination summoned up by the incredible German word *Vergangenheitsbewältigung* – the management of, coping with or reckoning with the past that came along on the heels of the Mitscherlichs' book and the 1968 student movement – subconscious mechanisms of repression continued successfully to keep the past at bay. Over four decades after the Mitscherlichs' revelations, many of the problems remain unresolved. In a book called *Die geheimen Ängste der Deutschen* [The Secret Fears of Germans] published in 2011, family therapist Gabriele Baring writes: "the idea that a normal person can process experiences such as those of war and dictatorships without consequences has survived to this day."

Drawing on her own experiences as a systemic therapist, Baring uses examples of her patients to elucidate the long shadows the war has cast on those that witnessed it firsthand, but also their children, and their children's children. "Only in the lived experience of grief lies the chance for reconciliation," she remarks. Her book is full of terms that signal the interruption of a flow of emotions: *Gefühlsstau, Blockaden, Abkapselung* – emotional congestion, blockage, detachment. There is *Schuld* – guilt – and most of all *Schweigen* – silence. Lives came to be shaped by the weight of family secrets, and the gloomy, oppressive burden of traumas that could find no outlet or expression. How many unexpressed memories and decades' worth of unshed tears are encapsulated in the fabric of Berlin's post-war wastelands?

As I begin to look further and examine the parts of the past that the window's view offers up, I realize its message is also about the house, the place, the land, the soul of the city. About the act of recognition in itself. In Berlin after 1945, when all but three houses on my block were gone, other losses were harder to visualize. The catastrophes held in the stones of the buildings. The streams of suppressed emotion that run in undercurrents beneath the city's streets. The untapped grief seeping into the groundswell of the elevated water table.

# 16

# Dead End

*In the first days* of May 1945, the Red Army sent town criers into the streets of Berlin calling all people aged between fifteen and fifty-five to report for duty and begin clearing debris. As there were barely any men left, the work fell largely to the women, lined up in long chains, passing bricks and stones one piece at a time from hand to hand. According to eyewitnesses, Berlin was now a city of women:

> Everywhere there were women alone, in pairs
> or groups, paying for their own drinks in cafés ,
> cutting wood, moving debris, doing men's work.
> As the winter wore on every third woman or girl

came out dressed in the trousers of her absent husband, brother or son.

These *Trümmerfrauen*, or rubble women, brought back some semblance of order to their surroundings. At the same time, Nazis were suddenly nowhere to be seen. "It happened very quickly," recalled an eyewitness. "They suddenly were dressed differently, all uniforms were gone, no insignia at all, and they'd all been 'forced' [. . .] The turnabout happened so fast, it was a joke." They were hiding in plain sight. Meanwhile, the Soviet occupiers began to dismantle workshops and industries, and seize property, currency and artworks, as well as books and whole archives from libraries. By the autumn of 1945, according to Alexandra Richie, "eighty per cent of machine-tool productive capacity and sixty per cent of light and specialized industrial production was removed, along with hundreds of railway cars and tracks."

Toy production had officially been put on hold during the Second World War. There cannot have been much demand for Sala-Spiele's printed paper games amidst falling bombs and mass evacuations, and certainly not for the *Führer-Quartett*. The Sala brothers were too old to be called up although in the last months, when whole generations were already dead or captured, older men

were rounded up along with teenage boys, and sent out
to defend the doomed Nazi Germany.

My attempts to find out more about the Salas' activities during the war years have drawn a blank. Having squeezed as much narrative as possible out of the
building documents regarding the house, I decide to
visit the *Landesarchiv*. Forty minutes north on the
S-Bahn from Anhalter Bahnhof, it is housed in a huge
nineteenth-century redbrick building that has recently
been subject to an unfortunate interior remake, with
glass insertions and ambitious signage. The reception
staff are helpful and accommodating and show me to
a desk in the reading room where I input my favorite
search terms into the database. The Landwehr Canal
brings up over a thousand entries plus another twelve
hundred images. There are police documents from the
1930s detailing suspected murders or suicides: more
dead bodies dredged out of the waters. An image from
1899 shows the Schöneberger Bridge, an arched stone
bridge with carved crenellations and boats gliding
along the water. The same bridge appears in an image
from 1945, this time its innards are trailing in the canal
and bombed out houses form the background. Is one of
them the Salas' house? It is impossible to tell. When I
give the name "Sala" into the database, the registration
of the family business comes up, dating all the way back
to 1848. But no detailed records of Sala-Spiele have been

kept. I have reached a dead end. There is one more archive I can try: the *Bundesarchiv*, Germany's federal archives. They hold the membership records for NSDAP,
the National Socialist Party. I fill in the online information request form, wire the fifteen Euro research fee
and wait to see what emerges.

When the war ended and Berlin was plunged into an
ongoing state of limbo, the status of the city changed
practically overnight, from the crosshair target of a violent conflict, to its ruthlessly fought-over prize. Geo-
graphical decisions about the splitting up of Germany
had already been sketched out by the Allies in 1943, but
the final lines were decided upon in a conference of the
"Big Three," the United States, the USSR and Great
Britain, held in July 1945. It took place in Cecilienhof
Palace in Potsdam, surrounded by Lenné's gardens on
the banks of the Heiliger See. A rough zigzag was drawn
on the map of Berlin, dividing the city into four distinct
sectors, one each for the United States, Great Britain,
France and the USSR, to be governed by a joint administration. Germany may still have existed in terms of
territory, but its sovereignty was gone.

I have a map from 1952 on which the sector borders
are marked with a thick red line. The erratic path this
line takes becomes more extreme as it approaches my

neighborhood. After cleaving close around the eastern edge of the Tiergarten and passing in front of the Brandenburg Gate, it swings a sharp right on Lennéstraße then a sharp left on Bellevuestraße in an aggressive triangle that came to be known as the Lenné-Dreieck. At the next corner, the line turns right again and proceeds to skirt around all three sides of the vacant block where the Potsdamer Bahnhof and its tracks used to be, before continuing along Stresemannstraße and then on east towards Kreuzberg. The detours of this jagged path make no clear sense when read on the map. Their logic was arrived at through territorial disputes and political wranglings over who got what at the end of the war. This area, which only a handful of years before had been the city's pulsing center, was now nothing more than the fraying edges between different occupiers' plots of land.

The Salas' house on the Ufer ended up in the American sector of West Berlin, but just two blocks up the British sector began, while across the canal behind the Anhalter Bahnhof was the start of the Soviet sector. The house was almost exactly at the apex of the triangle where these three zones meet. A short stroll in each direction and you would be subject to the rules of a different occupying force. The Railway Directorate's headquarters, which had escaped the war undamaged, also landed by a whisker in the American sector. But the railways themselves were under Soviet control. For the first years after the war, the Soviet military administration continued to use the building, but as the stand-off between the occupying powers intensified, it became a pawn in a territorial dispute. As with every event during these volatile years, an account of it depends on where your allegiances lie. There is an Eastern and Western version to each narrative of this time.

These disputes would have affected the Salas as they did all Berliners. Perhaps more so, given their particular proximity to the sites of its conflicts. But the only documents I have for this time are plans from the Chamber for Building Records, such as those from 1947 to separate the front-facing apartments from those in the side wing, turning one unwieldy apartment per floor into two more manageable ones.

When my ex-husband left the apartment never to return, he left all of its contents as well. The cutlery and crockery bought by his mother, the furniture and stereo, the sheets and towels, the ladder and toolbox, the washing machine, the books. At some point he came to pick up his clothes and a few of his favorite artworks, but that was all. At the time it felt like a brutal extraction, as if the cut-out hole in the shape of the father/husband he left behind would just close up and grow back together. The Zero Hour of our relationship.

Now I see it differently, more like being left a dowry
with which to begin a brand-new life chapter. In our divorce settlement, the apartment on Tempelhofer Ufer is
written over to me. As the Salas did before me, I close
off the side wing, dividing it into two apartments to
make it more inhabitable, and look into renting out the
separate side wing space. It is better to rely on walls
than words for income. I am now a propertied bourgeois
woman, living on the water.

By 1947 it was clear that the wartime alliance was over.
The Soviets began a campaign of intimidation and
disruption – cutting off water and electricity without
warning, kidnapping officials under the guise of denazification, killing and imprisoning tens of thousands – to
force the Allies to leave. As the violence escalated into
the following year, the American military threw the Soviets out of the Railway Directorate building, but when
the S-Bahn was disrupted in West Berlin as a result,
they quickly backed down. Shortly after, two hundred
striking railway workers stormed the Railway Directorate, demanding to be paid in Deutschmarks rather
than Ostmarks. Currency reform had been introduced
as a means to curtail the rampant inflation, bringing
Deutschmarks to West Berlin, allowing money to re-
sume its normal function and bringing the black market

under control. The Soviets finally relocated their railway management to East Berlin, but the animosity that had flared up lead to a strategy of hijacking American trains. The Soviets were encircling the city and there was little the vastly outnumbered Western Allies could do about it. The blockade on Berlin began.

Hovering over the rooftop of the German Museum of Technology two blocks down the Ufer from our house is a silver aeroplane, one of the *Rosinenbomber* used in the Berlin air bridge that began in April 1948 and supplied the city with essential rations. I can see it from my balcony if I look down the canal to the right. If it were to continue its imaginary flight trajectory, it would crash right into the tower of Hobrecht's pumping station. By the time the blockade ended in May 1949, the Allied troops were seen as a benevolent force of protection, while the Soviets were feared for their repression and tyranny. But West Berlin had also come to rely on outside aid in order to survive. Its own economy was unviable. On the day Stalin lifted the Berlin blockade, the constitution for the new Western government was published: the Federal Republic of Germany. A few months later, the German Democratic Republic was created. Berlin was now not only a destroyed city recovering from the effects of war, but also a potent symbol of Cold War division.

———

One evening in January, having spent all day at my desk trying to get to grips with this intransigently entangled post-war period and just about to cook dinner for the boys, I check my emails one last time and see that an email has come in from the *Bundesarchiv*. I had forgotten about my request for information regarding the Salas, and was not expecting to hear back from them. I open the email with trepidation. It contains a letter with two documents attached. In the letter, a Herr Schelter details his research relating to the Sala-Spiele Verlag and the Sala brothers Bruno and Curt. Two records have been found. I click open the first PDF. It is a scan of both sides of a grey-green index card: NSDAP Membership Number 1106760, Curt Sala, Tempelhofer Ufer, born 01.06.1890. Curt Sala joined the party on 1st May 1932. 1932! Before Hitler was even in the Chancellery! Curt Sala was a true blood Nazi. My heart sinks and I feel chilled, standing here in my kitchen, looking at this document on my computer screen. With even greater trepidation I open the second PDF. This time a smaller orange card, also for Curt, this time spelt with a "K," but with the same membership number. A small black-and-white passport photograph stapled to the reverse side is dated 16.06.1934. This was not the news I was hoping for. I feel let down, disappointed and somehow repelled. The unsmiling passport portrait peers out from my computer screen: an ordinary-looking balding man with a prominent nose in a suit and tie.

This sensation I have, the desire to discover an untarnished past, must be how people feel who look into the records of their family members. I remember this feeling from my visit to the Deutsches Historisches Museum storage, and my pointed questions about the *Führer-Quartett*, seeking confirmation that the Salas were coerced into making it, and did not print it of their own free will. The utter transparency with which the Federal Archives has simply and efficiently sent these records in response to my enquiry is impressive. It is a refreshing antidote to the desire to bury uncomfortable parts of the past. No membership card was sent for Bruno Sala, however – does this mean he was not a member? The following day I call Herr Schelter at the *Bundesarchiv* and ask him. Helpful and friendly, he confirms that he checked all of the party records in the two different archival systems and nothing for Bruno was found. It cannot be ruled out completely, but it is most unlikely that he was a member. That, at least, feels like a relief. But now another fault line has appeared, between the two brothers, the business partners, living together on the Ufer, on opposite sides of this ideological divide.

On July 3, 1952, at a quarter past midnight, Curt Sala dies. His death certificate is in the online ancestry register, and according to this he died "in the apartment," though it does not say if this was in the front building or side wing. The cause of death, confirmed not by his wife Charlotte, but by an "Ernst Otto," a salesman living at 1 Yorckstraße, is given as *Aderverkalkung, Herzschwäche*: hardening of the arteries and weakening of the heart.

The denazification of German society set into action by the Allied Control Council in 1946 was a fraught process with only limited success. There were practical difficulties to denazification, given that the Nazis and their doctrine had systematically permeated every area of life and all strata of society, and there were no clear criteria for distinguishing between who was and who wasn't a Nazi. Hannah Arendt writes:

> The injustices of the denazification system were simple and monotonous: the city-employed garbage collector, who under Hitler had to become a party member or look for another job, was caught in the denazification net, while his superiors either went scot-free because they knew how to manage these matters, or else suffered the same penalty as he – to them of course a much less serious matter.

In *The Inability to Mourn,* Alexander and Margarete Mitscherlich conclude that many old Nazis had returned to positions of prominence and responsibility in the course of West Germany's reconstruction, while not enough had been done to address the crimes of the Nazi era. All too often, the past was simply written off. Over in the Soviet zone, the authorities were quick to round up Nazi Party members, interning them in camps. This gave East Germany the prerogative to declare itself an "anti-fascist" state, though many political opponents were swept up at the same time and conveniently held at bay under the cover of denazification.

On both sides of the city there was demolition mania as war-damaged buildings were razed to the ground and their remains delivered to the outskirts, where they were piled up and turfed over, forming artificial hills in the relentlessly flat landscape. Post-war Berlin was seen by many as a tabula rasa on which a radical rethinking of the city could take place, enabling, in theory, a clean break with the past. In 1946 already, a group of architects including Hans Scharoun and Wils Ebert came up with the *Kollektivplan*. Scharoun treated the city as a *Stadtlandschaft*, an urban landscape with a design that followed the path of the *Urstromtal*, the glacial valley. The plan aimed to sweep away the narrow streets and heavy tenement buildings of Hobrecht's time, to break up densely-built areas with abundant green spaces, and lay a rectangular grid of fast moving traffic arteries over this new clean slate. It aimed to remove not only roads and buildings but all existing infrastructure including the nineteenth-century sewage system and tram and underground networks, disregarding the basic needs of an already battered citizenry. On this basis, the *Kollektivplan* was deemed "utopian" and ultimately rejected.

Despite the colossal damage incurred during the Second World War, from the point of view of architecture and urban planning, another terrible fate had been narrowly avoided: Germania, the newly construed capital city for the "Thousand-Year Reich," conceived by Hitler with his chief architect Albert Speer. If James Hobrecht had been laissez-faire about the nature of Berlin's terrain when he drew up his plans in 1862, Speer aimed for its outright domination. In reimagining the country's capital, he planned to shift its axis from east–west to north–south, winding back time to before the Berlin–Warsaw glacial spill carved its geological path across the region. His hubristic concoction of gigantist typologies, oppressive symmetries and relentless right angles intended to remove everything that stood in the way. Top secret scale models, locked in Speer's office at the Academy of Art, were visited daily by Hitler throughout the war, as both his battle plans and visions for the city became increasingly deranged.

A new square was to be built beside Potsdamer Bridge from which a ruler-straight line heading south was drawn. All existing buildings that happened to stand in its way, including the Salas' house and its neighbors, the Railway Directorate, and Hobrecht's pumping station, would be razed. The new North–South Axis – wider than the Champs-Élysées, as Hitler liked to boast – would obliterate the entire railway complex of the Potsdamer Bahnhof and the Anhalter Bahnhof, severing their tracks and yards. The plot on which my house stands would have ended up between the Ministry for Propaganda and IG Farben, the fascist-aligned chemical and pharmaceutical giant. Germania was to be a man-made city for eight million people: ready-made crowds for scenes of Nazi propaganda set against a backdrop of maximum scale and rigidity. By 1937, many plots of land had already been expropriated and by June 1938, Hitler had laid the first stone for the foundations of the North–South Axis. Its construction by thousands of forced laborers brought into the city by Speer continued until March 1943 and was only brought to a halt by Germany's wartime defeats and the Allies' relentless carpet bombing of Berlin.

———

In 1958, still struggling to decide how to reconstruct this half of the city, the West German government announced a new competition. Titled *Hauptstadt Berlin*, the brief itself was utopian, calling for plans to redesign Berlin as if it were a unified capital city. Scharoun and Ebert's entry, generally regarded to be the best design, again revealed the desire for demolition: this time nearly all surviving pre-war buildings were to be knocked down. It proposed in their place a broadly spreading inner city of widely distributed buildings and huge pedestrian zones, accessed by six- to eight-lane motorways. Vast underground car parks would keep the streets car-free: the largest, approximately 500 meters wide and 2 kilometers long, was to be built beneath Southern Friedrichstadt. Once again, nothing came of these plans, but one aspect of it struck a chord with Willy Brandt, Berlin's new mayor: the vision of an *autogerechte Stadt*, a car-friendly city.

After his brother Curt's death in 1952, Bruno Sala has become the sole owner of Sala-Spiele. It is not until 1956 that planning applications are made for the repair of the roof of the front-facing building, however. More than ten years have passed since the end of the war. How did they live here for a decade beneath a damaged roof? The apartments on the first and second floors are subsequently rented out to tailors, with separate rooms for ironing, storage, sewing machines and apprentices; the *Berliner Zimmer* is used for handiwork. In February 1958, Bruno Sala reports that the third floor of the backyard factory building is experiencing ongoing blockages of the drains. I am reminded of Klaus Theweleit's writings about the swamp, the mire, "the veil of mist over the lowlands." As he sees it, women were associated with all hybrid substances defined by their "ability to flow." They were the ones who worked with, and in, all things swampy and mushy. "The average bourgeois male of the Wilhelmine era would have let himself be shot rather than touch those substances in any context that was reminiscent of 'women's work,'" he wrote. It was the women who "cleared black muck out of stopped-up drains and cleaned toilets. [...] They wiped the floors and got their hands into liquid manure." They were the ones transgressing boundaries, flowing on, in, over and out.

Curiously, just as I am writing this, various sinks and drains in our apartment have become blocked. Not only the shower, which continues to emanate those unsettling swampy smells, but now the bathroom sink too. I put it down to our youngest who is growing his hair: long blond strands clogged up with wax form a tangled mass in the U-bend. But when the sink in the side wing bathroom blocks too, it starts to feel uncanny. This occurrence seems to suggest the exact opposite to the downward flows of leaking water that have troubled us until now. What sense is to be made of this? How can one read a blocked drain, a furnished room, an inhabited house, a broken family, an historical dilemma? Beyond its interpretive potential, however, this is a problem that needs to be solved. I set to with tools and rags and attempt to clear the drains.

Throughout the 1950s, the entrenchment of the Eastern and Western superpowers, as they came to be known in the new global alignments, etches Cold War delineations into the surface of the city. The movement of people from East Germany into West Berlin increases steadily, as the GDR's social restrictions become more apparent. By 1958, with one hundred people leaving every day, Walter Ulbricht, general secretary of the Socialist Unity Party, or SED, denounces "flight from the Republic" as a crime and spreads scare stories about West German depravities. This does nothing to stop the outward flow, however: escape is as easy as travelling two stops on the U-Bahn into West Berlin. The refugees are for the most part young skilled workers, professionals and new graduates – "the elite of East German youth," as Richie puts it, who can easily find employment in West Germany:

By 1961 over 5,000 doctors and dentists had left the GDR, as had hundreds of professors – including the entire Law Faculty of the University of Leipzig; over 2,000 scientists left, three-quarters of whom were under forty-five. Thirty thousand students fled, many only days after receiving their diplomas. Some defections were particularly embarrassing: in 1961 the East German Miss Universe came to the west, followed by 4,000 members of the SED.

On the night of August 12, 1961, Ulbricht gives the order to seal the border between East and West Berlin. By early the next morning, the line drawn on the map has been made physical, first with barbed wire, then with a hastily constructed brick and mortar wall, and then by a barrier of prefabricated concrete panels. The wall, four meters high and forty-three kilometers long, encircles West Berlin. It is surrounded on the east side by the death strip, a security zone accessible only to guards, and punctuated by watchtowers. The outward flow is dammed.

"It is forbidden to discuss the recognition of the present borders of the two German states as a fact from which one must first proceed," wrote the Mitscherlichs of the taboo that had arisen around the frontier. In West Germany, it was seen as a physical manifestation of Germany's defeat and loss of sovereignty. A permanent reminder of failure, it is called the "Wall of Shame" by some. But in the East, its official name was the "antifascist protection barrier." The GDR was a black spot on the Federal Republic's soul, but just as much, in keeping with the contrapuntal narrative of the time, West Berlin was a black spot on the map of Communist Germany. On the GDR's city maps it appears as a blanked-out area. Wherever you are in West Berlin, if you drive straight ahead, you reach a dead end.

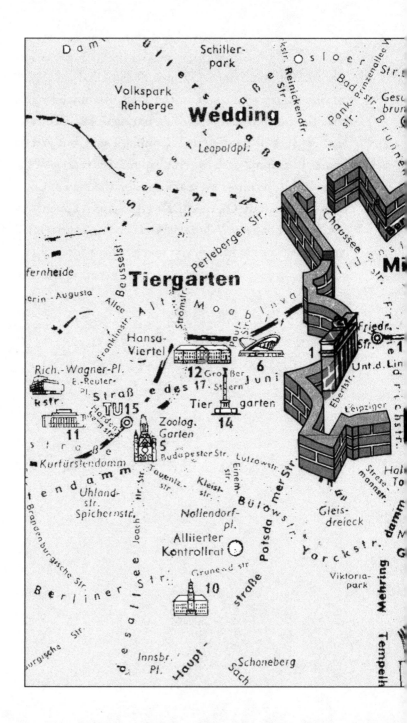

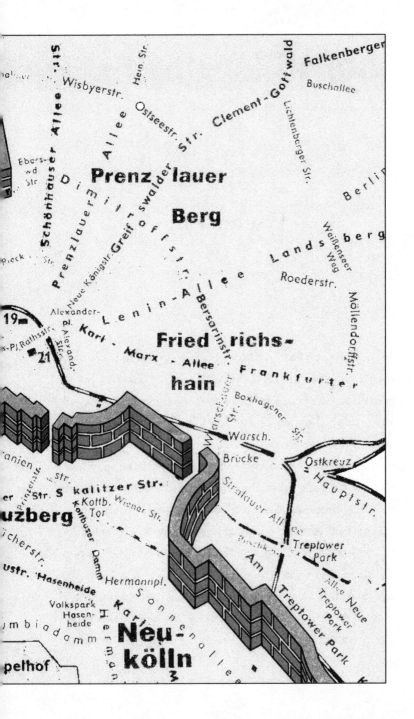

# 17

# Exception

*In 1964*, Bruno Sala replaces the coal ovens in his buildings with gas central heating. This is a kind of progress. But two years later, on September 16, 1966, aged seventy-six, he dies. His widow Charlotte is sixty-three years old when she inherits the house and business. Her daughter, Melitta, is thirty-two. By this time, production of the Sala-Spiele has been outsourced to a larger printing company. The years of fine craftsmanship, creativity and exclusive handmade products are over. As the 1960s draw to a close, the house on the Ufer is one hundred years old. The decades of urban development, acceleration and destruction it has witnessed have slowed down now, ground virtually to a halt. A Daihatsu car dealership has opened next door on the corner of

Schöneberger Straße. The Railway Directorate beyond
is quiet. Grey-mantled crows roost in the young trees
planted outside.

If Melitta and her mother Charlotte were to leave
the house early one morning, turn left at the Daihatsu
dealership and proceed towards the Gleisdreieck
U-Bahn station, they would come to a barrier. The former freight depot and goods yards are now an urban
wilderness surrounded by a high perimeter fence. The
land still belongs to the railways, which are managed
by East Berlin. Access to it is forbidden. Nevertheless, curious locals, nature lovers are drawn to this
site of romantic abandonment and find their way in
through the southern border, scaling the unused railway bridges at Yorckstraße. The "Gleisdreieck walkers," as they are known, investigate the terrain, where
wild-growing plants creep over the rusting railway
machinery and around the dilapidated redbrick engine
houses, as if it were a botanical garden. The wheels of
freight trains from decades past have imported exotic
seeds from the south. Now a great variety of types and
structures of biotope have developed, springing up
between the parallel lines of the north–south railway
tracks. "For decades," writes Janos Frecot, himself a
frequenter of this fenced-off terrain, "the Gleisdreieck
was regarded by artists, urban flâneurs, freaks and
bums as a synonym for a specific West Berlin state of

mind consisting of melancholy, depression and the will to be different."

This dozing wilderness idyll is threatened, however, by Governing Mayor Willy Brandt's vision of the *autogerechte Stadt*, the car-friendly city. Plans to create inner-city freeways to service six million projected future inhabitants had been seeded in Scharoun's *Kollektivplan* of 1946 and its 1958 revision, and were developed in the mid-1960s. However, both of Scharoun's plans had been devised with the whole city in mind. Now, in a territory full of dead-end streets, the urban flyovers are a future-driven fantasy, in denial of the actual present-day facts. Thousands of apartments in relatively undamaged parts of Kreuzberg are to be sacrificed for the motorways which some are now ironically calling "the fastest way to the Wall." The *Westtangente*, or West Tangent, will cut through the Gleisdreieck wilderness, and meet the South Tangent at the canal, two blocks away from the Salas' house. In 1974, a pressure group founded by local residents, those with a stake in this area, begins to organize and fight against these "senseless and threatening" plans.

The citizens activist group, *Bürgerinitiative Westtangente*, or *BIW* for short, worked for years to prevent this development, devising a detailed plan for an ecological alternative they called the "Green Tangent." It took until 1988, but finally the local government gave up the notion of a car-friendly city and the West Tangent plans were shelved. The citizens group continued to push for their Green Tangent, preventing the felling of trees on the Gleisdreieck and a decade later, in 1998, the first part of it opened to the public. It was this same activist group that prevented planners in the early 2000s from selling the Gleisdreieck land to real estate investors. Their awkward tenacity and vigorous insistence, demanding respect for existing nature and the land's local usage, slowed down the plans for development and helped shape the thoughtfully-designed and useful park that occupies this terrain now.

If Melitta and her mother were to walk out of their house in the early 1970s and take the other direction, following the Ufer downstream to the corner, they would come to the last of three houses that survived the war on this block. It is another four-floor *Gründerzeit* building, very similar to theirs, except for the curved room on the corner itself that conceals the street's sharp angle as it turns right and heads up to the Gleisdreieck U-Bahn. Today, a white enamelled sign with dark blue serif writing hangs on the front wall of this house. An official "Berlin Memorial Plaque," like that marking Hobrecht's pumping station. This one reads: "From 1971 to 1975, singer, lyricist, and composer Rio Reiser lived and worked here with the band Ton Steine Scherben."

Rio Reiser, a skinny wastrel in flared trousers with dark eyes and long straggly hair, lead singer of Ton Steine Scherben, remains a hero to Germans of a certain generation. The band's songs – simple compositions with catchy choruses sung in German – created the soundtrack to West Berlin's anti-establishment and anarchist movements. Songs like *"Keine Macht für niemand"* ("No Power for Anyone") were designed to sing along to, while *"Macht kaputt, was euch kaputt macht"* – "Destroy the system that destroys you" – was their mantra. The whole band lived in a six-room apartment in this corner house, which they called "T-Ufer." The address was even published on their records, and it became a crash pad for musicians, street kids, fans and girlfriends, who came and went with steady regularity.

Hundreds of Wilhelmine-era houses like this were standing empty in Kreuzberg and Schöneberg, often with only coal-oven heating and outdoor toilets in the backyards, and desperately in need of repair. Many were slated for demolition to make way for the city's new motorways and concrete housing blocks. In the meantime, they were rented out to badly-paid immigrant workers from Greece, Italy and above all Turkey, crammed into substandard living quarters and charged a per-capita rent. Squatters began to move in too, signalling the era of West Berlin's house occupations.

In 1972, as social change is rumbling, Charlotte Sala dies at the age of sixty-nine and her adopted daughter Melitta inherits both business and building. She is now the landlady of the house at the Ufer, and the proprietor of Sala-Spiele. She is also now a married woman, the wife of one Wolfgang Kozlowski. Thirty-eight years old and childless, she doesn't let go entirely of her independent status. Her name appears in the documents as Melitta Kozlowski-Sala.

I was born the year before, in 1971. My parents had moved from Edinburgh, where they had met as students, to Croydon, a suburb of London. My father, a research scientist, had been offered his first real job in a pharmaceutical company. My mother was stuck at home with a newborn baby and my brother, a toddler not yet two, far away from her friends and family in a semi-detached mock-Tudor house. While pregnant with me, she began reading Germaine Greer's *The Female Eunuch*, which had just been published. "Women must learn how to question the most basic assumptions about feminine normality in order to reopen the possibilities for development which have been successively locked off by conditioning," she read. She resolved to bring up her daughter differently. There would be no dolls or prams or other gender-orientated toys. I would have the same opportunities as my brother. A different future would be available for me than that which her own circumstances prescribed, where alternatives were being imagined, written down and shared amongst women, but for the time being female stereotypes prevailed and patriarchal structures kept wives isolated, at home with the children.

At around the same time, as the late 1960s were folding into the 1970s, a small girl moves from a village in the West German countryside to a house like the Salas' on Paul-Linke Ufer, farther down the Landwehr Canal in Kreuzberg.

> My parents had told us wonderful stories about the enormous apartment with its six large rooms that we were going to live in now. They would start earning a lot of money, my mother said. We would each have a room all to ourselves and she would buy beautiful furniture.

Six-year-old Christiane spins these words into fantastic visions of a beautiful bedroom all to herself, but what greets her on arrival is a different vision altogether:

> I have never forgotten what the flat we moved into looked like. I immediately felt a deep terror of this flat. It was so big and empty that I was afraid of getting lost. If you spoke loudly, it echoed spookily.

Her family lives in three sparsely furnished rooms; the other three rooms are to be used for her parents' new business: a marriage bureau. But the business plans come to nothing, and one day soon after a truck pulls up and the few pieces of furniture they own are loaded up and driven to a two-room apartment on the eleventh floor of a high-rise in *Gropiusstadt,* a brand-new development on the southern outskirts of the city, purpose-built for 50,000 people. "From far away it all looked very new and well maintained," remembers Christiane, "but if you got nearer, it smelt of piss and shit between the high-rise buildings, from all of the children and dogs that lived in the *Gropiusstadt.*" This girl would go on to become West Berlin's most notorious street kid and wayward youth of the 1970s, known as "Christiane F."

Groups of disaffected youths not much older than Christiane F. were beginning to move into the empty buildings in Kreuzberg and Schöneberg, experimenting with new forms of collective living. One of the squatters' anthems was Ton Steine Scherben's *"Rauch-Haus-Song"* about the raid of the Georg-von-Rauch Haus in April 1972. Georg von Rauch, a self-styled "city guerrilla," had been killed in an exchange of bullets with police. The building on Kreuzberg's Mariannenstraße that bore his name had been squatted since the previous December. *"Doch die Leute im besetzten Haus / Riefen: Ihr kriegt uns hier nicht raus / Das ist unser Haus, schmeißt doch endlich / Schmidt und Press und Mosch aus Kreuzberg raus!"* goes the chorus of Ton Steine Scherben's song: "The people in the occupied house cried you'll never get us out! This is our house! Throw Schmidt and Press and Mosch out of Kreuzberg instead!" Schmidt, Press and Mosch were notorious real estate speculators reviled by the squatters.

There was a darker side to the experimental new forms of living that took root throughout 1970s West Berlin, however. It was not only the capital of counterculture, but also the heroin capital of the Western world. An article in *Der Spiegel* from 1978 reported: "In no other major European city is the death rate, measured by the number of addicts at risk, so constant and so high. Even the drug stronghold of New York, with 49,000 addicts, falls behind." In New York, six to seven addicts out of a thousand died on an annual average, in Berlin it was more than twenty. The book *Wir Kinder vom Bahnhof Zoo* [We Children of Zoo Station] – follows the descent of Christiane F., now thirteen years old, into the club and music scene, and the consumption of ever-harder drugs. Within a shockingly short space of time, she has gone from taking marijuana and speed to engaging in prostitution to fund a heroin habit. I have never seen *Christiane F.* before, the film made in 1981, so I watch it now and am immediately seduced by night-time shots of the elevated U-Bahn travelling from Kreuzberg to Charlottenburg, and of the SOUND Diskothek on Genthiner Straße, in the once prestigious area of Tiergarten. Christiane F.'s story was recorded in salacious detail in interviews journalists Kai Hermann and Horst Rieck made when Christiane was sixteen years old. First published in *Stern* magazine in 1978, the story quickly acquired notoriety and was devoured by West German adolescents, more entranced than repelled by the scenes it depicts. Reading it now, I wonder about the fine line between empathy and exploitation in the male journalists' recording and publishing of the life story of someone still so young and vulnerable.

David Bowie's late 1970s music is the soundtrack to *Christiane F.* The night of the Bowie concert at the Deutschlandhalle in 1976, which Christiane went to, was the first time she took heroin. Bowie was living in West Berlin himself during these years and the albums he recorded here, *Low* and in particular *Heroes*, with its synthesizer undercurrents and dark guitar riffs, defined the sound of this time in Berlin. "I couldn't have made music like that back then if I hadn't been completely under the spell of Berlin, with its very particular structures and tensions," Bowie recalled some years later. In summer 1977, Bowie booked Hansa Studio's largest studio, the *Meistersaal*, big enough for a hundred-piece orchestra and known for its cavernous natural reverb, and began working on what would become *Heroes*. I feel another quiver of proximity when I realize that Hansa Studios is right here, across the canal just two blocks beyond the Hafenplatz. I can't wait to tell my sons, who both have David Bowie posters on their bedroom walls. The Weimar-era ballroom on Köthener Straße, which had initially housed Dada artist John Heartfield's publishing house and the gallery of George Grosz, and later hosted Nazi soirées, was one of those massive solitary buildings left stranded in the post-war wastelands of Southern Friedrichstadt. Its façade was pockmarked with bullet holes and it stood so near to the Wall that the musicians could look out over it as they were working.

Christiane F.'s doomed narrative spools out against this soundtrack and is graphically depicted in the film I'm watching: the descent from a fresh-faced girl with glossy lips and a lilac satin bomber jacket, to a pale skinny urchin, arms full of scars and rings under her eyes. As the film progresses, I am less seduced than distressed, and just keep thinking: Where is her mother? My sons are both teenagers now, growing up in a city where drugs remain easy to come by: this subject matter strikes a nerve. In the film, Christiane and her friends seem to simply drift into hard-drug use, as if it is an integral part of the music scene. There is little sense of a social context that might lead her towards this desperate escape route. The first-person transcripts in the book provide details that the filmed version elides. Christiane describes her childhood, growing up in the *Gropiusstadt* with no nature, nowhere for children to play, warning signs everywhere forbidding all kinds of activities, and gangs of children playing power games and bent on destruction. Shortly after arriving there, her survival instincts kick in.

Christiane's father's family had been well off but after the war, their property and printing business in the East of Germany were expropriated by the Communist state. He drives a Porsche but is unemployed and beats his wife and children. All of the families in the *Gropiusstadt*, according to Christiane, have violent alcoholic fathers. They belong to the generation that were children during the war and still carry the scars of those experiences, though this fact is not mentioned here. Her father is so full of shame for the situation he is in, wife and two children but no prospects, that he pretends to his friends that his daughters are not even his own. Christiane's parents separate and her mother, who is busy earning a living to support the family and has a new boyfriend, does not notice as her daughter goes off the rails. The search for alternatives to prescribed ways of living does not always have a happy end.

Already in 1950, Hannah Arendt had recognized exceptionalism in the behavior of Berliners compared with those in other parts of Germany. "I do not know why this should be so," she writes, "but customs, manners, speech, approaches to people, are in the smallest details so absolutely different from everything one sees and has to face in the rest of Germany that Berlin is almost like another country." Berlin is an exception, notes Arendt, "for the city is hermetically sealed off and has little intercourse with the rest of the country." She describes how in other parts of Germany there were also people who are "different," but they are forced to "use up their energy in efforts to penetrate the stifling atmosphere that surrounds them, and remain completely isolated."

Throughout the 1970s, those that feel "different" in other parts of the Federal Republic are drawn to the exceptional status of West Berlin. Alternative ways of living to the conventional nuclear family are tested. Nonconformist behavior and visible expressions of outrage are encouraged. Illegal nature lovers, grassroots community activists, radical musicians, artists, filmmakers, queer communities, students, outsiders and renegades are all at home here. West Berliners are exempted from the military service that male citizens in the rest of the Federal Republic are subject to and this fact alone is a draw for many. In the absence of sustainable local industry, this half of the city is kept alive by a financial lifeline from the new West German capital in Bonn, which underwrites over half of its annual budget. Meanwhile, West Berlin's cultural scene is bolstered by creative imports through the artists-in-residence program established after the Wall was built. In 1963, Austrian poet Ingeborg Bachmann had been the first visitor to the exchange program established by the Ford Foundation and eventually taken over by DAAD, the German Academic Exchange Service. It was during this residency that Bachmann began writing her only novel, *Malina*, an extraordinary fever-dream reflection on male-female relationships and subordination. Twenty years later, in the spring of 1984, Margaret Atwood, another DAAD visitor, would begin her novel *The Handmaid's Tale* while living in West Berlin. "The background was RAF, Germany's Nazi mother cult, and East Germany with its spy circles and discouragement of private friendships, like amongst the partners of the Handmaids," said Atwood about a book she calls "the literature of witness."

By the end of the 1970s, 10,000 apartments are empty, while 80,000 people are still in need of housing. The squatters begin to organize, renovating the houses they move into, demanding leases and asking for an end to the policy of keeping houses empty that are awaiting demolition. A *Besetzerrat* or "Occupiers Council," is established which meets every Sunday in a house on Anhalter Straße, behind the former station. It is the only old house left on this street and stretches over two backyards. Its exposed firewalls are painted with enormous brightly colored murals in stark contrast to the grey of the surroundings. One pictures three witches in black hats and cloaks sitting around a blazing fire. This occupied house became a center for art, alternative theater and film called KuKuCK, which stands for *Kunst Kultur-Centrum Kreuzberg*, but *Kuckuck* is also the word for cuckoo.

As I am reading my way around Berlin in the 1970s, I am wondering again about the female perspective. What happened to those capable heroines of the post-war years who had cleared the city's streets of rubble and kept their families alive? What were their daughters doing? The emancipations these women had experienced in the immediate post-war years were followed by a reactionary conservatism. A Federal government report from 1966 claimed that the chief roles for women were to be "caregiver and comforter, symbol of modest harmony, bringing order to the reliable world of the private sphere. Women should only engage in gainful employment and social commitment if the demands of family life allow it." Women were not allowed to work without the permission of their husbands, could not have their own bank account, and were legally responsible for housework until 1977, when new matrimonial laws were finally introduced. Such social conservatism had been sanctioned already in the *Kuppelparagraph*, a law introduced in 1950, which prevented unmarried couples from living together. Initially devised to prevent war widows with large apartments from renting out rooms to unmarried couples or allowing night-time visits to single women, it remained in place until 1969, threatening non-compliant landladies with fines. The only way around these laws were the *Wohngemein-schaften*, or shared apartments, which gradually became acceptable in the late 1960s and were one step in the direction of women's slow emancipation.

A "family start-up loan" of 4,000 Deutschmarks was introduced in 1962 to attract young families to West Berlin. But young single female students were coming of their own accord, drawn by the city's exceptional status and isolation, reachable only by the *Transitautobahn*, or the flights coming through the "West Berlin air corridor" to Tegel airport. Further education was still not a given for young women, who had to fight for this privilege and came looking for alternatives and a chance to stretch their wings.

Women's movements began to form around the universities, the Action Committee for the Liberation of Women in 1968 and an autonomous group set up at the Freie Universität at the same time. A few years later, in January 1973, Berlin's first women's center opened in a house on Hornstraße. (This short street, only one block long, is a remnant of what would have been Lenné's main arterial boulevard, which had been aborted by the railway takeover, and now ended abruptly at the perimeter fence around the abandoned Gleisdreieck.) The center on Hornstraße gave women a place to meet, to discuss the movement and its issues, but also to simply cook and socialize together, suggesting a communal way of life a world away from the lonely fate of the isolated housewife. The women's group initiated a *Kinderladen*, or childcare center, which took an anti-authoritarian approach to child-rearing, and more followed. By the late 1960s, five such childcare centers had opened and seven more were being planned.

The feminist branch of the anti-Vietnam war 1968 student movement was tolerated but not taken seriously by male students who saw it as petty bourgeois and marginal, the very things it was set up to criticize. Psychoanalyst Margarete Mitscherlich began to involve herself in questions of gender, turning her research towards understanding where the roots of women's oppression lay, and advocating for women's rights. Her 1985 publication *Die friedfertige Frau* [*The Peaceable Sex*] cemented her position as one of the main figures of West German feminism. She was critical of the 1968 student movement, seeing the "de-idealization of Americans" that lay behind the anti-Vietnam war movement as an alibi for the "de-idealization of parents, above all of the father," thus setting up an ideological binary between one generation and another, as she writes in *The Peaceable Sex*. Mitscherlich saw the aim of feminism to be in circumventing such binary conflicts by cultivating empathy, advocating critical thinking and questioning the ideology of obedience that hampered women's emancipation. The work of remembering and of working through difficulty towards self-acceptance in both sexes could encourage an attitude of tolerance, she believed, that would rein in the sadomasochistic structures underpinning patriarchal relations.

———

The situation for women in the West was just half of the picture in the divided city. On both sides of the Wall was a desire for change. In socialist East Berlin, women were accepted as members of the workforce and provided with state-run childcare, but the oppressive patterns of relationships rooted in patriarchy still remained untouched. In the secret-police ridden society, trust was eroded through the culture of unofficial informants or IMs, whose numbers peaked at 200,000 in the mid-1970s. Journalist and author Maxie Wander undertook a series of interviews with women living under socialism between the ages of sixteen and ninety-two. "We are all in uncharted territory and are still largely left to ourselves," she writes. "We are looking for new ways of living, in private and in society."

Christa Wolf wrote the introduction to the book of interviews, published posthumously in 1977, after Wander's early death at the age of forty-four. Wander "did not come to judge, but to see and hear," she writes. Her interest alone offers something other than the usual "formula of loneliness and self-disgust, of shyness and withdrawal," encouraging instead "touch, intimacy, openness, sometimes startling ruthlessness and an exhilarating courage to face oneself." It offered a chance for connection like that in the women's meeting house on Hornstraße, for community and shared experience rather than isolation. The women Wander interviewed were offered a rare chance for self-reflection and to become eyewitnesses of their own lives.

The social shifts taking place in this period, as one generation nudges up against the other, are reflected in the city's horizon line. In the view from our house on the Ufer, the first tall buildings begin to appear in rapid succession in these years. In the middle distance in 1964, a golden ribbed tower appears. In 1968, right behind the Anhalter Bahnhof, comes a massive rectangular block studded with rows of windows, the Excelsiorhaus, built on the eponymous hotel's foundations. Over the next dozen years, a group of grey concrete tower blocks appear one after another in the middle distance to the left. From the perspective of my view, these tall buildings appear like chess pieces on the political checkerboard that Berlin's terrain has become.

The Excelsiorhaus was an expedient solution to the housing crisis in the West, offering 500 apartments in one fell swoop, but the golden-ribbed tower had a more strategic goal in mind. It was built by Axel Springer, the head of the newspaper empire reviled by the student and feminist movements. It was to this tower that a crowd of 2,000 marched in April 1968 following the shooting of activist Rudi Dutschke, who had been branded "No. 1 Enemy of the State" by Springer's press. When construction began in 1959, the site was already very near to the border between the American and Soviet sectors – it was a calculated provocation. By the time its twenty-story corpus was completed, it butted right up against the newly-built Berlin Wall. Ulbricht's SED government answered Springer's gesture with a cluster of high-rises of their own on the other side of the Wall. One after the other, four boxy concrete apartment buildings rose up on Leipziger Straße, each between twenty-three and twenty-five floors high. In a military-style display of power, a square-shouldered stand-off was staged, one executed through architecture, that played out on the skyline of Melitta Sala's house.

· 18 ·

# Wide Field

*The binary suggested* by the dividing of Berlin is
misleading. As the distinct entities of West and East
emerge, the process is more like the division of cells.
Varieties of difference proliferate. Throughout these
diffuse post-war decades, every individual fact, event or
issue that comes up is like a many-sided crystal. It must
be turned, examined and re-examined from all sides to
account for complicity, political allegiance, subterfuge,
instrumentalization, gender bias, conformity or anti-
establishment tendencies. The most apparently simple
description must be considered and reconsidered to
understand its perspective and what aspects it may obscure. The narratives that belong to this time are not so
much contrapuntal as kaleidoscopic.

Seeking full immersion in a version of this period, I turn to the provocative and manically prolific filmmaker Rainer Werner Fassbinder. With three box sets of DVDs and another stretch of time alone as the boys are with their father, I settle in on the sofa in the *Berliner Zimmer* to immerse myself in Fassbinder's world. Watching his films in quick succession, the ensemble nature of his production is immediately clear. The same small cast of actors appears, assuming a different role in each film, their faces and gestures growing familiar from one piece to the next. His manic working-through of the troubled psyche of post-war German society offers up rich visual textures and psychological nuance, as outmoded social conventions play out over coffee, cake and copious cigarettes smoked in highly patterned living rooms. Most palpable though are the suppressed emotions that simmer dangerously beneath the surface and explode suddenly on-screen in moments of violent catharsis.

In his films from 1968 to 1982, Fassbinder casts a sardonic, unblinking eye on the environment and social structures around him. The women in his films are so entangled in class, family and social structures that they are rarely owners of their own destinies. They are not merely appendages to men, however, but drivers of the plot. His afflicted heroines are played by a cast of incredible women with whom Fassbinder had notoriously close and cruel relationships. He demanded love and submission from them while extracting compelling performances. Fassbinder had a dim view of relationships, and of marriage in particular, rooted in his parents' disastrous marriage: "No authentic relationship is possible," he said. "The answer: abolish first marriage, then all society based on property and the desire for possessions, the root of our ills. Till this happens, individuals and classes will go on corrupting each other forever." Despite this, and regardless of the fact that he was openly gay, he married actor Ingrid Caven in 1970, divorcing two years later.

Fassbinder had been turned down by the German Film and Television Academy, Berlin, in 1967 and began his career in Munich in the theater instead. Most of his films are set there but a handful take place in Berlin and, as usual, I find myself searching these out and combing the screen for familiar locations. *The Third Generation* from 1979 is set here: a satire about domestic terrorism, made just after the climax of the Red Army Faction's violent kidnappings and assassinations of 1977. The film's locations are typical West Berlin: Charlottenburg landmarks like the Kaiser Wilhelm Memorial Church and the Europa Center; vast, many-roomed nineteenth-century apartments, in which an assemblage of radicals, junkies, anarchists and leftist intellectuals converge. One scene plays out around the

Anhalter Bahnhof ruin, and the camera zooms in on my neighborhood's street signs: Anhalter Straße, Stresemannstraße. I can barely follow the plot of this film, however, with its spying, crossing and double-crossing. The version I am watching doesn't have subtitles and in almost all of its scenes, a TV is blaring in the background, manic news broadcasts cutting across the actors' words.

Fassbinder's main Berlin work is his thirteen-hour TV adaptation of Alfred Döblin's 1929 novel *Berlin Alexanderplatz*, an extraordinary tour de force, made from 1979 to 1980. While filming this during the daytime, Fassbinder spent cocaine-fuelled nights writing the script for *The Marriage of Maria Braun*, which follows the checkered story of Maria, a war bride, played by Hanna Schygulla. (In 1981, this was the first of Fassbinder's films to be shown in the GDR.)

*Berlin Alexanderplatz* was set in the late 1920s, and *The Marriage of Maria Braun* in the immediate post-war period, but in both films Fassbinder uses the past as a way of discovering the roots of present maladies. He suggests the politics, choices and ethics of previous generations are part of an inherited continuum. Fassbinder's attitude to contemporary social dilemmas is summed up in the lengthy subtitle he appended to his adaptation of Theodor Fontane's *Effi Briest:* "Many people who are aware of their capabilities and needs nevertheless accept the prevailing

system in their thoughts and deeds, thereby confirming and thoroughly reinforcing it." The hypocrisies of
nineteenth-century society equal those that bind the
present in a painful state of inhibition. *Effi Briest* was
the first film Fassbinder had ever wanted to make, but
by the time he made it in 1973, he already had twenty-
six other films under his belt. He titled it *Fontane Effi
Briest* as a clear tribute to the author, and took all of
its dialogue directly from the novel.

The film is shot in black and white, and Hanna
Schygulla again plays the lead: a soft-faced, ringlet-
ted Effi, ravishing in lacey white dresses, Wilhelmine
with a 70s flair. The freedom and gaiety we first see in
seventeen-year-old Effi, swinging in her parents' country garden, are quickly snuffed out once she marries
the austere civil servant Baron von Innstetten. Twenty
years older than her, he is stiff, formal, "as frosty as a
snowman," she says, unable to respond to Effi's natural
affection. Scenes play out in heavily-furnished interiors, with little physical contact or even eye contact between characters, who are arranged at angles to each
other like the chairs in Menzel's painting. They appear
obliquely, reflected in ornately-framed mirrors, seen
through windows, or filmed through screens of lace,
confined within a suffocating present. Even the emotional high points of the narrative are treated cooly:
Effi's affair with Major Crampas takes place off-screen

and Innstetten's duel with him, a challenge he calls long after the affair has ended, is a swift and unemotional (if fatal) transaction.

One phrase punctuates Fontane's novel and is used as a catch-all excuse for inaction, or refusing to touch upon a difficult issue. *Ein weites Feld* – a vast subject. This is repeated insistently in Fassbinder's film. "Quite, quite. But don't let's argue about it. It's a vast subject. And then people are so different," says Effi's father evasively. Effi is publicly disgraced following the revelation of her affair with Crampas, abandoned by society, her daughter taken from her, and she eventually leaves Berlin and returns to her parents' country house. Here she dies a tragic young death, unable even to broach the possibility that Innstetten's rigid and cruel behavior, or her parents' informal upbringing, could have contributed to her misfortune. In the last lines of Fontane's book, and of Fassbinder's film, Effi's grieving mother tentatively asks if it could have been *their* fault: if they should have brought her up more strictly, if she wasn't too young to marry. Her husband nips this firmly in the bud saying *"Ach, Luise, laß . . . das ist ein zu weites Feld"* – "Ah Luise, that's enough . . . that's *too* vast a subject." Guilt of any kind, or responsibility beyond the given social norms, is *far* too vast a subject, even to spare the life of an only child. "This is not a film that tells a story, but it is a film that traces an attitude," said Fassbinder of *Fontane Effi Briest*. "It is the attitude of someone who sees through the faults and weaknesses of his society and also criticizes them, but still accepts this society as the one that is valid for him." I later learn that the real woman on whom Effi Briest was based, Elisabeth von Ardenne, did not in fact die a tragic young death. After her divorce, she trained to become a nurse, reconciled with her adult children and lived a long, fulfilled life together with her companion Margarethe "Daisy" Weyersberg, a patient suffering from "melancholy" she had met while working in a sanatorium. She died only in 1952 at the age of ninety-eight. Though Fontane was affectionate towards his heroines, his fiction did not enact the social liberation that their real-life counterparts fought for and ultimately achieved. While revealing the damaging hypocrisies of social structures, Fontane accepted the prevailing system, as Fassbinder's subtitle to *Fontane Effi Briest* declares, "thereby confirming and thoroughly reinforcing it."

Ever since Fontane used the phrase *Ein weites Feld*, it has been adopted as a popular avoidance strategy. *It's too vast a subject*, I think to myself, as I try to get to grips with Berlin in the 1970s, so distant to my own upbringing, culture, chronology and place. But comprehension only comes through close attention, and the shadows of this time are still here, soaked into the city as much as are the previous eras. Until his early death in 1982, aged only thirty-seven, Rainer Werner Fassbinder dove straight into this *vast subject* with his multifaceted oeuvre, refusing to shy away from its dissonance, ambivalence and difficulty. His life's work was symptomatic of this period in post-fascist divided Germany, and of the exceptional potential for art to address psychological and social complexities head-on. As a chronicler of both Germany's past and present, Fassbinder explored the structures that allow people to oppress others, and the influence of power and money on ethics and behavior. He made an incredible forty-four films and television dramas during his abbreviated life, shooting by day and writing by night, before he died from a fatal mixture of cocaine and sleeping pills. Beside him when he died was the unfinished script he had been working on: a biopic about Rosa Luxemburg in which Jane Fonda was to play the lead role.

Fassbinder was not based in Berlin but in Munich, and in fact most of West Germany's cultural production took place elsewhere. The material that West Berlin produced was raw and rough-edged, driven by the exploding of social structures that the 1968 student movement brought about, but also heavily subsidized by authorities keen to recapture Berlin's place as a world leader of cultural production. West Berlin's richest work emerged from subcultural seams, not surprisingly, given the extreme living conditions of the island city. It remained in a state of exception. The most provocative and lasting works were made by outsiders, a bohemian scene of musicians, filmmakers, artists and fashion designers, living and working in communities like that of the *fabrikneu* loft in Kreuzberg's Zossener Straße. Filmmakers Ulrike Ottinger or Rosa von Praunheim, fashion designer Claudia Skoda, one-offs like actor, singer and costume maker Tabea Blumenschein, Ottinger's muse for several years. Do-it-yourself punk bands like Einstürzende Neubauten, Die Tödliche Doris and Malaria. The attitude was not slick but self-made. Scrappy but radical in content.

Attempting to find a footing in this wide field, I narrow my focus again and return to the house itself. The first time I visited the Land Registry Office on nearby Möckernstraße and Frau Lier handed me the pile of fading folders relating to the house, I had found a document from 1999 listing the names of all of the tenants who lived there at that time. On the first floor was a urologist who had been there since the early 1980s. On the second floor was *Martinswerk*, an organization that had been renting the apartment as shared accommodation for students since 1974. (When we first came to see the house, a peek into the four small windows of this apartment's *Mädchenkammer* on the way up the stairs revealed that it was still being used as two half-height sleeping quarters.) Then there is the name of the person who in 1981 moved into our third-floor apartment.

A document in a faded green folder in a room in an administrative building has led me to this name, but it is the internet that leads me to her person. I have fished countless valuable historical remnants out of the internet up until now, and followed them up in libraries or archives and stitched them into my narrative. But this is the first time it provides me with an actual living woman. She is an architect, a partner in a firm in Berlin. I write an email and introduce myself, sending a tentative enquiry. Within two hours she has replied. "How funny," she writes, "I lived in that building from 1981-2008, in the top floor of the front building." She agrees to meet me the following week for tea. A real inhabitant has appeared, crossing my path like an apparition.

We arrange to meet on Saturday at three o'clock at Café Einstein on Kurfürstenstraße, a short bike ride from the Ufer, westwards across Gleisdreieck Park. I find a table against the wall in the grand Viennese-style coffee house and a few minutes later she walks in, a slight woman wearing a red coat, with pale watery eyes and red lipstick. She walks straight over, recognizing me, having looked me up on Google beforehand.

Settling into the banquette opposite, she launches straight in, generous, open and clearly excited to share her memories from her time spent on the Ufer. She had come to Berlin in 1972 as an eighteen-year-old from the Rhineland, to study architecture at the Technical University. Initially she lived in a shared apartment on Kurfürstenstraße, just beyond Potsdamer Straße, before it reached what was still then the dead-end perimeter fence around Gleisdreieck. At that time, Potsdamer Straße was full of bordellos, she tells me, and prostitutes would be sitting outside on the streets. She spent many evenings here at the Café Einstein, drinking wine until deep into the night.

I barely need to ask any questions as the architect talks and talks, freely reminiscing about this period of her life to me, a perfect stranger, connected only by the fact of the house. In 1981, she had fallen in love with a fellow architect, and they had found the third-floor apartment in the house on Tempelhofer Ufer. The landlady, Frau Melitta Kozlowski-Sala, asked to visit the prospective new tenants at home, to ascertain their living standards. Sitting in their living room, Melitta smoked one menthol cigarette after another, lighting one up, taking a drag and stubbing it out before lighting the next. She agreed to rent the apartment to them on the condition that they hang curtains in the windows. They said they would, but never did.

Melitta was living in a side wing apartment when they moved into the house on the Ufer. When they arrived, their apartment was slick with black, sticky oil, having previously been rented to a company producing small parts for electrical engines. In the decades following the war, many such huge apartments had been split up and rented out room by room to small businesses and cottage industries. Considering her remark about the curtains, their landlady was clearly more concerned with outward appearances than the appalling state of the flat's interior. The architect and her partner restored the original floor plan, knocking out walls to reinstate the enfilade of four front-facing rooms. In 1985, their son was born, and she would take him for walks around the neighborhood, pushing his pram along the path of the Wall.

I ask her what it was like there in the mid-1980s. *"Unbelebt,"* she says – uninhabited. There was a petrol station two houses down, as there is now, where she would go every morning to buy a newspaper. The man that ran it always asked why she didn't just get a subscription, but she liked him, she told me, and she enjoyed the daily ritual. He was the only man she had come across that looked good in shorts, she says. There would often be people sitting and drinking on the low wall in front of the petrol station. The same woman was there every morning and would greet her as "Prinzessin" when she came down to get the paper. In the evenings, she would cross the canal to the Excelsiorhaus and drink Lambrusco in the top floor Saskatchewan bar, which only sold sparkling wine and coffee with condensed milk.

Other architects and writers were living in the house at the time, and together they decided to found a publishing house for pamphlets about architecture. Later I find some of the pamphlets in the Berlin State Library. One is on Kafka and architecture, and another on Hermann Henselmann, an architect born in 1905, a committed socialist and friend of Bertolt Brecht. Henselmann had come to Berlin to study in the 1920s and was building radical modernist villas and small houses in and around Berlin in the early 1930s until forced to give up his architecture office by the Nazi authorities. His involvement with Communist resistance fighters during the war enamored him to the occupying Soviets and during the post-war years he quickly rose to become the GDR's most prominent architect.

Henselmann, a visionary and idealist, is remembered chiefly for his involvement in the GDR's first architectural project from 1951: Stalinallee, a grand boulevard built in neoclassical Soviet style that began at Alexanderplatz and headed straight east. The street design was shared between several architects, but

Henselmann was responsible for its most striking elements, the symmetrical tiered towers with ornamental façades that frame the boulevard at Strausberger Platz. Despite its Soviet era credentials, Stalinallee's broad, stern sweep was recognized by the international architecture community and hailed by some as Europe's "last great street." Its spacious and attractive apartments were East Berlin's most desirable, home to the GDR's top-ranking officials.

From 1953 until 1959, Henselmann was chief architect of Greater Berlin and designed the Haus des Lehrers and the Congress Hall at Alexanderplatz. His 1958 plans for a signal tower, a tall needle spiked with a glittering silver ball, became the template for the *Berliner Fernsehturm*, the GDR's TV Tower. This silvery symbol of the future, visible all across Berlin, immediately became an icon when completed in 1969. It punctures the horizon line in the view from my window.

"Hermann Henselmann transforms the question of the city and the question of its form, into that of housing," writes the architect in her introduction to the pamphlet of Henselmann's selected writings. A drawing of one of the Strausberger Platz towers is pictured on the cover. It was published in 1982, when she was living in the house on the Ufer. Would she have been sitting here beside the window as she wrote this text, looking out at the TV Tower, visible across Berlin's divide? Her essay emphasizes Henselmann's conscious relation to social questions: that the city could be the place in which to openly express a collective consciousness and develop a new form of social coexistence. In an essay from the pamphlet called "Generation without an Heir," Henselmann calls for a rejection of the *Lebensangst* – the fearful life – conjured by the Nazi era and for a radical new critique instead. "To be radical – someone once said – means to get to the root of things. And the root for the human being is the human being himself."

The architect's eyes sparkle across the table in the Café Einstein as she tells me about her visits to Henselmann, across the border in East Berlin. Henselmann had founded an *Ost-West Salon* in the apartment in one of the Strausberger Platz towers that he shared with his wife and eight children, inviting architects and urbanists from the western part of the city to come and discuss ideas. At that time West Berliners could travel east with a day-trip visa, crossing the border at Checkpoint Charlie, but East Berliners were forbidden from going west. The architect lived for over two decades in the apartment on the Ufer. At some point, she and her partner separated, and she remained there with her son, renting extra rooms to young architects to work in. Hers seems an uncanny precursor to my life now, living here alone with my two sons. Finally in 2008, she left and moved from west to east across the axis of the city, into a two-room apartment on Karl-Marx-Allee, as Stalinallee was renamed in 1961.

Berlin was a site for ideological debate about urbanism and architecture, but both halves of the city suffered from a shortage of housing. The socialist goal in the East was that by 1990, every citizen should have access to an apartment with kitchen and bathroom and an affordable rent. Enormous prefabricated housing blocks, the *Plattenbauten*, were erected across East Berlin and the GDR. (Henselmann had been one of the first to investigate the industrialization of the building industry.) Meanwhile in West Berlin, many plans were made but few were realized. An International Architectural Exhibition, *Interbau*, had been held in 1957, centering on the reconstruction of the *Hansaviertel* in western Tiergarten. The most acclaimed architects from the world over built high- and low-rise residential buildings, as a model city of the future. In my area, however, little had been built besides the Excelsiorhaus, which within ten years had already fallen into such a terrible state of disrepair that an investment of ten million Marks was needed to improve the dire living conditions of its tenants.

In 1979 another West Berlin architectural showcase was called into being: the International Building Exhibition, or IBA. "The city is not merely a purpose-built phenomenon," wrote architect Josef Paul Kleihues in the project's mission statement, "it is also a symbol for existence, self-assertion, Zeitgeist." The project aimed to rethink the tabula rasa approach that had prevailed until then, and began a new development strategy known as "critical reconstruction," that would go on to become the bane of Berlin's post-Wall redevelopment efforts.

Four of the six areas earmarked for redevelopment were along the Landwehr Canal, from the borders of the Tiergarten down into Kreuzberg, running close to the westerly path of the Wall. Housing was the imperative, as it was across Europe at that time, with architects trying out new solutions to house growing urban populations. In Berlin, where so much housing stock had been destroyed and not yet replaced, the situation was acute.

All of the bourgeois apartment buildings around the Hafenplatz, where Fontane's fictional heroine Cécile had lived a century before, had been destroyed in the war, and in 1961 the harbor was filled in and turned into the Mendelssohn-Bartholdy-Park. All around the former harbor, state-subsidized energy-efficient social housing was to be built. Small apartments and larger ones for families, with winter gardens and solar panels. Integrated kindergartens were built along with a primary school across the street on Schöneberger Straße, screening off the exposed hulk of the Anhalter air raid shelter. Heterogeneity was encouraged and dozens of architects were employed, each with different visions. The apartment blocks and buildings that resulted, mostly four stories high, are variously successful, but they do articulate a thoughtful analysis of the local population's needs. In 1987 the "IBA 84/87" exhibition in the Neue Nationalgalerie displayed the results of the project, just as another exhibition titled *Bauen zum Wohle des Volkes*, "Building for the People's Benefit," was opening in East Berlin.

As well as constructing new forms of architecture, the IBA latched onto the ethos of the squatter movement. Architects developed plans to preserve and modernize decrepit old buildings, supporting the self-determined ways of living that had emerged in the previous decade, while administrators attempted to negotiate favorable leases for previously illegal tenants. The KuKuCK on Anhalter Straße was singled out for IBA support, as was Tommy-Weisbecker-Haus, a refuge for young people who had run away from home, on Wilhelmstraße. There, the inhabitants participated in converting the building into communal apartments, workshops, offices and a youth café. They painted brightly colored murals on its gable wall, but shortly after these were painted over by the local authorities. One problem of enlightened urban planning strategies was that other administrative bodies did not always see eye to eye. At KuKuCK, despite the IBA's efforts to negotiate a lease with the building's private owner, a change of ownership came in 1984 and the police cleared the building.

The Tommy-Weisbecker-Haus is still there on Wilhelmstraße today and is still run as a self-organized youth collective and emergency hostel for homeless runaways. A solitary remnant of pre-war architecture on this block, the building's façade has been painted again with a brightly colored mural. But what has become of the KuKuCK? I walk over from my house and find 7 Anhalter Straße – also the only old building on its block. It has been cheaply renovated now, its façade painted yellow and ochre with plastic window frames, and is flanked by bland new buildings, lined up flush in a row. Each one is a different brand of budget hotel: number 7 itself is now Relaxa Hotel, followed by Imbiss Budget, Imbiss Hotel and Novotel. Directly opposite on the other side of the road is a fenced-in expanse of land with no buildings on it at all. The Prinz Albrecht Palace once stood on this plot, and was used during the Nazi years by the SS and Gestapo. Designated the "Topography of Terror" in 1987, this is now a memorial as excavation site.

If I were to turn right at the corner of Anhalter Straße and Wilhelmstraße, I would come to the

Tommy-Weisbecker-Haus a couple of blocks down. But I turn left instead and there ahead of me is the Wall, or a part of it at least. It used to run right across the street here, and a section still stands in front of the Topography of Terror. Approaching it from a distance, the barrier of prefabricated concrete segments is not so high as to appear threatening. It seems rather short and flimsy in fact, as if it is only a gesture, which this small section is, in effect. The real menace of the Wall was its relentless horizontality, its impenetrability, its guards and watchtowers, and its complete encirclement of West Berlin.

Despite the intransigence of the Wall, during these years in the late 1980s change can be felt in the air. The architect is living with her young son on the third floor of the house on the Ufer, the students downstairs come and go, and new social housing projects are cropping up along the left side of Schöneberger Straße. Frau Kozlowski-Sala is in her side wing apartment, able to keep a close eye on her tenants. (Steeped in Fassbinder as I am right now, I imagine her as the lead character in one of his films – *Melitta* – with her menthol cigarettes and penchant for curtains.) Her business, Sala-Spiele, continues to design new games that respond to the changing social environment. *Berlin-Bummel* – A Stroll through Berlin – comes onto the market in 1987, a nostalgia-awakening board game which pictures the city as it was in 1900. The same year another game appears: *MONEY: Geld regiert die Welt* – Money Rules the World – the perfect game through which to celebrate West Germany's economic miracle, not that much of it is visible here in the still struggling corners of West Berlin. The short description on the box calls it "A game of shares and loans, in which the winner is, of course, the one who accumulates the most capital."

A year later, a real change occurs in the house on Tempelhofer Ufer. On September 26, 1988, so the papers in the Land Registry tell me, Frau Melitta Kozlowski-Sala sells the "apartment house and factory building" for nearly two and a half million Deutschmarks. The deed of sale stipulates that she may remain in her second-floor side wing apartment, for a fixed rent of 536.55 Deutschmarks per month. It will be modernized but care must be taken "not to disturb the fixtures." These include in particular, "the fitted kitchen and luxury bathroom with gold-plated taps, air conditioning and central heating."

The next document in the files at the Land Registry archive is another deed of sale, dated only a few months later. On February 14, 1989, the building is sold again, this time for over three million Deutschmarks, a tidy profit of half a million. Had Melitta perhaps been ill-advised when it came to her capital losses and gains? Once again in the contract is the stipulation that she may, for the rent agreed, remain in her second-floor side wing apartment, with its fitted kitchen and golden taps. With the benefit of hindsight, given the changes ahead on that year's horizon, she could not have chosen a less opportune moment to sell her inherited property. The real estate speculators would soon be coming to the city, smelling money to be made.

· 19 ·

# Turn

*The streets around my house* are largely uninhabited –
*unbelebt* – just as they were when the city was divided.
When the kitchen window is tilted open, I can hear the
steady stream of traffic below, but there are rarely people to be seen. The canal waters simply offer back rippling reflections of sky, trees, passing birds, the buildings
lined up on its banks. For a period of just over a year at
the end of the 1980s, however, just as the tectonic plates
of the Cold War were beginning to shift, waves of people started washing in. They were coming to the disused
wasteland where the tracks of the Potsdamer Bahnhof
once were – to the *Polenmarkt*, the Polish market.

In 1988, the Polish government changed the law to
allow its citizens freedom of travel and by early the next

year it was easy for Poles to get a passport, the only document necessary to enter West Berlin. Every day, tens of thousands of Poles, compelled by economic precarity, boarded overcrowded trains with goods to sell. Arriving at Bahnhof Friedrichstraße, they would walk to this muddy patch of wasteland beyond the Wall. Traders crouched on the ground between huge rubbish-filled puddles, selling Polish sausages, meat, eggs, butter, mushrooms, clothing, cigarettes and even live animals. The *Polenmarkt* grew rapidly, becoming wild and chaotic and was soon difficult to control. Criminality, vandalism and prostitution proliferated, according to the press of the time, as did *Fremdenhass*, or xenophobia, and aggressive clashes between Germans and Poles. The police attempted to shut down the market by fencing off the land, but the traders simply moved north, settling by Scharoun's Philharmonie until the fences were removed and they returned. The first cracks in the dam that separated East and West were beginning to appear.

One by one, the Eastern European countries that formed the border separating East and West Germany from the USSR – Poland, Hungary and Czechoslovakia – were beginning to resist Soviet control. Poland was a front-runner, followed by Hungary, which in early May 1989 began dismantling its border with Austria. When Hungary declared in September that GDR citizens would be allowed through this border, they left in droves for

West German embassies in Prague and Warsaw to apply for visas and begin their passage to the West. An artist I know left Prenzlauer Berg for Hungary in the summer of 1989 aged twenty-one, carrying just a suitcase and her portfolio. Arriving in West Berlin was like landing in another century, she told me, in a society still functioning according to obsolete conventions, particularly when it came to women and children: nineteenth-century protocols in a twentieth-century world. Since that summer, a popular protest movement had been growing in the GDR – the *friedliche Revolution*, or peaceful revolution. In October massive demonstrations were held in Leipzig, Dresden and eventually East Berlin.

On November 4, 1989, four days before the Wall is breached, a crowd of 500,000 has gathered at Alexanderplatz. Christa Wolf is giving a speech: "I have my difficulties with the word *Wende*," she says. This is the first authorized public demonstration not organized by the government in the history of the GDR. Wolf berates the *Wendehälse*, the "long-necked ones" who are already turning away and abandoning socialism. Those that "adapt quickly and easily to a given situation, move skillfully in it, know how to use it." Turncoats, would be the English word. Wolf and many others in the East are not interested in such smooth accommodations to the ideologies of the capitalist West. Instead, she and the half a million she is speaking to are searching for a new democratic form, in which socialism is not renounced but rather flipped head over heels, setting its foot soldiers at the top. Such ideas have been brewing over the preceding months when a new political group, *Neues Forum*, had formed, demanding a dialogue about political reforms. "Revolutions happen from the bottom up," declares Wolf emphatically. "Let's dream with our eyes wide open. Imagine this, it is socialism and no one wants to leave."

Wolf's speech is well-known to West and East Germans over a certain age, but to outsiders like me, the significance of this time is all tied up in the single act called "The Fall of the Wall." The events that led up to it and those that followed are less clear-cut. On November 9, 1989 when the Wall came down, I was eighteen and living as an au pair with a family in Italy. We gathered around the television in the living room as the news was announced. It was clearly a momentous occasion, the sense of euphoria was palpable. But I can't remember what happened next. The following summer I was inter-railing and took trains heading south to Sicily and boats across to Greece, but I did not travel northwards to see for myself what was happening in Berlin.

Curious now about how this decisive moment was being reported here, I search for the West German TV news programs from that period. I wonder if Melitta

Kozlowski-Sala would have been sitting in her living room in the side wing apartment on the second floor of the house on the Ufer, smoking and watching the eight o'clock news on ARD on November 9, 1989. The news anchor reports on the East Berlin press conference held that evening in which SED official Günter Schabowski announces the opening of the GDR's borders with the Federal Republic of Germany. Visas will be issued immediately to anyone wanting to travel. A journalist at the press conference asks if this also goes for "Berlin West." Schabowski, clearly caught on the fly, shrugs and looks through his papers. *"Doch, doch,"* he says: Yes yes, this border will be opened too, immediately. The ARD anchorman then moves on to report further news items of the day: Chancellor Kohl's visit to Warsaw fifty years after the invasion of Poland; the 11,000 East Germans who have crossed the Czech border into West Germany; pension reforms and train ticket price rises; lead poisoning in milk and human rights troubles in Turkey. It is nerve-wracking, watching this footage with the benefit of hindsight. While the anchorman calmly reports from his West German TV studio, East Berliners have begun heading to the Brandenburg Gate and are beginning to scale the Wall.

ARD's eight o'clock news program the following day is no longer business as usual. The anchorman can barely suppress a grin as he reports the momentous events of the night before. Footage in the background shows crowds of people standing on top of the Wall and cheering. Chancellor Kohl has hastily returned from Warsaw and is giving a speech at the town hall in Schöneberg: "The border between the two German states is a terror no more. Today we Germans are the happiest people in the world," says West Berlin's mayor, Walter Momper. Thousands of GDR citizens have already visited West Berlin and the Federal Republic, rushing uncontrolled through now open borders to collect their official *Begrüßungsgeld*, or Welcoming Money, of 100 Deutschmarks per head. The shopping mile of Kurfürstendamm is "one single great big party zone." Thousands more have gathered at the Brandenburg Gate. Brass bands are playing, car horns are honking, as all of these people, in jeans and anoraks or short leather jackets, with large wire-framed glasses, perms and moustaches, celebrate jubilantly around the Berlin Wall.

Would middle-aged, settled West Berliners like Melitta have welcomed this historic change after decades of division? Would they have embraced this disruption of the status quo and celebrated as East Berliners poured through the now open Checkpoint Charlie? The images distributed by mainstream media did not represent the more differentiated experiences of locals. For many, the populist nationalistic character of the celebrations was problematic, as *Der Klang der Familie: Berlin, Techno and the Fall of the Wall,* a scintillating oral history of the rise of techno in 1980s and 1990s Berlin, plots out. In this book, accumulated eyewitness accounts from insiders in the techno scene suggest a range of opinions from both sides of the Wall. "They acted as if we had been eating bricks in the East," says one, complaining about the patronizing gestures of West Berliners who showered the newcomers with bananas and coffee. Another is disappointed by what awaited them on the other side of the Wall: "West Berlin was such an unbelievably stuffy and penny-pinching city" full of "catastrophically badly dressed people. Kurfürstendamm was anything but glamorous." Meanwhile a West Berliner living in Kreuzberg finds all of the East Berliners that have rushed over "dumb": "They looked like shit, behaved stupidly and all the shops were sold out of fruit by the evening."

Come eight o'clock on November 11, the ARD news anchor tells us that 2.7 million visas have been issued by midday that day. The footage now shows people with hammers and pickaxes chipping away at the surface of the Wall. This impenetrable barrier is now a piece of history.

The momentum that led to the fall of the Wall continued in a series of rapid-fire decisions which set the two halves of Germany on a track towards unification that in retrospect seems inevitable, but which in reality had the effect of quickly closing up gaps of opportunity – eradicating the very desires for freedom for which the peaceful revolution had been fought. Almost 1.2 million citizens sign a petition titled "For our Country," drawn up by a group of East German signatories including Christa Wolf. It proposes an independent GDR, the development of a society of solidarity rather than "selling out our material and moral values" in a takeover by the Federal Republic of Germany. Despite this, on March 18, 1990, in East Germany's first free elections since 1949, a resounding majority of the East German population votes for unity. In July currency reform is introduced – one for one, Ostmarks for Deutschmarks – and on October 3, a formal ceremony is held to celebrate the unification of Germany. This is not the new start that many were dreaming of before the Wall came down, but in less than a year it has become reality.

It took Christa Wolf twenty years to write about this period in Germany and in her own life. Her final novel, *City of Angels*, a sequel of sorts to *Patterns of Childhood*, was published in 2010. From the distance of geography, culture and language offered by a residency in Los Angeles, Wolf can reflect on what she calls "the events." "The whole process, from the demonstrations to the fall of the Wall to unification, became known as *die Wende*, the 'Turn' or 'Turning Point,'" she writes. "But what exactly had 'turned'? Away from what?" By herself or with her German colleagues, she can ruminate on the complexity of "so-called Reunification," but when socializing with Americans she does not admit her reservations. "I didn't want to disappoint the people here, who expect to hear that everyone was happy in unified Germany. No, there was nothing in their newspapers about disappointments. Nothing about losses. It would have seemed petty for me to talk about them here." In the book, Wolf lays out the contradictions between her internal impressions about the transition and how it was portrayed by the media, played out in public and compressed into the insufficient term *die Wende*. "That's a long-standing concern of mine," she writes, "the intensity and speed with which the political class and its media push a name that suits them onto events that have surprised, maybe even overwhelmed them."

The thirtieth anniversary of the fall of the Wall was celebrated last year, and Berlin's newspapers were full of analysis and interviews. A friend of mine, a costume designer my age, more or less, who grew up in the former GDR, was interviewed in the *Süddeutsche Zeitung*. She talks about moving to Berlin in 1996, about the freedom, the excitement, the potential it offered for *Selbstentfaltung*, personal growth. But also about how she is still reminded on a daily basis of her "migrant background" – "I am often told 'You've really come a long way for an East German,'" she says. "The message is always: What are you complaining about? Be happy that you are allowed to take part here!"

Christa Wolf read the forty-two volumes of files the Stasi had kept on her that documented the minutiae of her comings and goings from 1969-1989, and commented on "the brutal way they took your lives and made them trite over hundreds and hundreds of pages." But she also lived out the revelation that became public in 1993 that she had been enrolled as an informant herself from 1959 to 1962, something she claimed to have no recollection of. Like the repressed memories Wolf ascribed to her ancestors in *Patterns of Childhood*, she had repressed difficult memories of her own. "An unused memory gets lost, ceases to exist, dissolves into nothing – an alarming thought. The faculty to preserve, to remember, must be developed," as she wrote in that earlier book.

When the Wall is breached, the energy trapped within the city for twenty-eight years can flow again and with it comes an enormous wave of potential. Berlin will be the center of Europe again! Regardless of this momentous change, the view from the window of the house on the Ufer does not change much. A canopy of trees above the Landwehr Canal. A crenellated redbrick chimney.

A massive rectangular housing block and the silver pin of the TV tower. The Berlin Wall is being taken down, chipped away at by people who save chunks as souvenirs. The stage is set for another chapter of development. But development never happens in a void. Built structures like the Berlin Wall or the bombed-out buildings in 1945 contain a special type of energy, known to architects as "grey energy." Grey energy is intrinsic to the materials that make up our built environments, to all materials in fact, and it accumulates over time. There is no such thing as empty space. Something energetic is always left behind.

Less than a year after the Wall comes down, a new building is in development, one which I catch a glimpse of now, its top right corner peeking out from behind the Excelsiorhaus. It is one of my favorite buildings in Berlin: a high-rise that, despite its height and breadth, is not a solid boxy mass, nor a rigidly rectangular power statement like the Axel Springer building. Its wide body (thirty-five windows across) is slim (only eight narrow windows deep) and curves in a gentle ellipse. The façade is not a fixed grid of wall and window, but a patchwork of colored blinds in shades of liver, salmon, beige and red, that constantly change throughout the day in an animated color-field composition. Rather than being planted firmly in the ground, this colored curving plane balances on a long horizontal street-level pedestal of shops and office spaces. With color, curvature, elegance and wit, it stands out from everything else around it. It was the first building to be commissioned in the undivided city.

In autumn 1990, a competition had been called to design a new headquarters for Berlin's largest housing association, the GSW. The new building was to be on Kochstraße in Southern Friedrichstadt (later renamed Rudi-Dutschke Straße, after the activist shot in 1968, an action which galvanized the student movement). It was in such close proximity to where the Wall had until recently stood, that the building inevitably came to address the rejoining of the two halves of Berlin. Six architects were invited to apply, among them Matthias Sauerbruch. Sauerbruch was living in London at the time, where he had just established his own practice together with his British partner Louisa Hutton, but before that he had lived in West Berlin, studying architecture here in the 1970s.

I have met Matthias Sauerbruch and Louisa Hutton in art-related circles, and ask if I can talk to them about the building of the GSW. In their offices not far from the new Hauptbahnhof, they regale me with insights into Berlin's complex urban history. They make a compelling duo: Hutton statuesque, with thick waves of grey hair swept back from her face, and a plummy tone that no doubt commands attention in the male-dominated architecture industry; Sauerbruch slender and thoughtful with a nimble intellect. Their approach to the design of the GSW complex, they tell me, was rooted in the "English landscape garden tradition." "We wanted to work with the 'as found' in a positive way," Hutton explains. "Instead of an idealistic strategy that imposes rules and regulations, it is a thinking that comes out of the situation." Their winning proposal chose to work with the intrinsic "grey energy" of the site, adopting everything on it as "existing matter" – including an awkward and unintegrated seventeen-story tower block from the 1950s that had previously housed the GSW offices – and creating a new ensemble that could connect all of its constituent parts. Energy conservation was considered throughout their design and the high-rise slab was orientated towards the west: its multicolored panels are solar shutters designed to exploit the low angle of the afternoon sun. The emblematic *Slab* is just one part in an ensemble of five different volumes, each with a different form and dimension, that frame the leftover 1950s high-rise and anchor it back into the street plan. This playful architectural concoction responds to the heterogeneous urban structure around it with a remarkable levity, inserting itself suggestively between an inherited past and an unknown future.

My own understanding of architecture is founded less in hard facts than in certain sensations that have to do with how a building acts as a meeting point between place and person. The feeling that something sits right or not is hard to explain precisely. It concerns proportion and surfaces, but also a respect towards the "grey energy" of a city's existing material and resonances accumulated over time. An open attitude, ready to work with the intrinsic conditions of the site, historical as much as physical.

Although Sauerbruch and Huttons's competition entry for the GSW building was chosen unanimously by the jury in May 1991, it took four more years to receive planning permission. A new city building director, Hans Stimmann, had been appointed two months after it was selected. He was vehemently against their design and spent his first years in office employing every means possible to prevent its construction. "He filibustered the project for four years," Hutton tells me, but in the end, he could not stop it. The first foundation stone was only laid in June 1995 and it was not completed until 1999.

Hans Stimmann was not an architect but a planner and his aims for rebuilding the unified city had less to do with creating an inviting urban environment than with regulating its development. He set stringent building codes that shaped its evolution by favoring uniform heights of twenty-two meters, fixating on façades (preferably clad in stone or ceramic rather than made of glass or steel) and adhering doggedly to the city's pre-war street patterns. He rejected grand architectural visions in favor of a pragmatic city planning that stuck to historical precedent, in particular James Hobrecht's 1862 street plan. Ignoring the years of conflict and barbarism, division and oppression, experiment and wild difference that had preceded this moment in Berlin's narrative, he envisioned a homogenized and normalized architectural capital.

In a video interview from 2018, part of a series of interviews which examines Berlin's architectural identity, Stimmann appears uncomfortable. His thinning face is obscured by a large white moustache, and he taps his fingers impatiently on the desk while being questioned by the three young architects who put together the series. He blocks their questions and looks repeatedly at his watch while insisting on the role of *Städtebauplanung*, urban planning, at the cost of architecture. "Buildings should be instruments that are regulated in order to construct a controllable city," he says, declaring at one point, "it has nothing to do with architecture!" This too is *ein weites Feld*, another vast subject.

Stimmann remained at the helm until 2006, steering these vital years of Berlin's reconstruction into a cul-de-sac of conservativism. The result, according to architecture critic Niklas Maak, is a street like Friedrichstraße which "looks like a filing cabinet." A city filled with "countless façades of overwhelming cowardice," as journalist Georg Diez puts it. To adopt Matthias Sauerbruch's words, it is dull, unloving and disconcerting. The rebuilding of reunified Berlin is seen by many as one of the greatest missed opportunities in recent architectural history.

Reunification itself is a disputed term. How could the discrete entities of East and West Germany *re*-unify when they had never existed before? As the GDR's past was increasingly discredited and denied, West Germany was accused of approaching the process with a *Siegermentalität*, a victor's mentality. The division of Germany was one more shame-filled chapter whose lumpy fragments were swept under the rug. The potential of and opportunity for a slow, organic development that could accommodate ambiguity were displaced through shortcuts, compromises and a rush towards economic growth. The flaw in the "reunification" process was the belief that the clock could be wound back and that the whole that had existed a century ago could be rebuilt from this pile of remnants.

It takes eleven hours of debate on June 20, 1991 to reach the decision that Berlin will become the nation's new capital – many in the West are suspicious and resistant: Berlin is so worryingly close to Eastern Europe. Once the decision is made, plans follow for Potsdamer

Platz to become the triumphant face of the unified nation. The death strip is sold off to corporate investors. Daimler Benz buy 60,000 square meters at a tenth of the regular price. Sony buy another swathe. A fistful of renowned international architects swiftly deliver a plan and the cranes and diggers move in. The atmosphere of the finished Potsdamer Platz today is not lively or welcoming, exciting or desirable, however. The wind blows harsh along Leipziger Straße, between the rigid façades of buildings locked in a bitter face-off. Most of its visitors are tourists, checking it off on a list of must-see landmarks. There is such palpable resistance in the atmosphere around here that I wonder if this area can be inhabited at all. The streets behind Potsdamer Platz, between the high-rises flanking Leipziger Straße and the borders of the former Potsdamer Bahnhof, feel unsettled. It is here that I find the plaque on the wall of what used to be Theodor Fontane's house, where he lived and wrote his novels set in Wilhelmine Berlin. A couple of years ago this was a Starbucks, but that has gone now too.

"There is a blankness to Berlin, to the experience of walking through its streets, amongst its buildings," I find in notes I've written on my phone at some point in the last two years. "A flatness, a drabness, that does not just have to do with colour. The sky is also not so much grey as uniformly blank. *Eine Leerstelle*. A void." No one wants to come here. Parvati, the feng shui master, tells me she performs little private healing ceremonies every time she passes through.

Twenty-five years have passed since the Wall came down when I move with my family to the house on the Ufer, but the situation around here still feels unresolved. Our apartment is also reluctant at first to allow itself to be inhabited. Some of its parts are holding onto the past, a dingy history that clings to corners and shadows its walls. Following her initial appraisal, Parvati returns to the apartment and performs small rituals room by room, lighting matches, making gestures and drawing invisible marks on the walls. Once she is finished, she invites me back in, and I have to admit that the rooms do seem different, especially the *Berliner Zimmer*. Whereas previously the air seemed thick and subtly tinged with grey, now it is diaphanous and bright. Looking out of the window, I notice for the first time the tops of the buildings on the street behind. Despite the ambivalence outside, our apartment's interior is being coaxed into life. The swampy feeling has been lifted and I can now move freely, setting the stage for inhabitation by our newly consolidated family. When Parvati was on the balcony of the *Berliner Zimmer*, as she tells me later, performing her ritual to seal the apartment's outside walls, her box of matches caught fire in an energetic flare-up. She shows me the singed ends of her fine wavy hair.

The missed opportunities of the Wilhelmine era that resulted in Werner Hegemann's *Stone Berlin* and the "sea of houses" that Benjamin laments, are repeated a century later. The mistakes that Karl Scheffler complains of in 1913 happen all over again: "There is no rhythm to be felt in the city." A brief period between 1960 and 1966 had provided relief from the short-sighted bureaucratic tendencies of Berlin's city planners when Werner Düttmann became the chief urban planning director. A Berliner born in 1921 and a practicing architect, Düttmann acknowledged the heterogeneity of the city. "Berlin is many cities," he wrote, its different versions coexisting "one behind the other and side by side." Decrying *Gleichgültigkeit*, or indifference, in architecture, he spoke for the necessity of embracing change: "True vitality is the virtually unplannable quality, for which we must nonetheless plan."

A seam of culture at the former Potsdamer Platz had already been proposed by Scharoun in his 1958 plan and Düttmann (Scharoun's former student) picked up on it in 1962, persuading Mies van der Rohe, who had left Germany in 1937, to build his only post-war German building here. The Neue Nationalgalerie, a pavilion of glass and steel beside the Potsdamer Bridge, on the very site where the first stone of Speer's Germania had been laid. Scharoun was chosen to build his magnificent golden Philharmonie and in 1964, he also won the competition to build the Staatsbibliothek, the Berlin State Library, one of his final buildings, completed posthumously in 1979. Düttmann left his mark on this windswept territory by commissioning this visionary triumvirate of cultural architectures, a statement at the brink of the no-man's-land of Potsdamer Platz.

In Stimmann's version of the early twentieth century, however, any instincts for liveliness are displaced by rules, regulations, policemen and civil servants. Only cherry-picked parts of the past are let in, and grey energy is wantonly squandered. Post-Wall optimism is replaced by regret in Berlin's emotional energy chambers.

A book I find in Scharoun's Berlin State Library titled *Feng Shui and Architecture*, documents an academic conference held in Berlin in 2010 and extrapolates some of the failures of Potsdamer Platz. Florian Reuter, a Sinologist from the Humboldt's Department of African and Asian Studies, begins his paper by carefully acknowledging the perceived "inconsistencies and conflicts, arbitrary or subjective interpretations, lacking in empirical models for accurate prediction" that hamper the recognition of feng shui. Nevertheless, he defends it as a practical art, one based in "the Chinese habit to formulate comparisons" and to respond sensitively to the conditions of the atmosphere: wind and water, light and shadow, shelter and openness. No different from the considerations, in fact, that Sauerbruch and Hutton took in designing their GSW ensemble. Regarding Berlin, writes Reuter, "we may wonder whether the ubiquitous presence and menace of underground water and the various open waterways altogether qualify Berlin as a site for auspicious constructions." No site is empty after all and Berlin has always had problems with its water table.

Reuter disparages the Potsdamer Platz development in relation to feng shui principles, not least because it did not take up on the possibility of connecting with the nearby waterway: "The architectonic ensemble at Potsdamer Platz ignores the existence of the Landwehr Canal with its Qi or atmospheric potential and influence." Instead, attention is shifted to roads, avenues and cars which, in replacing the open energetic flow of water, constitute devastating drainages for any positive energy that architecture may create. The difficulties that Berlin inevitably experiences, due to its inauspicious swampy site and the menace of underground water (not to mention its recent history), may be circumvented by the intelligent application of observation – by looking, reading the land, the buildings, the atmosphere and the instances of the past that come together to form the present. By recognizing, for instance, the value of Scharoun's and van der Rohe's buildings, as well as the nearby Tiergarten and the Landwehr Canal beyond.

In these terms, Potsdamer Platz is the greatest failure of all. "The horrible architectural "triumph" of corporate towers so spitefully angled they seem to slice your body in two every time you pass them by," wrote my late friend the artist and curator Ian White, in his inimitable acid script. "So much for reunification."

In the rush to fill up the empty spaces on Berlin's cartography in the years after the *Wende*, decisions were made to plug its holes with the usual late-twentieth- or early-twenty-first-century services of shopping, dining and entertainment. Later came blandly slick and badly proportioned apartment buildings with names like High Park. The apartments in this building on the corner of Gabriele-Tergit-Promenade are still over half empty, five years after completion. *Wohnen auf höherem Niveau* – "living on a higher level" – the promotional signs had boasted during construction. Unusual buildings like Sauerbruch and Hutton's GSW ensemble allow questions to remain and to flow in the present, exposing historical juncture and letting it be. Turfing over the Potsdamer Bahnhof and lining it with soulless boxes has the opposite effect. The area feels somehow ungrounded, unanchored, as if it has not docked into our space-time coordinates and remains hovering, hesitant, unmoored, unsure of its own transition from architect's rendering to reality. Both landscape and discourse are muffled in a kind of non-site. What is visible somehow barely registers, despite having been here by now for over two decades.

Berlin's accidental memorials in the form of wastelands and unbuilt plots are disappearing for good. Meanwhile, the inert geometries that surround the ex–Potsdamer Bahnhof are barely inhabited. The shops in the Potsdamer Platz Arcade are vacated one by one until it finally shuts down, in a limbo while considering reinvention with another form of consumer content. In 2007, Daimler sells the nineteen buildings it owns at Potsdamer Platz to a Swedish investment bank, at a substantial loss according to the press. In 2008, Sony sells up too, to an international consortium who two years later sell it on – this prime and historical central Berlin location – to a Canadian investment company. The Sony Center's international cinema closes. There is more moving out than moving in. As if lives and capital are flowing backwards.

N

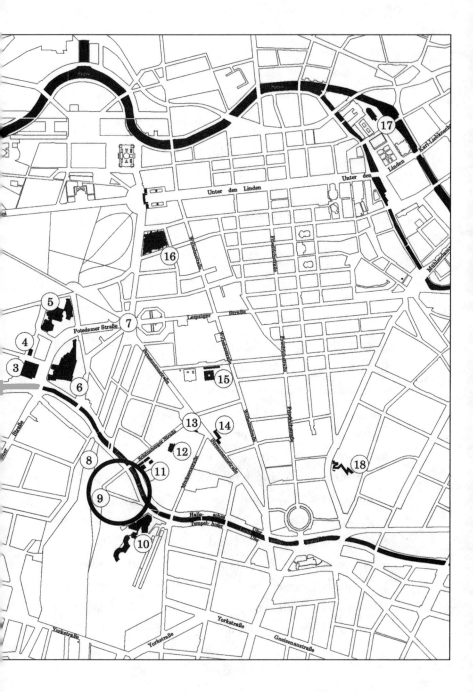

## · 20 ·

# Displacement

*It is a Sunday afternoon* in May, fresh green leaves
have just unfurled from the buds on the thousands
of trees across Berlin. I am still trying to get to grips
with the un-dividing of the city, to grasp it in a material sense. The best approach, I decide, is to walk the
path of the Wall. My eldest son agrees to join me: he
is seventeen now and has emerged from puberty just
enough to be seen in public with his mother again. We
begin by the Oberbaumbrücke that crosses the river
Spree in Kreuzberg, and head to the East Side Gallery,
a kilometer-long remnant of the Berlin Wall, famous for
its brightly colored friezes and always swarming with
tourists. The Wall ran along the north bank of the river
here, but the Spree itself belonged to East Berlin. Only

when it reached the Reichstag and Tiergarten did the river switch allegiances and become part of the West. When the city was still divided, as I find out later, five children drowned in the river Spree between 1966 and 1975, in separate incidents near the Oberbaumbrücke. The GDR border patrol guard on the bridge did not respond to help the West Berlin children that fell into the water. Adults on the banks in Kreuzberg were afraid to jump in and help them in case they would be shot. Following the death of five-year-old Çetin Mert in 1975, over a thousand people, mostly Turkish, gathered on the banks of the Spree to protest the murderous policies that allowed for this to happen. Only after this was an emergency procedure agreed on between the East and West.

Once my son and I are beyond the East Side Gallery, the tourists dissipate, and the path of the Wall becomes harder to find. The purpose of our expedition feels completely detached from the streets we are walking along, as if this invisible wall, this history, and all its tragic consequences, were something I had just dreamed up. At times I can only determine its path by tracing my finger along the red line printed on the map I brought with me. Occasionally a double row of cobblestones appears laid into the asphalt, as evidence of where the Wall once was, like a scar in the vernacular of the street. Sometimes, a bronze plaque in the ground announces its absence with the words BERLINER MAUER 1961–1989. But these markings are erratic, they trail off as if this once historical border shies away from being seen. As we continue southwest through Kreuzberg towards Moritzplatz, the territory we are in feels increasingly ambiguous and tentative. It as if the activities taking place on the street surfaces and in the buildings don't penetrate somehow, are not really connected and cannot attach. What should attach in a city? Lives to streets? People to buildings? One person to another?

In the post-war years, this area of Kreuzberg was full of dilapidated Wilhelmine tenement buildings, rented out at a price per head to newly arrived immigrant workers. Initially Italian and Greek, and later Turkish immigrants came to Berlin from the 1950s onwards, labelled with the unhelpful term *Gastarbeiter* which suggested both that their presence was temporary, and that West Germany was a gracious host to whom the guests should be grateful. The concept of the "guest worker" dated back to labor agreements drawn up in 1955 and one such agreement with Turkey had been in place since 1961. Within the rhetorical structure of the "guest worker," migration was proposed as an entirely transactional one-way street. The possibility that migration could be a driving force for social change was never suggested. A reactionary binary of "German" versus "Other" quickly established itself instead and lead to an anti-immigration movement. An article from *Der Spiegel* in 1973 headlined *"Die Türken kommen, rette sich wer kann!"* – The Turks are coming, run for your lives! – is full of racist clichés and discriminatory attitudes. By that time, 20,000 Turkish people were living in Kreuzberg, an "invasion" as *Der Spiegel* put it. "Ghettos are emerging, and sociologists are already predicting urban decay, crime and social impoverishment like that in Harlem," reads the article, reciting prototypical racist tropes. Fassbinder was one of the few who could be counted on to address this fear and hypocrisy directly, in particular in his 1974 film *Ali: Fear Eats the Soul*. In this film, the sixty-year-old widow Emmi falls in love with Ali, the younger Moroccan "guest worker," played by El Hedi ben Salem, Fassbinder's lover at the time. When I arrived in Berlin in the early 2000s, one of many so-called cultural workers drawn from other parts of Europe and the US by its openness and affordability, I was struck by the casual discrimination still directed at the immigrant population, thrown into sharp relief by my own ostensibly immigrant status. But as a northern European with fair hair and pale skin, I appear to belong, passing superficially as German, while English as my mother tongue affords me linguistic privilege. The legitimacy of my presence here has never been called into question.

———

My son and I walk past a construction site where a new housing block appears to be being built right on the path of what once was the Wall. Is this even allowed, I wonder? We continue on through northern Kreuzberg, where strangely slick apartment and office blocks crowd the streets in all directions, past the Axel Springer building, onwards to Checkpoint Charlie and Mauerstraße where my son's father used to live, and farther to the Topography of Terror in Southern Friedrichstadt. My son leaves to meet some friends and I am walking home alone, along Schöneberger Straße towards the canal. Almost at the bridge, passing in front of the two-story redbrick primary school, the one built by the IBA in 1987, I happen to look down and notice a small brass plaque laid into the pavement: ten centimeters square, words are engraved into its dull brass surface:

HIER WOHNTE
ADOLF REICH
JG. 1884
DEPORTIERT 1.3.1943
ERMORDERT IN
AUSCHWITZ

"Here lived Adolf Reich, born 1884, deported 1.3.1943, murdered in Auschwitz." It is a record of the inhabitant of a building that is no longer here. A single instance of disappearance, one life plucked out of the city's weave. Square brass plaques like this one have become another element in Berlin's pavement vernacular since 1996. The *Stolpersteine*, or stumbling stones, are Berlin's most effective memorial to loss. Embedded into the surface of the streets we walk on every day, they are reminders of the other ordinary citizens who once lived here too, before being abruptly uprooted and sent to their deaths. The internet assists, offering biographical details for each plaque's subject. Adolf Reich was the son of a Jewish salesman, unmarried and without children, a textile wholesaler who lived at Bahnhofstraße 2, a street that is no longer here, directly behind the Anhalter Bahnhof. In 1941, he was made to work as a forced laborer in an armaments factory until arrested and deported in 1943 and sent to Auschwitz where he died.

Inserted flush into the sidewalks of ordinary neighborhood streets, the *Stolpersteine* create a vast but antimonumental memorial. They are a reminder that the atrocities began right here, amongst neighbors in the city's streets and buildings. In Berlin alone 8,786 *Stolpersteine* have already been laid, and there are now over 75,000 in thousands of locations all over Europe.

Conceptually sharp and potentially expansive, this memorial was not a state-devised initiative but rather a grassroots program begun by artist Gunter Demnig, a "68er" born in 1947 whose artwork was rooted in protest, originally against the Vietnam War. Beginning with a project to commemorate Sinti and Roma victims of the Holocaust, Demnig went on to invite descendants of the Holocaust's victims or local historical groups to nominate recipients of *Stolpersteine*. Each stone is laid at the threshold of the "last voluntarily chosen address" of the commemorated individual.

How to remember in a city, in a city with a past like this? The question comes up again and again here, cut through as it is with conflicting desires, politics and priorities. You can see it in the Topography of Terror at the site of the Prince Albrecht Palace. During the Nazi era, the former palace was used by the SS and the Gestapo and prisoners were held, interrogated and tortured in its cellars. The bomb-damaged remains of the building were blown up in 1949 and the land was cleared and levelled: another tabula rasa. A debate between local citizens and government authorities emerged about whether a memorial should be built, or the site simply left as is. Architectural competitions and altercations followed, but when a symbolic dig in 1985 uncovered Gestapo cells, a government sponsored archaeological excavation ensued. The temporary exhibition *Topography of Terror* set up in 1987 became permanent, inviting visitors to explore the overgrown site, where signs indicated what had once been there and had taken place. The legacy of SS and Gestapo brutality was situated in the actual geography of Berlin's terrain, an open wound for all to see.

Berlin's two official sites of remembrance – the Jewish Museum and the Holocaust Memorial – were the subjects of even more passionate debates since the late 1980s. How to commemorate the victims of the Shoah? Here, in the city of its perpetrators? A site adjacent to the Brandenburg Gate was eventually chosen and in 1999 architect Peter Eisenman's design was accepted by the *Bundestag*. The "Memorial to the Murdered Jews of Europe" that opened in 2005 did not rely on information but on the physical sensation of a body in space as a means of remembering atrocity. Entering what appears to be a forest of geometrical stone blocks of regular heights, the undulating nature of the terrain underfoot leads you lower and lower. The stele around appear higher and higher. It is increasingly disorienting. Fear sets in.

The first time I came to Berlin in 1997, the Holocaust Memorial was still being debated, the Jewish Museum was under construction, and Potsdamer Platz was a vast open crater being billed as "Europe's largest building site." I had come for the opening of an exhibition at the DAAD's gallery on the first floor of the Café Einstein villa, and it was here that I first cast eyes on my future husband. I first saw him springing lightly down the villa's staircase, half-way down he turned around to speak to someone on the stairs behind him. I was struck by his unencumbered sense of levity. Three years later, when I began to get to know him, I fell for this lightness and flexibility of spirit. He was not interested in control, in holding things tight or fixing them down. He was adaptable and spontaneous. The apartment he lived in on Mauerstraße had been his home for several years, first with a group of friends and then on his own as they gradually moved out. Besides its enormous bathroom, one of the apartment's highlights was that it backed right onto E-Werk, a techno club in a former electric substation that was famous in the 1990s. Another legendary techno club, Tresor, in the vaults of the former department store Wertheim, was only a stone's throw away on Leipziger Straße. These buildings' empty shells in the former East were reinhabited, adapted and used by a curious and energetic new population. But by the time I moved here in 2001, E-Werk had closed, and for me, the nights of clubbing until the early hours were over. In a matter of months I was pregnant and our lives took a different curve.

My lived experience of Berlin in those years was
initially exploring by bike, and then, after our son was
born, pushing him through the neighborhood in a big,
sprung pram. Like other young mothers in Berlin, I
was navigating the notion of the *Rabenmutter*, a de-
rogatory term for mothers who go to work and neglect
their children, imported from West Germany. It dates
back to the eighteenth century, although it turns out
to be a myth that raven mothers neglect their young.
(Several years later, as I was deep in writing a book, I
remember our youngest son asking me, "What do you
like better, your work or being with us?") I had begun
to write about art just before our first son was born,
and by visiting galleries, museums and project spaces I
learnt the city's streets. Berlin felt unique in the world
at that time, as creativity seeped in to fill up its many
gaps. From the mid-1990s to the mid-2000s, as foundations were being laid in construction sites across the
city, a parallel seam of activity was taking place, and
ad-hoc bars, techno clubs, exhibitions or DIY galleries
sprung up in every imaginable space. People like me arrived here and felt like the city belonged to us. We didn't
have to dress or behave in a certain way, and we didn't
have to *be productive*. But as art was being made and
shown, and clubbers headed home in the early hours
of the morning, believing in the freedoms that Berlin

seemed to offer, deals were being made in boardrooms. Whole buildings and empty plots of land were bought by investors at cut-rate prices. *Grund und Boden* – land and property – were being sold off. By 2010 or so, it was visibly apparent that commerce had gained the upper hand. The constructed results of Stimmann's lattice of regulations and the governing mayor Klaus Wowereit's investor-friendly policies were taking shape all over the cityscape.

The loaded narrative of constructing and remembering during Berlin's post-unification years finds its most contentious and symbolic form in the narrative around the Palast der Republik, and the Berliner Stadtschloß, Berlin's City Palace on the river Spree. The Palast der Republik, a horizontal modernist slab clad in reflective panels of gold and bronze, had opened in 1976 on Marx-Engels-Platz as the seat of the *Volkskammer*, or People's Chamber, of the GDR. Post-unification it was slated for demolition, along with other administrative buildings of the former GDR. In the interim period, blockbuster shows were staged in the building's gutted shell. I saw the final exhibition there in December 2005, not a blockbuster this time, but a last-minute self-organized show of thirty-six local artists. Although it only ran for eleven days, ten thousand visitors came, not only to see the show, but to visit the building for one last time. The exhibition, as journalist Niklas Maak wrote, was not pro or contra the Palast debate per se. Rather it attempted to demonstrate "what constitutes the wealth of notoriously cash-strapped Berlin: smart improvisation within the ruinous; the temporary; and a system of chaotic creativity."

A shifting assortment of reasons for knocking down the Palast der Republik were given, most prominently asbestos, but the underlying motivations were ideological in nature: an eradication of this part of recent political history. Bruno Flierl, a revered East German historian of architecture and urban planning and member of the Commission for Berlin's Historical Center formed after the Wall came down, proposed that the Palast be left standing for twenty years. During this period, it could be used as a place for both East and West Germans to think critically about the past, formulate desires and discuss the future of the city, slowing down the pace of change.

Neither idealistic planners nor improvisational artists were able to prevent this chapter in the ideological reconfiguration of Berlin's *Stadtbild*, however. In 2002 the decision was made to tear down the Palast der Republik. Dismantled from the inside out, its constituent parts became collectors' items. The modular system of glass globe lamps that used to illuminate its vast open foyer was now being used to light the walls of the small French restaurant on Torstraße we used to go to. You can still find a gold-rimmed plate with ornamental "PdR" monogram online for sixteen euros. It took two whole years to demolish the building itself. According to Wikipedia, 78,000 tons of building materials were removed. Its grey energy alone would have been enough to power a small city. Following its demolition, the foundation stones of the building were daubed in white paint with the words: *DIE DDR HAT'S NIE GEGEBEN* – the GDR never existed.

The Stadtschloß, built in the early 1700s, had originally stood on the same plot of land but, like so much around it, was damaged in the Second World War. In 1950, GDR General Secretary Walter Ulbricht had its remains torn down, rather than rebuilt, although it was not irreparable. This decision scandalized those in the West – even Gabriele Tergit comments on it in her memoirs, furious at the "monstrous barbarism" with which Ulbricht flattened it, simply because "he wanted a parade ground." "This has nothing to do with Communism," she wrote. "Russians, Poles, Czechs all cultivate their national heritage. This is rather a mixture of complete ignorance and Prussianism." The decision fifty years later to tear down the Palast der Republik is revenge for Ulbricht's destructive act, while the rebuilding of the Schloß attempts to draw a neat trajectory from the present day back to a prelapsarian past, skipping over the uncomfortable truths and experiences of the twentieth century.

Dieter Hoffmann-Axthelm, a contentious historian and urban planner, one of the early instigators of the Topography of Terror, made an alternative proposal to the destructive double bind of removing one building and reconstructing a ghost from the past. "The Palast der Republik doesn't have to be torn down," he said. "As long as it is still standing, it remains an object of discussion." He suggested leaving it there and beginning excavations around it to rediscover the remains of the former Schloß, thus allowing both buildings and both parts of history to be visible in the present.

As it is, the voices of historical revisionism prevailed. Marx-Engels Platz has become Schloßplatz again and the doors to the rebuilt Schloß have opened. It is a colossal simulacrum in three dimensions, architecture as photorealist reproduction. "A meaningless, functionless picture of the past," according to Bruno Flierl. The Humboldt Forum, as it is called, is not only a misrepresentation of the past, but also a misreading of the present. Attempting to suture distant historical relics into the textures of the present times results in awkward junctures. Too much has happened in the interim.

The Humboldt Forum houses the Ethnological Museum and Museum for Asian Art, relocated from the suburbs of Dahlem, a decision made two decades ago when the project's advocates were grasping around for ways to fill this huge space in the heart of the city. The insertion of this collection of artifacts acquired from other cultures, sometimes through dubious means, has brought up unwelcome issues regarding Germany's colonial past. Art historian Bénédicte Savoy deemed it a disaster waiting to happen and resigned from the Humboldt Forum's expert council in 2017. Without undertaking research into the provenance of the works in its collection, she said, the institution would render itself invalid. Indeed, when the Humboldt Forum is ready to open in December 2020, a controversy ignites as Nigeria calls for the restitution of the sixteenth century works known as the "Benin Bronzes" in the Humboldt's collection. The streets are lined with protestors and press headlines declare it "dead on arrival." The final decision to crown the dome of the museum housing an ethnographic collection with an enormous cross, justified in the name of historical verisimilitude, is the ultimate cultural non sequitur. "The Schloß – that's really painful to see," says Louisa Hutton. "Plus there is so much concrete there it will never be blown up!'

Plots of land and buildings are being bought and sold all over the city as the forces of gentrification shift up a gear, and the house on the Ufer changes hands once again. Melitta Kozslowski-Sala is no longer living in the side wing by now. She left her apartment with its golden taps and central heating in 1992 and moved to a detached house with a garden in the wealthy middle-class southwesterly suburb of Steglitz, far away from Berlin's center of action. The same year, she sells the business to the printer who has been producing the Sala-Spiele products for many years. They hand the distribution of Sala-Spiele on to a different company a year later and by 1994 most of the games have disappeared from the market. In 1999, a Swedish real estate investor buys the building, and in 2008 he terminates the rental contract with the architect who lived in my apartment, after discovering that she is subletting rooms to other architects. He claims the lease is strictly residential only. In the house on the Ufer, one by one the apartments are taken back from their tenants and sold off to people like me and my ex-husband, a common situation in the city now where rents are raised and tenants forced out under the guise of modernization. After evicting the architect, the new landlord moves into the apartment himself: we buy it directly from him.

Only after moving in did I realize there are two camps in our building. In the front-facing apartments we are all newcomers: the young family on the Bel Étage, and the painter on the first floor. On the second floor, all of the students moved out and a company took it over as office space (so much for the landlord's claim of residential usage only). The company is somewhat mysterious, it has something to do with mail-order cosmetics and its staff is made up entirely of young women, with straightened hair and manicured nails. The DHL man is there every day and my main interaction with them is to pick up the packages they take for me when I am out. Our apartment is the next floor up, and finally above that, the newly developed rooftop penthouse, where another architect-developer now lives. In the side wing are almost all long-term renters. The front building / side wing divide inscribed in the architecture when the house was built continues to assert itself a century later. In the factory building in the backyard that housed the Salas' former printworks, different varieties of sporting activities are stacked up floor by floor: an aikido studio on the ground floor, followed by Cross Fit, yoga, boxing and Zumba.

When we move in, the house is shrouded in scaffolding and the common parts are being renovated: new windows in the staircase and linoleum on the floor. The façade is replastered and painted now a muddy grey tone. The Salas' name, written in huge capital letters across the entrance to the backyard, is painted over grey.

----

One late afternoon in autumn three years after we'd moved in, the police are driving up and down Tempelhofer Ufer announcing with a megaphone that everyone must evacuate. An unexploded bomb weighing 250 kilograms has been found in the construction site behind the petrol station where the foundations for a new hotel are being laid. Four hundred people have to evacuate their homes, offices or hotel rooms; the U-Bahn line has been shut down, the bridges blocked off and the street is closed to cars. Every time the ground is broken open and foundations are dug for a new building, energy is released and remnants of the past appear. Had this bomb gone off when it was dropped back then in the 1940s, what would it look like around here now? Would my building still be standing? Would the Salas have survived? Would I have ended up on the Ufer and be sitting here writing this book? There is no getting away from the war in this city. The ruins may be swept away, new-old palaces reconstructed, craters filled in with banal new buildings, but the war's traces remain.

"The past was all around us, but was nevertheless a taboo of utmost secrecy," writes Sabine Bode, a journalist known since the early 2000s for her groundbreaking research into the experiences of *Kriegskinder* and *Kriegsenkel*, the children or grandchildren of the war. According to her research, of all the Germans who survived the war, those born between 1939 and 1945, who were babies or small children during the bombings, fires, evacuations and deaths, were the most severely traumatized but the least equipped to come to terms with their experiences. Their entire mechanism was trip-wired for survival. Bode was a war child herself, growing up in the destroyed city of Cologne. She recounts the case of four-year-old Gudrun Baumann, in her bedroom during an air raid, terrified of the flames she can see bursting from the windows of the houses opposite. She cries out for her mother who comes in and tells her to turn to face the wall and to close her eyes tight. "You didn't see anything," her mother says, before leaving her alone. These children, now elderly, have buried their eyewitness memories, like the bombs lying untouched beneath the city's surface.

In 2009, German psychotherapist Michael Ermann published a large-scale research paper into the legacy of the trauma experienced by children during the war. He discovered that the *Kriegsenkel*, the war's grandchildren, inherited all the unaddressed emotions of their parents:

> the feeling of uprootedness of the displaced persons, the anxiety of the trapped, the fear of those hunted by low-flying aircraft, the loneliness of the children evacuated to the country, the distrust of the resistance fighters and persecuted

children. And, last but not least, the feelings of
guilt felt by those who cannot alleviate distress
and confusion.

When memories are supressed, pustules of shame
develop, fostered in silence and passed on in chains
of inheritance to children and grandchildren. I am a
grandchild of the war myself. Both my parents were
born during the war years, but geography was on their
side. Fewer bombs were dropped on Scotland, and none
at all on Ellwood City, Pennsylvania. The father of my
children is another grandchild of the war; the proximity
is far greater for him. His own father was a young teenager during the early 1940s, and stepped over dead bodies in the streets of Cologne on his way to school in the
morning. I knew him as a dignified man who lived his life
with stoic reserve. When he recently passed away and I
took my children there for his funeral, I noticed an aerial
photograph of war-ravaged Cologne framed on the wall
of his study. He may not have talked about this part of
his life, but it was never far away. Family secrets of any
kind exert an oppressive weight. The flip side to being
unencumbered is the ease with which one can detach.

Advances in epigenetic research show that inter-
generational trauma is communicated socially and affects the genes, but that these changes can be reversed
when the trauma itself is recognized. Melitta was a

*Kriegskind,* an eyewitness right here during the war. What happens when there are no heirs, as seems to be the case with her? Do her experiences and traumas sink instead into her environment? Seeping into the surfaces of the house she inhabited for fifty years of her life? Can they be inherited or rather picked up on by its future inhabitants? Can they leak spontaneously into the present and make themselves be known?

Along with the intermittent water damage we have experienced, I have been having recurrent dreams of water dripping through the ceiling of the apartment, sometimes in secret rooms I cannot access, or parts of the apartment I have forgotten all about. I ask an astrologer about these dreams and she says that these should be read symbolically. She asks if there is one room in the apartment that feels especially touched by the past, and suggests putting dark stones in the corners of the room. So now in each of the eight corners of the octagonal *Berliner Zimmer* is a small rough rock of black tourmaline. Once a week I rinse them under running water to cleanse them of accumulated debris. The astrologer also mentions a daughter whose energies seem to be invested in the building. Do I have a daughter? she asks.

———

Gabriele Baring, author of *The Secret Fears of Germans*, has experienced firsthand the developmental difficulties of *Kriegskinder* and *Kriegsenkel* through her work as a therapist specializing in the technique of "family constellation." The case studies in her book reveal the roots of present-day problems in inherited experiences based in the past. I look up Baring online: she lives in Berlin too. I write asking to meet her and she replies, inviting me to take part in an upcoming family constellation seminar. Two weeks later I am in the front room of a ground-floor Charlottenburg apartment, one of a dozen people sitting on chairs around the walls, the room's only window obscured with ivy.

Baring, an elegant woman in her early sixties, is stern and schoolmistress-like in introducing us to the subject and sketching out the parameters of the practice. But once the constellation begins, she is radiantly alert. The constellation is personal, designed to address the issues of one participant at a time – the analysand – who outlines his or her issue, and then chooses participants one by one to be a *Stellvertreter*, or stand-in, for various family members and sometimes, on Baring's suggestion, abstract entities like "Money," "Love" or "The Past." Another stand-in represents "The Self" allowing the analysand to observe the evolving scenario from a distance. Each stand-in is guided to a place in the center of the room by the analysand, after which Baring begins to pace around, circling and looking at the arrangement – this constellation – from all angles and asking each participant how they feel.

In the first constellation of the day, I am not picked to be a stand-in, and am sitting in my chair against the wall watching the scenario unfold. Suddenly I notice that my heart is beating fast, and I am getting goose-bumps on my arms. I feel the need to stand up and participate, and Baring invites me in. I don't know where to stand at first, but find a spot and intuitively look away from the other people standing there. My heart is still beating fast, I am full of anxiety and fear. I sense that I am standing in for a persecuted person. Baring asks me how I feel. "Terrible," I tell her. "Cold all over with sweaty palms, as if I were dead." We plunge straight into the heart of the war, and this continues all day.

I cannot explain how it happens, but when standing there in these constellations, you do feel certain things. Heat or shivering cold, a desire to move, to stay rooted to the spot, or to fall down to your knees. You may turn your back on one participant, or be particularly drawn to the side of another. All of this takes place with only the barest knowledge of the background or circumstances of the analysand's case. The energetic feelings that the setup arouses are strong and specific: surges that determine behavior and emotion. The stand-ins act as conduits to access buried information and connections appear, secrets make themselves apparent, through emotions expressed at a high pitch in order to make themselves legible.

"Magic is the application of resonance, whether it takes the form of thought-reading, projecting images, prophesying, faith-healing, or causing inexplicable death and disaster to an enemy," writes T. C. Lethbridge, originator of the Stone Tape Theory. Its potential lies in channelling areas that are otherwise hard to access, excavating long-buried experiences, or inherited traumas that may appear long-forgotten but are nonetheless twisted into the epigenetic code. The "family constellation," an esoteric discipline, allows open questions to assume an embodied form. It is another kind of reading: a diagram drawn with people in space to represent a situation whose traces can no longer be seen. I can sense the adrenaline Baring feels when she starts to detect a pattern and attempts to solve it like a riddle, steering the narrative towards reconciliation.

When it comes to my turn to be the analysand and present my own issue, the diagram isn't about the war but it is about my heritage. My matriarchal ancestors are staged in a living-room dramaturgy which allows me to realize that the feelings of inauthenticity I have been troubled with are not simply to do with an unhappy marriage, living out a role I felt I hadn't chosen, but are also to do with my grandmother. I have unwittingly adopted her unfulfilled social aspirations, a feeling of being better than the others. Her hair-sprayed chignon, the pearls and the cigarettes. The smart war-wedding suit and cut crystal glass from which she drank her daily whisky. The apartment my grandparents lived in always seemed too small for my grandmother. She married a sheepskin salesman and was a school maths teacher herself, but her aura was far grander than that. The life I have fashioned for myself is the life she would have liked to have. "Living alone in 200 square meters," is how Baring put it, having no idea of the truth in this statement. This is the root of my feelings of disorientation, swinging between two opposite poles like a magnet that cannot settle. The one who wants a grand façade, and the other who is happy with a simple, modest life. I cannot abandon either part, they both belong to me. I am living in ambivalence, made up of both these sides. Images from this and the other constellations fill my mind for days afterwards and a question starts to form itself. Could Baring help me with the blind spots in my story? Could we stage a constellation for the house itself?

## · 21 ·

# Constellation

*On all sides of the house* on the Ufer, construction sites are in operation. Night and day, through the window of the *Berliner Zimmer* I can see large cursive letters illuminated in red, spelling out "a-l-e-t," from the sign that crowns a new building behind our house. An Aletto hotel stands on the site where the bomb was defused a few years ago. Out of the front window, two bright yellow cranes are pivoting on the skyline. Between Hobrecht's pumping station and the Anhalter Bahnhof, on a plot of land that I didn't even know was there, an office block is being conjured into being. It remains to be seen if it will rise high enough to be visible from here. But in the meantime, every morning this winter a blinding light from one of these cranes has shone directly in through the kitchen window, casting night-time shadows on the wall. The pumping station was decommissioned back in 1972. For thirty years it was used as a *Lapidarium* and statues of long-forgotten dukes and counts, in tricorn hats and buckled finery, assembled in the engine room. Figures from an obsolete past, performing their stony gestures while awaiting an unknown future. Now the pumping station has been renovated and is the office of a well-known Berlin art collector who keeps a few of the statues on display, along with the original pump engine, a highly polished relic of industrial chic.

The old pits itself against the new, and the new against the newer, as Berlin turns into a "transit city," the party capital of Europe. The relatively meagre population of only 3.5 million is constantly swollen by incoming waves of transient pleasure seekers. Rents rise and hasty developments catering towards the night-time needs of a temporary population are prioritized: more budget hotels and hostels, cheap fast-food joints, and apartments let as short-term tourist rentals. What does this mean for the city, when its visitors' interests are catered to before those of its residents, and when those interests are in nightlife? Every year, as rents go up, there are more sleeping bags and shopping trolleys on the banks of the Landwehr Canal, shambolic camps set up by homeless people beneath the shelter of the overhead U-Bahn tracks.

New plans are afoot at Gleisdreieck, where a borderline sliver has been sold off to investors intent on planting seven new high-rise buildings here. The brick archways of the former railway bridge have now been levelled flat. The Gleisdreieck Park feels like our backyard. An enormously popular inner-city redevelopment, its success lies in its suggestions of activities but non-prescriptive layout: a hoop but not a whole basketball court, a landscape of gentle rubber-covered hillocks for kids to roll down on scooters or bikes, overgrown patches of meadow amongst stretches of mown grass, allotment gardens around its edges, and a terrace of shallow steps for sitting on, seeing and being seen. My sons have visited almost daily since we moved here, now primarily for the honing of skateboard skills or hanging out in the evening doing teenage things. I come for early morning walks, taking in the brambles growing wild between the rusting rail tracks and greeting the local, black-hooded crows. In a fenced-off area not far from the German Museum of Technology, broken statues can be seen amongst the tangles of undergrowth: a lower torso on its side, forward foot just visible, a headless eagle stretching its wings. Cross-strutted pylons and enormous bells without their clappers are lying around in wild terrain that is home to families of small grey rabbits. Teams of park attendants arrive early every morning, clearing

away the rubbish strewn across the grass by thought-
less revellers the night before.

Now that new building plans are underway – an
unwieldly development of commercial high-rises which
would ruin the park with stark shadows, wind tunnels
and brutal aesthetic intrusion – the Gleisdreieck activists are on alert again. Signs are posted all over the
park and everyday my inbox is full of email petitions
and protest letters.

Grassroots agitation has deep roots in Berlin, as a
way of combatting local government policies. A law is
introduced to control the city's rising rents: a five-year
rent freeze that sees money flowing backwards from the
landlords into the pockets of tenants across the city. It is
overturned a few months later, to a clamorous uproar, but
the effort cements widespread support for rent controls
and even *Enteignung*, the expropriation of properties belonging to Berlin's biggest private housing companies.
Rumblings are being made about the canal bank opposite my house, to turn a stretch of the Hallesches Ufer
that runs from Kreuzberg past the pumping station and
up to Potsdamer Straße, into a green pedestrianized
zone. A possible return of Lenné's "green shore"?

The water damage in our apartment woke me up to my
predicament of an unhappy marriage, displaying the

crisis I had refused to acknowledge. I had been stuck in a holding pattern and had slipped into a dependency that was both comfortable and humiliating. Now, although I am living in the shell of my former married life, it is not an empty shell, we like it here and now that it is smaller, we can start to fill it with our lives.

But then it happens again: another incident. In the hallway that leads to the *Mädchenkammer*, the former maid's room which we use now for laundry and storage, a brown patch appears on the ceiling. An appliance has been faultily connected in the penthouse apartment above. A few months later, damp appears in the *Mädchenkammer* and soon water is running in fast blue rivulets down the wall. Somehow it finds its way into the washing machine's central control panel, trickling along the minute channels of its circuit board, and three weeks later it dies. Not long after, several small puddles of water appear on the floor. With no visible source or cause, they seem to have emerged upwards out of the concrete itself. Anti-gravity pools, not dripping down but rising up. I check all the pipes but there is no sign of damage. They evaporate as mysteriously as they appeared. Then on the balcony of the *Berliner Zimmer*, where Parvati's matchbox caught on fire and burned her hair, a broken drainpipe begins dribbling water which appears as a bruise of green mold on the interior wall.

At the beginning, all of this compulsive architectural leakage seemed to point with increasing urgency and dramatic flourish to an emotional dead end, describing a chain of logical consequence: *blockage–leakage–overflow*. But since that dam of emotional repression has ruptured and the relationship's rubble cleared away, the meaning of the water damage is no longer so clear. I try to channel a different kind of attention so that other patterns can emerge. A porous, permeable state of mind and a loose, sifting methodology in order to determine cause and orientation. Which brings me back to the starting question. What is the house trying to tell me?

The adopted daughter, Melitta, sole heir of the Sala family remains the biggest enigma in this narrative. I have been trying to fill in her outline since I first found her name in the files in the Land Registry Office. Nothing comes up when I search her name online, so I turn to the local authorities instead. The *Anwohnermeldeamt*, the Resident Registration Office, is my first port of call, as it is for any new resident in the city, who has to register their address. I fill out the forms requesting information and receive a terse typed-out response several weeks later by post. Melitta Kozslowski-Sala, born 7th May 1934, died in Steglitz on 18th October 2013. (By then we had bought the apartment and were starting the renovation.) I try to reach the Resident Registration Office by phone with no luck, so I pay a visit to their offices in person. I manage to talk my way past the porter, despite not having an appointment, and am soon sitting opposite a clerk. She simply advises me to fill in another form, which I do and several more weeks later receive an even terser response. Only family members are entitled to receive further information. But what if there are no family members, if this person is the end of a family line?

I call the number on this letter and speak to a Frau Buske who tells me they do not have any more information there. She suggests I contact the *Sterbeamt*, the Office of Deaths. Frau Lobrecht, at the Office of Deaths in Steglitz, after requesting proof of my profession as a writer, sends more scraps of information. Melitta was widowed when she died, her husband, Wolfgang Kozlowski, had passed away three months earlier. They had married in the Kreuzberg Registry Office in 1958. I try asking some more questions but that is as much as Frau Lobrecht can tell me. She suggests I contact the *Eheschließungsamt*, the Marriage Registry Office in Kreuzberg. I call them – no answer – but keep trying and eventually reach a man who tells me to send an email, which I do. I am still waiting to hear back from him. The life of this person – Melitta – remains elusive, dispersed in biographical fragments in bureaucratic offices across the city.

Despite the few vivid anecdotal flourishes provided by the architect who used to live in my apartment, I still know very little about Melitta. The architect told me she used to refer to herself as an *angenommenes Kind*. Unlike the word *adoptiert*, the word *angenommen* seems to me to have something reluctant about it. The DHL parcels that my downstairs neighbors accept for me are *angenommen*, taken on.

I don't know what leads me to it, but one Sunday afternoon in June – the day of the summer solstice in fact – I decide to visit the nearby graveyard, the Dreifaltigkeitsfriedhof on Mehringdamm. It is enormous, three separate graveyards brought together at some point in the past. I suppose the idea in the back of my mind is that I might find the Salas here, or perhaps even the Zimmermann family, but there are so many graves, so much space, so many possible paths to take. How to conduct a search like this? It is exhausting reading all the names on the graves and I quickly realize that my task is futile. I take out my notebook and start copying down the names from the headstones instead, to suggest a sense of the terrain and of this literal task of reading.

Röseler, Schwarz, Hensel, Braumüller, Vogt, Schulz, Klein, Neumann, Hoffmann, Salewski, von Graefe,

Krause, Gerlach, Meyer, Baugarten, Wolf, Günzl, Schmidt. Right at the very back I come across the grave of Rahel Varnhagen, who I have just discovered was an early-nineteenth-century salonist, the subject of Hannah Arendt's first book. I am about to start writing down singular female names – Liselotte, Marianne – and turn a corner and then suddenly there it is: a headstone marked with the names Bruno and Charlotte Sala. A dark red marble stone, rectangular and low, with letters engraved and filled in with gold leaf. Beside it is a tall black monument inscribed with the names Anton and Louise, Adolf and Marie, and Annelise Sala. The Sala family grave. I have found it. It is not far in fact from the entrance I came in by. I have circled all the way through the graveyard and had given up hope, thinking instead about how to write about not finding the grave. That exact moment of giving up lead me to discovery.

Three generations of the Sala family are here: Anton Sala, founder in 1845 of the Sala printing company, the year that Adolph Menzel painted his *Balcony Room*. Adolf Sala, Anton's son, who married his cousin Marie in 1888. (Her maiden name, Sala, is also written on the gravestone.) Their daughter Annelise, who, I find out now, died in 1923 aged only thirty-four. Adolf was Bruno Sala's uncle, it is surprising that he chose to be buried here rather than with his father Fortunato. There are no graves here for Fortunato, nor for Bruno's brother Curt. And no grave either for Melitta. She must have chosen not to be buried with the parents who took her in. Though she would have been the one to have her mother Charlotte Sala's name inscribed on the headstone when she died, fifteen years after her husband. On my way out, I read on a sign at the entrance that the graveyard would have been destroyed had Speer and Hitler's Germania been built. The founding Salas' final resting place was almost lost for good.

But still no Melitta. Where can I go from here? I contact Gabriele Baring and tell her about the apartment, the house, the Sala story. She is all for it, agreeing at once that we can use the family constellation method to look into this puzzle. "I once did a constellation on a pair of shoes," she says. I sign up for another seminar and a few weeks later I am back in the ground-floor room in Charlottenburg, with ivy growing over the window.

Once again, this odd group of a dozen or so people, sitting on an assortment of spindly wooden dining chairs and upholstered armchairs pushed back against the walls of the room, leaving an open space on the parquet floor in the center. Several constellations are staged addressing personal crises of various kinds, and then we come to mine. By now we have got to know each other in an oblique but intense manner, given all of the

roles we have adopted in these excerpted dramatur-
gies of each others' past and present lives. We are like
Fassbinder's ensemble cast, adapting ourselves to each
melodrama that comes up. But it is also an empathetic
process. I present my case to Baring and the group: it
does not have to do with my history, but with that of
the house I live in. With my feeling that it is trying to
tell me something, but I don't know what it is. I sketch
out the outlines of the problem: the water damage, my
broken marriage, the Sala family, Melitta. Everyone is
up for my unusual proposition and curious about how
it will unfold.

The constellation begins with five stand-ins: one
for Melitta, one each for Bruno and Charlotte, one for
the house, and one for me, as the instigator of the enquiry. Eyes closed, I guide each of them to a place in
the center of the room and then return to the sidelines,
where Baring and I remain, observing the action from
a distance. The stand-in for the house, a youngish man,
portly in a scarlet pullover with slicked-back black hair,
starts saying "I am not standing well, I can't find any
right angles." He feels bad, as if he is wrongly placed
on the wrong site. "There are only triangles here," he
says. We bring in a stand-in for Herr Zimmermann, the
landowner who originally built the house in 1869. There
is something unidentified here it seems, a problem of
some kind. So we bring in a young woman to represent

"The Problem," who sits straight down on the floor. She clearly has something to do with the sadness and fate of the house, but it takes us a while to identify what. At first, she is cowering between Herr Zimmermann and the house, but then she moves to stand behind Zimmermann. I ask if she is his wife and she says that she thinks she is. Her health has suffered as her husband neglects her and invests his energy into the building. He does not notice her suffering and just carries right on with building the house.

When the house is eventually sold to Adolf Sala (for whom I quickly find a stand-in), Zimmermann is happy, relieved to be rid of this burden. They shake hands, Sala delighted at this purchase for his company. But by then it is already too late for Zimmermann: his wife has died and the whole enterprise has brought only unhappiness. (It is only much later, researching the Zimmermanns, that I discover that Anna Zimmermann had married at seventeen and may have lost an illegitimate baby.)

Bruno Sala, Adolf's second-eldest son, who has been in the constellation from the beginning, has spent the whole time standing behind the house, worry written on his tense, serious face, as if shielding himself from these goings-on. Melitta, his adopted child, (played by a hearty Austrian woman) shrinks back, unwilling to stand too close to either her father or the house. A young, open-faced woman who is the stand-in for me is watching the activity from a distance, somewhat off to the side. At one point, Melitta moves up very close to her – "I feel connected," she says. "She is so nice, we are friends. And she has such lovely hair." She doesn't know why I am showing such an interest in her, but is flattered and enjoys the attention. It is curious to witness this from my position at the edge of the room.

Curt Sala, Bruno's younger brother, is brought in. He can't stop smiling, laughing, hopping from one foot to another. He shows no interest in his wife, the other Charlotte, but keeps saying how much he enjoys women in general and *vögeln* – shagging – as he light-heartedly puts it. Meanwhile the house keeps saying, worriedly, "there are triangles everywhere." It's true, there is a triangle between Curt, Bruno and Bruno's wife Charlotte, and another one between Melitta, the house and the stand-in for myself. Bruno observes my stand-in critically, impatient with my interrogation of the house, of Melitta, and Curt. He doesn't want so many questions asked.

Baring is director and interrogator of the enigmatic scenario that presents itself. Through asking questions of the participants, she teases out a narrative that suggests Melitta to be the illegitimate daughter of Curt, who carries on smiling, laughing, hopping from one foot to another. Brothers Bruno and Curt had made a deal: Bruno would take on Melitta, Curt's daughter, and would get the house and business, which would end up as Melitta's inheritance.

As we reach the end of the constellation, the stand-in for the house begins crying uncontrollably. He stands there and cries and cries. He – the house – is sorry, he is in pain and didn't realize that his tears were raining into my apartment. It's not my fault, he says. (The man in the scarlet pullover says later he hasn't cried so much for years.) It is fascinating to see this unhappy house, that feels unsettled and badly sited, concerned about all of these triangles and responding with the tears that keep flooding my apartment. The Zimmermanns' unhappiness, where all of the attention is directed towards the building of the house at the expense of the marriage, seems weirdly to mirror my own situation. It is as if that is why the house played a role in revealing to me my own damaged circumstances. As if we were unwittingly playing the Zimmermanns, replicating a past unknown to us.

The story of Melitta and her family relations is a conjecture that cannot be verified, it could well be entirely wrong. The family constellation method is susceptible to inventing false narratives and tying up loose ends too neatly. I do notice, however, in the days after the seminar, that she loosens her grip on my imagination. Strangely, the water damage seems to have stopped now too.

# Coda

*My eldest son* is sitting at our kitchen table making notes on white index cards. Six years have passed since we woke up to the flood on the kitchen floor. This child of mine is eighteen now and is studying for his history exam. The Second World War and the Cold War – the same subjects that I have spent the last year and a half wading through, immersed in the turgid history of my adopted home. Though not my own history, it is that of my son and of his younger brother. And through my children, through genetic and cultural inheritances, I too am twisted into this past. I have a stake in Berlin, the place where my children were born.

The view from this kitchen window has led me on a search that felt at first like retrieving memories that

belonged to someone else, but it has brought with it
a compassion for this place that I hadn't quite antic-
ipated. There are opportunities for revelation all over
in this city – this view, this vantage point that I have,
is just one single possibility. Once you start to pick at
the surface and ask awkward questions anywhere here,
the past begins to reveal itself. An active, lively understanding of the past, written and rewritten as attitudes
and perspectives shift and widen. A past that is called
to life through the act of reading.

In surveying the matter of the world, the hydromancers
instruct us to clear the mind and focus on what we want
to know when gazing at the water. To narrow this to a
single statement or question. My question was about
the undercurrents and the downward pull that seem
inseparable from Berlin's identity. Instead of avoiding difficulty and looking away, I have scrutinized surfaces, topographies, distinguishing features, buildings,
photographs, documents, literature. Paid attention to
blank spaces and interrogated isolation. Not just looking at what surrounds me, but trying to find out what
lies beneath it, and recording it in real time.

In this frame of mind, every minute detail speaks
of something larger. Standards, rules, and generalizations, like those in the history books my son is studying,

are set aside in favor of the fragment, the incident, the little patch of observation. Less tangible conditions are detected: the current, the drift, the invisible traces, recovered voices and disappearances made seen. Intellect is partnered with divination; perception outstrips memory. A place of conjecture is established where one is free to wander.

With these tools, partial images of the past can be pieced together. Not to reconstitute past lives, or repair the broken pieces. There is no whole to reconstruct and no complete view to be had. Lives remain half-glimpsed while any knowledge or understanding is a patchwork matter of information plus intuition. Monolithic notions of Berlin – from the peaceful brinks of industry to accelerated mechanization, the short-lived golden Weimar years or the totalitarian city of war, from division to unification – have given way to a splintered and prismatic vision. To the minor conflicts of lived experience. The firsthand accounts of eyewitnesses. There are no tidy endings or neat summations here; it is sprawling and unruly, as is the city itself. The place may not change, but a shift in perspective and input can shade your understanding of what you thought you knew. Making things visible that have been hidden, of which we are ashamed to talk. To recognize the violence, trauma and political contrivance that have forged Berlin's identity and seep into its water table.

———

One of the most unusual elements in the view from my kitchen window is a hot-air balloon that rises up intermittently above the tree line. It is patterned in green and blue to look like planet earth and DIE WELT, the name of a popular Berlin newspaper, is written across its girth in huge block letters. This enormous globe – *die Welt* itself, the world – bobs up just to the left of the Leipziger Straße apartment blocks. It occurs to me that if I were to take a ride in this balloon and rise up into my own skyline, I could see the whole view of this place, of my house within its entire environment.

I arrange to go there with a friend, and we meet one Monday morning in early spring. According to my phone it is going to be bright and sunny, the view will be clear. Biking along Stresemannstraße and past the Topography of Terror, I can see the top of the hot air balloon's enormous round form. Tethered with dozens of ropes and cables, it is "the largest captive balloon in the world." It rises to a height of 150 meters, wind allowing, while remaining anchored to this piece of ground. But approaching its site on the corner of Zimmerstraße and Wilhelmstraße, I realize the gates are closed. A sign tells us that due to high winds, the balloon will not be operating today. My friend and I don't think it seems windy at all, the wispy clouds in the blue sky are not even moving, but perhaps that feels different at 150 meters up. The overview remains out of reach and I am still earthbound. My friend and I have a coffee instead and then I go back home.

The view I have from the kitchen window is just a snapshot, a momentary image of a changing skyline. Another new skyscraper is in planning, to be built on a scrap of land behind the pumping station. A signature project for the Kreuzberg planning department, it will be built of wood, a hundred meters high, the highest wooden building in the world, with a mixture of social housing, private apartments and public viewing platforms. If the building goes ahead, it will rise up, floor by floor, and obscure my view of the ruined Anhalter Bahnhof, of the apartment blocks on Leipziger Straße, the TV Tower and the Rotes Rathaus on the horizon with its tiny fluttering flag.

When we first moved into the apartment, the view's insistence caught me off guard. It was as if the place – the house – was not only delivering me a project – this book – but was also giving me advice. It seemed to suggest that the crisis in which I found myself, if harnessed in the right way, could become an opportunity for redefinition. Not an easy movement towards wholeness, but a recognition of loss and pain, and an acknowledgment of what it is to live with ambivalence. The jagged edges of our broken family have been smoothed by time and the incremental work of reconciliation. Our family structure has been recalibrated and its schedule synchronized through an online calendar which regulates the children's movements – with me, with him, with me, with him. I am no longer the gravity-stricken counterweight to an opposite force of levity and free-ranging upward movement. The house has been teaching me the art of inhabitation, of the apartment itself but also of this city, this time, my body, my life. Reminding me that with inhabitation comes responsibility: to witness, to document and to act.

There is still one leaky drain from an upper floor balcony that drips along the exterior wall of the *Berliner Zimmer*, causing the paint to buckle and the plasterwork to crumble. It looks atrocious, like a virulent skin disease. It is only on the outside wall, however, it hasn't found its way in yet and I am trying hard to get my neighbor to fix it. Since unearthing the family tree of the building, my relation to the house has changed. It no longer needs to interrupt my daily life with weird apparitions that goad me along interpretative tangents. The house has less of a hold over me and we can live here unperturbed, my sons and our cats, navigating the frictions of everyday family life more or less harmoniously.

I am inscribed now into the official history of the building on Tempelhofer Ufer: my name appears in the *Grundbuch* as the owner of the third-floor apartment, front-facing and side wing. I have my place in the historical lineage amongst the names of former inhabitants. I have stood at the window and cast my mind back over the lives of the architect who lived here in the 1980s, of Melitta Sala, the Charlottes, and Frau Zimmermann, and tried to imagine a female perspective living on the Ufer over a span of time. Now the builders are back, starting necessary renovations in the side wing so that we can rent it out. But the boys and I agree that our apartment is still too big. At some point soon we will look for something new. Something smaller, more manageable, and less temperamental.

# Index of Maps and Illustrations

# Author's Note

When I set out to write about Berlin, in particular the part of it that I can see from the window of my apartment, I imagined it would be a fast, slim text of a few thousand words. I soon realized, however, that once you begin to scratch the surface of this place, a narrative begins to emerge of unknown depths. It pulls you in. There is no simple version of this city. The end result of my concerted scratching – this book – is a partial and particular narrative of this place. Its subjective viewpoint and autobiographical lens are as much a framing device as is the window itself – both are deployed to suggest this view to be not definitive, but just one possibility amongst many.

I count myself as a reader rather than a historian but this book inevitably rubs shoulders with various difficult kinds of history in my adopted home. My approach began initially with the material of the city itself – its streets, buildings and municipal archives – but soon widened to look at eye-witness accounts, letters and diaries, journalism, literature or art of the time. Diving into these sources was one of the great pleasures of this project: examining Adolph Menzel's drawings or Theodor Fontane's writings, Rosa Luxemburg's letters, Gabriele Tergit's journalistic reportage, Christa Wolf's memoirs and novels, and Rainer Werner Fassbinder's films for evidence of the periods in which they were made. But in order to reach an understanding of these temporal contexts and then write about this city, I have leaned heavily on the scholarship of several notable historians. Alexandra Richie's impeccably researched and beautifully written *Faust's Metropolis*, published in 1998, has been my bible of Berlin. I turned to Richie's engaging narrative to understand the complex social and political backgrounds to many past versions of this city – from its founding in the twelfth century to its Wilhelmine incarnation, the aftermath of the Second World War and the fraught counter-narratives of the divided city – and have quoted from it extensively. Peter Gay's and Eric D. Weitz's insights into the Weimar period were essential, as was Antony Beevor's account of the fall of Berlin, Brian Ladd's 1997

analysis of the intersections of history and architecture, and Klaus Theweleit's incredible synthesis of the
German psyche in the late nineteenth and early twentieth centuries. Historical sources are inevitably subject
to change and reinterpretation and as far as possible I
have tried to reference the most up-to-date discourses
regarding contested historical events, particularly those
around the Second World War (see Helke Sander and
Barbara Johr's research into rape in the war's aftermath,
or Christian Goeschel's examination of suicide). Numbers can vary depending on who is doing the counting,
and how. Sabine Bode's research from the early 2000s
into the so-called *Kriegskinder* and *Kriegsenkel*, the generations who inherited their parents' war traumas, was
an illuminating turning point in my understanding of the
resonance of the past in present behaviors, as was Alexander and Margarete Mitscherlich's ground-breaking
1967 research before that, and Hannah Arendt's still illuminating analytical essays. The digital archives of local
newspapers or publications such as *Der Spiegel* were in-
valuable in sourcing the contemporary textures of Berlin's post-war years.

Where my sources were only in German, I have used
my own translations, and in some cases where English
translations exist, I have stuck with my own perhaps
more idiosyncratic renderings, as these were formative
in my understanding of a situation or period.

I am indebted to several individuals for their generosity and patience with my enquiries, including Parvati, the feng shui master; the architect who lived in my apartment in the 1980s; architects Louisa Hutton and Matthias Sauerbruch; Gabriele Baring, author and family therapist; and not least Melitta Koszlowski-Sala, whom I never found, but who nevertheless became the unwitting protagonist of my book.

# Sources

## Books and Essays

Dawn Ades, Daniel F. Herrmann (eds.), *Hannah Höch* (London: Prestel, 2a014)

Anonymous, *Eine Frau in Berlin: Tagebuch Aufzeichnungen vom 20 April bis 22 June 1945* [Published in English as *A Woman in Berlin: Eight Weeks in the Conquered City*] (Munich: Random House, 2008)

Ingo Arend, *"Das Erinnerungsprojekt: Gespräch mit Dieter Hoffmann-Axthelm über den Kampf um die Berliner Stadtmitte"* [The Remembering Project: A conversation with Dieter Hoffmann-Axthelm about the battle for Berlin's Stadtmitte], Kunstforum International (1993)

Hannah Arendt, *Eichmann and the Holocaust* (London: Penguin, 2005)

Hannah Arendt, *Essays in Understanding 1930-1954: Formation, Exile, and Totalitarianism* (New York: Schocken Books, 1994)

Margaret Atwood, "Margaret Atwood on how she came to write The Handmaid's Tale," *Literary Hub* (August 2018)

Gaston Bachelard, *The Poetics of Space* (Boston: Beacon Press, 1994)

Gabriele Baring, *Die geheimen Ängste der Deutschen* [The Secret Fears of Germans] (Munich: Scorpio Verlag, 2011)

Vicky Baum, *Grand Hotel*, trans. Basil Creighton (New York: New York Review of Books, 2016)

Antony Beevor, *Berlin: The Downfall 1945* (London: Penguin, 2003)

Walter Benjamin, *Berlin Childhood around 1900*, trans. Howard Eiland (London and Cambridge, Massachusetts: Belknap Press, 2006)

Walter Benjamin, *Gesammelte Schriften III (1912-1940)* [Collected Writings III: 1912-1940] (Frankfurt am Main: Suhrkamp, 1972)

Barbara Beuys, *Die neuen Frauen: Revolution im Kaiserreich 1900-1914* [The New Women: Revolution in the Empire 1900-1914] (Bonn: Bundeszentrale für politische Bildung, 2014)

Sabine Bode, *Die vergessene Generation: Die Kriegskinder brechen ihr Schweigen* [The Forgotten Generation: The Children of War Break Their Silence ] (Stuttgart: Klett-Cotta, 2004)

# Sources

David Bowie, Lars von Tröne, *"Ich denke oft, Brecht hätte das so gemacht"* [I often think, Brecht would have done it that way], *Der Tagesspiegel* (January 2001)

Arno Brandlhuber, Florian Hertweck,Thomas Mayfried (eds.), *The Dialogic City: Berlin wird Berlin* (Köln: Verlag der Buchhandlung Walther König, 2015)

Renate Bridenthal, Atina Grossmann, Marion Kaplan (eds.), *When Biology Became Destiny. Women in Weimar and Nazi Germany* (New York: Monthly Review Press, 1984)

Marie von Bunsen, *Die Frau und die Geselligkeit* [Women and Society] (Leipzig: Seemann & Co., 1914)

Marie von Bunsen, *Die Welt, in der ich lebte: Erinnerungen aus glücklichen Jahren 1860–1912* [The World in Which I Lived: Memoirs of Happy Years 1860-1912] (Leipzig: Koehler und Amelang, 1929)

Ralf Burmeister (ed.), *Hannah Höch: Aller Anfang ist DADA!* [Hannah Höch: All Begins with DADA!] (Berlin: Berlinische Galerie, 2007)

Florian von Buttlar (ed.), *Peter Joseph Lenné: Volkspark und Arkadien* [Peter Joseph Lenné: People's Park and Arcadia] (Berlin: Nicolaische Verlagsbuchhandlung, 1989)

Andrea Büttner, *Shame* (London: Koenig Books, 2020)

Felix Denk, Sven von Thülen, *Der Klang der Familie: Berlin, Techno und die Wende* [Published in English as *Der Klang der Familie: Berlin, Techno and the Fall of the Wall*] (Berlin: Suhrkamp, 2014)

Georg Diez, "Missed Opportunities: Berlin's Architectural Wasteland," *Der Spiegel* (March 2013)

Jenny Diski, *Stranger on a Train: Daydreaming and Smoking Around America with Interruptions* (London: Virago Press, 2002)

Jenny Diski, *Why Didn't You Just Do What You Were Told? Essays* (London: Bloomsbury, 2020)

Catherine Leota Dollard, *The Surplus Woman: Unmarried in Imperial Germany* (Oxford, New York: Berghahn Books, 2009)

Marguerite Duras, *Practicalities* (New York: Grove Press, 1990)

Jimmie Durham, *Between the Furniture and the Building (Between a Rock and a Hard Place)* (Köln: Verlag der Buchhandlung Walther König and München: Kunstverein München, 1998)

Werner Düttmann, *Berlin ist viele Städte* [Berlin is Many Cities] (Berlin: Archibook, 1984)

Christiane F., *Wir Kinder von Bahnhof Zoo* [We Children of Zoo Station] (Hamburg: Carlsen Verlag, 2017)

Rainer Werner Fassbinder, "Rainer Werner Fassbinder," *Arsenal* (August 2015)

Theodor Fontane, *Cécile* (München: dtv, 2011)

Theodor Fontane, *Effi Briest*, trans. Hugh Rorrison (London: Penguin Books, 2000)

Theodor Fontane, *On Tangled Paths*, trans. Peter James Bowman (London: Penguin Books, 2013)

Michael Fried, *Menzel's Realism: Art and Embodiment in Nineteenth Century Berlin* (New Haven: Yale University Press, 2002)

# Sources

Dieter Fuhrman (ed.), *Profession ohne Tradition: 125 Jahre Verein der Berliner Künstlerinnen 1867–1992* [Profession without Tradition: 125 Years of the Association of Berlin Women Artists 1867–1992] (Berlin: Kupfergraben, 1992)

Peter Gay, *Weimar Culture: The Outsider as Insider* (New York: Norton, 2001)

Christian Goeschel, *Suicide in Nazi Germany* (Oxford: Oxford University Press, 2009)

Peter Gosztony (ed.), *Der Kampf um Berlin 1945 in Augenzeugenberichten* [The Battle for Berlin 1945 in Eyewitness Accounts] (Düsseldorf: Karl Rauch Verlag, 1970)

Germaine Greer, *The Female Eunuch* (London: MacGibbon & Kee, 1970)

Annett Gröscher, *Berolinas zornige Töchter: 50 Jahre Berliner Frauenbewegung* [Berolina's Angry Daughters: 50 Years of the Berlin Women's Movement] (Berlin: FFBIZ, 2018)

Harri Günther, Sibylle Harksen (eds.), *Peter Joseph Lenné: Katalog der Zeichnungen* [Peter Joseph Lenné: Catalogue of the Drawings] (Tübingen/Berlin: Ernst Wasmuth Verlag, 1993)

Peter Hannemann, *"Tag eins nach Stunde null"* [Day One after the Zero Hour], *Der Spiegel* (October 2011)

Benny Härlin, Michael Sontheimer, *Potsdamer Straße* (Berlin: Rotbuch Verlag, 1983)

Werner Hegemann, *Das Steinerne Berlin* [Stone Berlin] (Braunschweig: Friedr. Vieweg & Sohn Verlagsgessellschaft, 1979)

Gisela Heller, *Unterwegs mit Fontane in Berlin und der Mark Brandenburg* [Travels with Fontane in Berlin and

Brandenburg] (Berlin: Nicolaische Verlagsbuchhandlung, 1993)

Franz Hessel, *Walking in Berlin: A Flaneur in the Capital*, trans. Amanda deMarco (London: Scribe Publications, 2016)

Merle Hiblk, *"Die Versöhnung"* [The Reconciliation], *Der Spiegel* (May 2013)

Gerhard Hinz, *Peter Joseph Lenné: Das Gesamtwerk des Gartenarchitekten und Städteplaners* [Peter Joseph Lenné: The Complete Works of the Landscape Architect and City Planner] (Hildesheim, Zürich, New York: Georg Olms Verlag, 1989)

Dieter Hoffmann-Axthelm, *Berlin Testament: Beiträge zum Berlin des 21. Jahrhunderts* [Berlin Testament: Essays on 21st Century Berlin] (Detmold: Verlag Dorothea Rohn, 2013)

John Horgan, "Scientific Heretic Rupert Sheldrake on Morphic Fields, Psychic Dogs and Other Mysteries," *Scientific American* (July 2014)

Gerald Hüther, *The Neurobiological Preconditions for the Development of Curiosity and Creativity* (Berlin: Jovis Verlag, 2015)

Christopher Isherwood, *Goodbye to Berlin* (London: Vintage Classics, 1998)

Stuart Jeffries, "Claude Lanzmann on why Holocaust documentary *Shoah* still matters," *The Guardian* (June 2011)

Barbara Johr, Helke Sander (eds.), *BeFreir und Befreite: Krieg, Vergewaltigung, Kinder* [Liberator and Liberated: War, Rape, Children] (Frankfurt am Main: Fischer Taschenburg Verlag, 2005)

# Sources

Claude Keisch, Marie Ursula Riemann-Rehyer (eds.), *Adolph Menzel: Briefe, 1830-55* [Adolph Menzel: Letters, 1830-55] (Berlin: Deutsche Kunstverlag, 2009)

Irmgard Keun, *Das kunstseidene Mädchen* [Published in English as *The Artificial Silk Girl*] (Berlin: List, 2004)

Elke-Vera Kotowski, *Gabriele Tergit. Grossstadtchronistin der Weimarer Republik* [Gabriele Tergit. Urban Chronicler of the Weimar Republic] (Berlin: Hentrich & Hentrich Verlag, 2017)

Brian Ladd, *The Ghosts of Berlin* (London: University of Chicago Press, 1997)

T. C. Lethbridge, *Ghost and Ghoul* (London: Routledge and Kegan, 1961)

Ruth Leys, *From Guilt to Shame: Auschwitz and After* (Princeton and Oxford: Princeton University Press, 2007)

Andra Lichtenstein, Flavia Alice Mameli, *Gleisdreieck/Parklife Berlin* (Bielefeld: transcript, 2015)

Rosa Luxemburg, *The Letters of Rosa Luxemburg*, Georg Adler, Peter Hudis, Annelies Laschitza (eds.), trans. George Shriver (New York and London: Verso, 2011)

Rosa Luxemburg, *Rosa Luxemberg: Selected Political and Literary Writings*, Mike Jones (ed.) (Pontypool, Wales: Merlin Press, 2009)

Niklas Maak, *"Das Ausstellungswunder von Berlin"* [Berlin's Exhibition Miracle], *Frankfurter Allgemeine Zeitung* (December 2005)

Janet Maslin, "Rainer Werner Fassbinder," *The New York Times* (June 1982)

Karen Meyer, *Die Flutung des Berliner S-Bahn-Tunnels in den letzten Kriegstagen* [The Flooding of the Berlin S-Bahn Tunnel in the Last Days of the War] (Berlin: Kunstamt Kreuzberg, 1992)

Alexander Mitscherlich, Margarete Mitscherlich, *Die Unfähigkeit zu trauern: Grundlagen kollektiven Verhaltens* [Published in English as *The Inability to Mourn: Foundations of Collective Behavior*] (München, Berlin: Piper Verlag, 1967)

Margarete Mitscherlich, *The Peaceable Sex: On Aggression in Women and Men* (New York: Fromm International, 1987)

Gernot Nalbach, Johanne Nalbach (eds.), *Berlin Modern Architecture: Building Activities 1954–1988* (Berlin: Senatsverwaltung für Bau und Wohnungswesen, 1989)

Helmut Nürnberger, *Fontanes Welt* [Fontane's World] (Berlin: Siedler Verlag, 1997)

Alison Owings, *Frauen: German Women Recall the Third Reich* (New Brunswick, New Jersey: Rutgers University Press, 1993)

Michael Paton, *Five Classics of Fengshui* (Leiden and Boston: Brill, 2013)

Florian C. Reuter (ed.), *Feng Shui (Kan Yu) and Architecture: International Conference in Berlin* (Wiesbaden: Harrassowitz, 2011)

Gabriele Reuter, *Aus guter Familie* [From a Good Family] (Marburg: Verlag LiteraturWissenschaft, 2006)

# Sources

Alexandra Richie, *Faust's Metropolis: A History of Berlin* (London: Harper Collins, 1999)

Joseph Roth, *What I Saw: Reports from Berlin 1920-1933*, trans. Michael Hofmann (New York and London: Norton, 1996)

Gerhard Sälter, Manfred Wichmann (eds.), *Am Rand der Welt: Die Mauerbrache in West-Berlin in Bildern von Margret Nissen und Hans W. Mende* [At the Edge of the World: The Wall Wasteland in West Berlin in Pictures by Margret Nissen and Hans W. Mende ] (Berlin: Christoph Links: 2018)

Hans Dieter Schäfer, *Berlin im Zweiten Weltkrieg: Der Untergang der Reichshauptstadt in Augenzeugenberichten* [Berlin in the Second World War: The Fall of the Reich Capital in Eyewitness Accounts ] (Munich/Zurich: Pieper Verlag, 1985)

Karl Scheffler, *Berlin: Ein Stadtschicksal* [Berlin: A City's Destiny] (Berlin: Suhrkamp, 2015)

Wolfgang Schivelbusch, *The Railway Journey: The Industrialization of Time and Space in the Nineteenth Century* (Oakland: University of California Press, 1986)

Michael Schmidt, *Berlin nach 45* [Berlin after 45], Ute Eskidsen (ed.) (Göttingen: Steidel, 2005)

Michael Schmidt, *Waffenruhe* [Ceasefire] (Berlin: Dirk Nishen Verlag, 1987)

W. G. Sebald, *On the Natural History of Destruction*, trans. Anthea Bell (London: Penguin, 2003)

Marie-Josée Seipelt, Jürgen Eckhardt (eds.), *Vom Himmel an das Reißbrett ziehen: Hermann Henselmann, Baukünstler im*

*Sozialismus: Ausgewählte Aufsäatze 1936-1981* [Dragging the
Sky to the Drawing Board: Hermann Henselmann, Archi-
tect under Socialism: Selected Essays 1936-1981] (Berlin:
Verlag der Becken, 1982)

Senat von Berlin (ed.), *Berlin: Kampf um Freiheit und Selbstver-
waltung 1945-46* [Berlin: Struggle for Freedom and Self-
government 1945-46] (Berlin: Spitzing Verlag, 1961)

Gitta Sereny, *The German Trauma: Experiences and Reflections
1938-2001* (London: Penguin Books, 2000)

Rupert Sheldrake, *Morphic Resonance: The Nature of Formative
Causation* (Rochester: Park Street Press, 2009)

Rebecca Solnit, *Wanderlust: A History of Walking* (London:
Penguin, 2000)

*Der Spiegel* (no author), *"Hauptstadt der Fixer"* [Capital of junk-
ies], *Der Spiegel* (January 1978)

*Der Spiegel* (no author), *"Die Türken kommen: rette sich, wer
kann"* [The Turks are coming: save yourselves], *Der Spiegel*
(July 1973)

Gabriele Tergit, *Atem einer anderen Welt: Berliner Reportagen*
[The Breath of Another World: Berlin Reportages] (Frankfurt am Main: Schöeffling & Co, 2018)

Gabriele Tergit, *Etwas Seltenes überhaupt: Erinnerungen* [Some-
thing Altogether Rare: Memoirs] (Frankfurt am Main:
Schöeffling & Co, 2018)

Klaus Theweleit, *Male Fantasies* (Minneapolis: University of
Minnesota Press, 1987)

# Sources

Andreas Tzortzis, "Berlin's Post-Wall Master Builder Retires," *The New York Times* (September 2006)

Paul Virilio, *Bunker Archeology* (New York: Princeton Architectural Press, 1994)

Maxine Wander, *Guten Morgen, du Schöne* [Good Morning, Beautiful] (Berlin: Suhrkamp, 2007)

Eric D. Weitz, *Weimar Germany: Promise and Tragedy* (Princeton and Oxford: Princeton University Press, 2017)

Ian White, *Here is Information: Mobilise* (London: Lux, 2016)

Petra Wilhelmy-Dollinger, *Die Berliner Salons* [The Salons of Berlin] (Berlin and New York: Walter de Gruyter, 2000)

Leslie Wilson, "Diary," *London Review of Books* (May 1994)

Christa Wolf, *City of Angels*, trans. Damion Searls (New York: Farrar, Straus and Giroux, 2013)

Christa Wolf, *Patterns of Childhood*, trans. Ursula Molinaro, Hedwig Rappolt (New York: Farrar, Straus and Giroux, 1980)

Virginia Woolf, *A Haunted House and Other Short Stories* (New York: Harcourt Brace Jovanovich, 1972)

Clara Zetkin, *Clara Zetkin Letters and Writings*, Mike Jones, Ben Lewis (eds.) (London: Merlin Press, 2015)

Peer Zietz, *Franz Heinrich Schwechten: Ein Architekt zwischen Historismus und Moderne* [Franz Heinrich Schwechten: An Architect Between Historicism and Modernism] (Stuttgart, London: Edition Axel Menges, 1999)

Hans Zischler, *Berlin ist zu groß für Berlin* [Berlin is Too Big for Berlin] (Berlin: Galiani, 2021)

## *Films*

Anne Carson, "On Corners," *Visualizing Theory* (University of
New York: 2018), The Graduate Center, CUNY, May 10, 2018

Ulli Edel, *Christiane F.* (1981)

Rainer Werner Fassbinder, *Berlin Alexanderplatz* (1980)

Rainer Werner Fassbinder, *Fontane Effi Briest* (1974)

Rainer Werner Fassbinder, *The Marriage of Maria Braun* (1979)

Rainer Werner Fassbinder, *The Third Generation* (1979)

Claude Lanzmann, *Shoah* (1985)

Walter Ruttmann, *Berlin: Symphony of a Metropolis* (1927)

Wim Wenders, *Wings of Desire* (1987)

## *Art*

Marie von Bunsen, *Theodor Fontane's Study* (1898)

Juan Garaizabal, *Memoria Urbana Berlin* (2012)

Hannah Höch, *The Beautiful Girl* (1920)

Käthe Kollwitz, *Pregnant Woman Drowning Herself* (c.1926)

Adolph Menzel, *Balcony Room* (1845)

Adolph Menzel, *Berlin-Postdam Railway* (1847)

Adolph Menzel, *The Schafgraben Flooded* (c.1842)

Adolph Menzel, *Soirée at the Schleinitz Salon* (1875)

Adolph Menzel, *Travelling through the Countryside* (1892)

Adolph Menzel, *View over Anhalter Bahnof by Moonlight* (1846)

# Acknowledgments

My heartfelt thanks go to Dominic Eichler for his tireless encouragement and critical reading of drafts at all stages; to Maren Lübbke-Tidow and Kito Nedo for their indispensable insights, many of which appear in this book; to Jason Dodge for his inspired map renderings and Silke Haupt for her meticulous cartography; and to Nina Sillem, Jacques Testard, Tamara Sampey-Jawad and Gunnar Cynybulk for their trust and commitment.

Love and gratitude for all kinds of ongoing daily support go to the relatives and friends that make up my cut-and-pasted family: its core of Oscar, Emil, Tony and Burkhard, and its incremental layers including Judy, Christine, Jason, Claudia, Leszek, Clarissa and all the many others with whom I have talked about this city.

**KIRSTY BELL** is a British-American writer and art critic based in Berlin. She has published widely in magazines and journals including *Tate Etc.* and *Art in America*, and was contributing editor of *frieze* from 2011 to 2021. She was awarded a Warhol Foundation Grant for her book *The Artist's House*, and her essays have appeared in more than seventy exhibition catalogues for major international museums and institutions such as the Whitney Museum of American Art, The Stedelijk Museum Amsterdam, and Tate, UK.